ALL THE FORGOTTEN PLACES

by Hunter James

PEACHTREE PUBLISHERS LIMITED
Atlanta, Georgia

Published by
PEACHTREE PUBLISHERS LIMITED
494 Armour Circle, N.E.
Atlanta, Georgia 30324

Manufactured in the United States of America

Text and Cover Design by David Russell

First Edition

Library of Congress Cataloging in Publication Data
James, Hunter.
All the forgotten places.

1. Southern States—History—Fiction. I. Title.
PS3560.A384A68 813'.54 81-12143
ISBN 0-931948-21-5 AACR2

For Lee, Michael, and Ellen,
with the hope that they will
find enduring value in the
heritage that remains so
much a part of their lives.

This book is not fiction; it is based primarily on personal observation and on dozens of exhaustive taped interviews with both whites and blacks. Although most of the events on which it is based actually occurred, particular incidents are not necessarily to be taken as literal or the characters as representative of actual persons. The resemblance, if any, is coincidental.

Research for this work was funded in part by the National Endowment for the Humanities.

CONTENTS

FOREWORD

The "forgotten places" of Hunter James' narrative about Southern racial change are certain towns and hamlets in the Black Belt of west central Alabama, places little known before 1964, little regarded since 1974, but very much in the nation's eye the decade in between. Yet the author is not so much concerned with the public side of the civil rights movement—the story that appeared on CBS and in the New York *Times*. He is concerned rather with some people who happened to be Southern and also happened to find themselves in the midst of racial revolution. His people are not the abstractions of the TV screen—the bull-necked sheriff, the moss-backed politician, the decadent aristocrat, the heroic black crusader. Rather they are common-enough people, some well-meaning, some seriously flawed, most both, all bearing in different fashions what C. Vann Woodward has called the burden of Southern history, all venturing, whether consciously or not, into what Robert Penn Warren has called "the awful responsibility of time."

If this book is about the Southern racial revolution of the nineteen-sixties, it also explores a theme that transcends the American South, goes beyond particular time and place. That theme, more ancient than Greek tragedy and just as universal, is the decline of an old order, the rise of a new. What we have here is not only the story of blacks battling whites for political power in one semi-fictional Black Belt Alabama county but the story of a people — the Southern white planter class, represented largely by the members of a single family on which the author focuses — who believe they represent civilization, whether they do or not; and believe they are being threatened by barbarism, whether they are or not. That single landed family thinks *classically:* the aging planter-storekeeper, Little Brother, knows Tacitus and Herodotus, has book shelves lined with Gibbon and Macaulay. He fears cultural fragmentation, as a classicist normally does, and he venerates the old order whether that order was just or not — and in many ways, it assuredly was not.

But the author makes no such judgments. He is, in truth, more nearly the novelist than the historian or sociologist, preferring the individual to the general, the concrete to the abstract. The best of his characters live — Little Brother, reciting verses from the *Rubaiyat* as his civilization crumbles around him; Calloway, the good ol boy planter who prefers Jack Daniels to Herodotus; the gentleman lawyer Meads, the "William Alexander Percy of Catalpa County"; Eula, the indomitable black servant; Cyrus Blue, the Bible-toting black preacher who becomes sheriff; the "old captain" — not so much a character as a presence, a force, now half a century dead — who had studied under Stonewall at VMI and had come to Alabama in the early eighteen-sixties bringing with him that noblesse oblige of earlier Virginia; and, as intriguing as any of the others, Edisen, the *Newsweek* correspondent, the Quentin Compson of the narrative, finding himself so close to his story he cannot adequately tell it.

If Mr. James has not fully escaped the shadow of Faulkner, we cannot really regret it. The cadences, the speech rhythms, the mastery of physical detail, the author's obvious gifts for tone and mood and description of landscape: these draw the reader into the story. And the author creates — or *is* — a fully realized narrator-persona, himself a journalist who ventures down into the Black Belt every few months, then returns to Atlanta or Baltimore to view Alabama from afar — at once involved and aloof.

I do not believe Hunter James set out precisely to write history when he undertook this book. I think, rather, he undertook to write a creative work, something approaching the novel his friend Edisen could never quite bring himself to write. But in his telling he does indeed write a kind of history—part oral history, based on numerous interviews with Black Belt inhabitants white and black; part the sort of "history" inspired by personal vision not unknown to the readers of William Alexander Percy and Wilbur J. Cash; but most of all, a very human book, wary of sociological abstraction, committing itself to the validity and dignity of the individual experience. What happened in the Alabama Black Belt in the nineteen-sixties and seventies was, after all, social history as well as political, and what the people thought and said and did—how, in their private lives, they reacted and responded to change—*is* the story.

Fred Hobson
Tuscaloosa, Alabama

The Ritual and the Taboo

August 1964

From the railway station in New Mt. Gizeh it is only a short drive up the hill and around a curve into the village proper —something more or less than a mile from New Mt. Gizeh, where the pulp train still stops, into old Mt. Gizeh, where almost nothing stops anymore. Even the road signs are gone now. There remains only a faded metal standard —*Holston Bros. Gen. Mdse.* — that for many years has marked the southern boundary of this tiny west Alabama farm community. The old store operated by the two brothers is about all that is left of what was once a flourishing trade center, and soon even that will be gone. Only one of the brothers is able to be up and about. The other, my father-in-law, has been out of the business and in steadily declining health ever since a 1963 operation that cost him his right leg. So now both the store and the post office that is its principal reason for existence have fallen under the supervision of the younger man, who in earlier years spent most of his working hours in the field, looking after the tenants and cotton. He, too, is in his last years and in rapidly declining health, considerably weaker and more withdrawn than when we last saw him. Yet he seldom neglects the store and is always there at an early hour, a shrunken man in faded khaki, looking out from behind a postal cage hung with yellowing "Wanted" posters and federal job notices that date back almost to World War II years.

From seven-thirty until a little after nine each morning there is a constant going and coming of community folk, people waiting for their mail mostly—field hands and Negro domestics, landlords and tenants, matronly farm wives in freshly starched cottons, and just plain morning idlers, a raucous and sometimes exasperating throng beyond which looms a murky and indiscriminate clutter: dusty counters piled with calico and cheap denim and tall going-to-church hats and shoes a bit too shiny for discreet wearing; apothecary jars crammed with sticks of peppermint and horehound, other jars stuffed with gingersnaps, or with boxes of alum and asafetida; bins of nails, scattered heaps of farm implements, plow lines, horse collars, saddles, trace chains, drums of kerosene; and in the midst of it all an elegantly stained cabinet labeled J. and P. Coats BEST SIX CORD THREAD; beside that, another large cabinet from which you still might purchase a seventy-five-year-old box of Velvet Bloom face powder or a vial of Little Tut cologne; and a little farther on, way back where even the morning sun does not reach, a maze of wall shelves lined with canned goods and soda crackers and breakfast cereals, with cartons of liniments and laxatives, with bottles of Lydia Pinkham and Hadacol and SSS tonic — an infinitude of ageless and nondescript merchandise which affords the old man only the leanest of profits.

By nine o'clock, or by nine-thirty at the latest, the store would be empty and the old man — "Little Brother" the family called him —would have stationed himself behind the giant coal stove, himself now a part of the clutter, the decay. During my last visit there he indeed seemed much weaker than before, lethargic and unmoving, yet somehow faintly alarmed, holding in his lap a recent edition of the *Birmingham News* and talking again, as so often before, of the civil rights movement—of Birmingham and Albany and Montgomery and all the other towns where the protestors had been, of the sit-ins and the freedom rides and the march on Washington.

And why was it, he wanted to know, that every time somebody got Martin Luther King salted away in jail somebody else had to come along and let him out?

No, he had not thought at all well of King's influence on the younger generation of black people. It did seem such a pity somehow, the number of "decent young nigras" who'd had their heads turned by King's false promises and hypocritical proclamations. "It's a mighty pitiful thing to think about all the lives he has ruined. Some of our best young nigras, the ones that used to be so peaceful and polite and decent—they all got to be out marching now and insisting on their 'rights.' " And it had all happened so quickly, too. Why, just a few short years ago they had been as hearty and compliant as always, and then, for reasons he still could not adequately explain, there had come of age a whole generation of black men who, like Faulkner's peremptory Lucas Beauchamp, "did not even bother to remember not to call him mister."

"Sometimes I'll be riding along and see one of our young nigras out walking and I'll just go ahead and throw up my hand—just like always—and like as not he'll just keep on walking. He won't even speak. He just walks right on past, just like he is Mister Somebody. You can tell what they're thinking: 'Nawsuh, boss, ain't no need to throw up yo hand at me. I is Mister So and So now.' And he just keeps right on walking. They all think they've got to act so *dignified* now. They think they've got to show off all their learning."

And so on in this fashion for another hour or more, no longer trying to read the paper but just holding it, looking out at the road, the sunlight, the pine forest. . . .

Decadent? Perhaps. Yet, at seventy-nine, he could hardly be aware, could hardly be expected to be aware, of the low state to which he had fallen. To him decadence would have been no more than an abstract idea, like B.O.: an affliction found often enough in your neighbor but one from which you remain strangely immune. Perhaps he was not even aware that the store was badly in need of a coat of paint, that the suckers and gumdrops needed dusting, or that the forty-nine-star flag over the porch roof was more than five years out of date; perhaps his ties were at once too garish and threadbare, his suits much too old-fashioned—all those wide lapels and floppy cuffs and everything—and his chin never quite free of stubble.

Still, if we looked closely enough we might have found

something more than mere decadence—an attitude, a manner, that stamped him as a man of some education and upbringing even if in these latter days he continued to share the prejudices common to his country and time. He had gotten through most of Dumas and Dickens and all of Scott by the time he was thirteen, and was accomplished in Latin even before he left home for two years of prep school at Sewanee Institute. He completed those two years and four more at the University of Alabama (plus another year of reading law in Birmingham) before returning home to help run the family farm and to take over half interest in this now-decrepit country store.

For more than half a century he and my father-in-law had run the store and farm as a joint enterprise, the older man spending most of his time behind the counter and tending to the "advancing" while Little Brother acted the part of plantation overseer. But was that really the best of all possible arrangements? Little Brother sometimes doubted that it was. One hesitated to impugn the Old Gentleman for his good heart. But it could be something of a problem at times. The old fellow, it seemed, was much too easygoing, too lenient with his customers, much too slow to collect the money that God knows was never in any hurry to come in on its own. Yet he was himself a man of no mean ability, with a facility of mind that belied his ignorance of Greek and Latin, and—yes, it was certainly true—with a compassion that led him to extend credit much too easily.

"Always talking about so and so needs a little help," Little Brother said. "So and so ain't gonna make it—ain't gonna get by—if we don't let him have a little something. If only he'd just gone on out and tried to collect some of those old debts. . . ."

Little Brother was right, of course. Storekeeping—tenants—cotton—such had been the making of many a fortune in Black Belt Alabama. But the Old Gentleman somehow had a way of letting all the money-making opportunities pass him by. In the immediate aftermath of the Civil War, stores much like this one had cropped up all across the rural South, sometimes as many as three and four to a single crossing, and with them a furnishing system that kept whole generations of black tenants—whites too—tied to the soil—often, if black, to the same soil worked by their parents and grandparents as slaves. The furnishing system, or the "advancing" as it was called hereabouts, had begun almost as a makeshift, a means of getting a crop out of the ground that first year after Appomattox, at a time when there were no solvent banks, no money. Few could have guessed that it would manage to hang on almost to the present day. But so it had, impervious to the clamor of social critics and political reformers, as omnivorous as kudzu, shaping the habits, folkways and literature of an entire people. But the "advancing" in itself meant nothing. It took a hard man—often a callous and even ruthless man—to make it pay. And the Old Gentleman, it seemed, was none of these.

"Always felt like he had to let folks have whatever they wanted — whenever they wanted it — money, too, sometimes—when he knew they had no security for it, when he and I both knew they wouldn't be able to bring in a crop that would pay the bill." He sat there with the paper on his lap, watching me. "Just never could understand it. Never could understand why the old boy did so hate to go out and ask a nigra to pay him what he owed. . . ."

But sometimes the Old Gentleman forced himself to do even that. We could all of us remember those hot dead Sunday mornings when, in order to get some of the money back, we would set out through the river country in my 1958 Hillman or — on the good days — in my brother-in-law's air-conditioned Cadillac. We would stop first at one shack and then the next, aimless really, surprising the black people in their own Sunday morning aimlessness. It would be the same at each stop: the Old Gentleman climbing out, squinting up at the house (his eyesight had never been good) and calling:

"Willie? Where are you, Willie?"

Then Willie appearing in the yard, servile, quite abject, promising to come in "first thing next Thursday" with the money. And so on to the next shack, the next promise that both he and his client knew would never be kept, for the simple reason that there would be no money, no means of making good the credit which the old man would have extended in any case.

"If only he hadn't felt so *bound* to accommodate folks," Little Brother said. "I just always would want to know why he didn't try a little harder to get some of the money back." He looked at me, ruminant, without stirring, brooding again on the missed opportunities, the lost wealth. "Just never could understand why he felt like he was bound to be so accommodating."

And there was something else too: the matter of all those slaves the Yankees turned loose during the war. Did I realize that the government had never paid a dime for those slaves? He had talked of it often, of Lincoln's promise to pay for the freed slaves, wondering if Washington had simply forgotten about it and whether it might be worthwhile trying to reinstate the claim. Even now the Holstons might regain much of their lost status in the world if the government would only make good on that old debt. Why was it that the politicians never talked about the important issues anyway?

"Yup. It was sure mighty hard on grandpa just to have to sit back and watch while the Yankees relieved him of every little thing he'd been able to accumulate. Always seemed like a right pitiful thing to me—the way the Yankees came in and scattered all those slaves to the four winds like that, and never a minute's thought about all the money tied up in them."

* * *

Little Brother, though something of a gallant in his younger days, had never quite gotten around to thinking of matrimony. Neither had my father-in-law until he was almost fifty. The Old Gentleman's marriage, to a girl not much more than half his age, was something that might be forgiven him—but certainly there was no thought of forgiving his wife Lurellia. She was different from the others, alien to the ways of Black Belt society, even though there was nothing in either her speech or manner to betray her hill-country upbringing. The small north Alabama town where she had grown up was only a little more than an hour's drive from Mt. Gizeh, yet much further than that in spirit, lying altogether outside the history of the cotton South, a mill town where there were few black people and where there had never been slaves. Her father, a bookkeeper by trade and an evangelist by calling, had regularly filled the pulpit of many a little country church unable to afford a fulltime minister. And she herself, after her marriage, had remained an uncompromising Baptist in a house full of Episcopalians.

She had first come to Mt. Gizeh as a schoolmarm of seventeen, staying only briefly and surprising even her own people by going back years later, after college and a stint of teaching in Birmingham, to become the storekeeper's wife. She had spent the first years of her married life in the old plantation house that had been home to three generations of Holstons. But she had never felt really welcome in that house, where, as she later explained in one of her frequent letters to my wife, "All were so much older than I. . . and had studied Latin." She had never read Xenophon and knew not Herodotus, even in translation, and could never shake the feelings of inadequacy that life among the Holstons had instilled in her. Her dark good looks were no help, nor was her college degree or refined manner of speaking. It was almost as if the sectional rivalry that had existed in Alabama from the time of its founding was to live on in her relations with her in-laws. And perhaps it could not have been otherwise. The land from which she had come was the ancestral home of free soilers, unionists, scalawags, farmers alliancemen, populists, and free silver Democrats, in pretty much that order, a world entirely apart from plantation society and one which her father-in-law, a small cotton planter and ex-Confederate army officer, treated with a contempt that came from reading too much Gibbon and Sallust.

He had been dead for almost fifteen years by the time Lurellia began life in the Holston home. But the mood he had evoked still hung about the place like a melancholy smell of old flowers. One day soon after her marriage some of his relatives from the Virginia Tidewater had come. Among them was a pleasant graying woman who, as the time grew near for departure, startled the postmaster's bride by drawing her aside and declaring, "My dear Lurellia, I feel exactly as my son told me he felt last evening. He said, 'Mother, *I* don't see anything wrong with cousin Lurellia. . . .'"

She had lived in the captain's house for more than a dozen years, among all the cotton snobs and Latin scholars, before finally moving into a white green-shuttered Cape Cod built in the late forties on a triangular patch of land directly behind the Holston store. Two of her three children were in high school by then, and her husband had just celebrated his sixty-fifth birthday. The old fellow would go back to his homeplace once more, after his 1963 operation, to place himself under the care of Little Brother's live-in maid, Eula Sides. He would stay there for about six months, a happy interlude in a way, because, of the nine children who had grown up in that house, the three who had spent most of their lives there were together again: Little Brother, now sole manager of the store and all-purpose keeper of the Alabama tradition; the Old Gentleman, bedridden, one-legged, still alert much of the time yet doomed forever to the shuttered room; and their sister, Miss Angie, a onetime Latin teacher and failed poet, disabled by an old hip injury and suffering from a paralytic speech tremor that had worsened with age.

Miss Angie was herself barely mobile, moving about the uncarpeted halls with great effort and only then with the help of her metal walker. After many years as a teacher at Sidney Lanier High School in Montgomery, she had come back to preside over the house with a graciousness undiminished by advancing age and not even diminished to any considerable extent by her hip injury or faltering speech. The real pity was that she'd had to rely so heavily on Eula for even the most rudimentary of her needs. Eula had been helpful enough in her own way. But to be perfectly truthful, she did seem to be getting somewhat above herself lately. No one had made a secret of it. Even Miss Angie had begun to notice and to say "little things." One might almost have assumed that the maid had never heard of our Southern way of life or how necessary it was for all the old customs to endure in spite of the civil rights "rout" and the agitations of Martin Luther King. "Frankly," said Mrs. Lurellia, "she couldn't stay with me till the water got hot."

* * *

Yes! And soon there would be others like her, in the schools, on the trains and buses, even in the streets of New Erie: marchers and agitators whose insulting signs and preposterous demands would be the talk of the county. Even now — already — there was talk that in the near future the black people would insist on their right to run for public office and actually to sit in the counsels of the white man. But till now we had given little thought to these matters. It had all seemed so remote somehow, so improbable, in spite of the clamor in the cities and the unchanging drone of the headlines.

For the moment there was only the enduring calm of the land itself: hills lonely with summer, a tableau of bright meadow and sunlight, of canebrake, backwater, and undulant prairieland. It was cattle country mostly, but with plenty of cotton left too, and an occasional dense stand of pine or hardwood; a country lush and sensuous even in the dog days of late August, the sunsets wildly luminous like the splashed bright colors of an untutored Tintoretto, the cottonwoods now completely free of the lint that not so long ago blanketed in one thick carpet the roadsides and waste places. Sometimes on these hot August afternoons, soundless except for the incessant buzzing of the jarfiles, you get the feeling that if there had never been secession or war or white-suited planters astrut on galleried verandas, if there had never been talk of all those marvelous antebellum balls with officers newly returned from battle toasting their girls under glittering chandeliers or on terraces fragrant with the odor of jasmine and wisteria and moonvines — that if none of this had ever existed, the land would still assert its dominion over us, casting a spell no less haunting or tragic, no less intoxicating, no less primordial in its power to lull, to sway, to float us off on a cloud of summer sleep, of winter sleep. . . .

Even now we remain aliens in a land shaped not so much by pioneer and broadax, and not even so much by the cotton gin or the imperatives of the international textile market, as by sorcery itself — a land chained by ritual and taboo, fraught with latent terrors and mysterious Caribbean echoes, Gothiclike myths as frail and evanescent — and as darkly ominous — as shifting threads of swamp mist; the swamps themselves a part of us now, the old rivers and bottomlands, the marshes out of which might come strange gargoylelike creatures to share the unspoken fancies and half-mad passions that lurk behind our easy smiles and reassuring handshakes.

Yes, all of it so much more real on these sultry afternoons than the news out of Washington and Birmingham. And so you sit there, thinking about the night less than two weeks ago when you went for a swim down at the old block manufactory and heard a long succession of eerie tribal-like chants coming up out of the Tombigbee river bottoms. The evening had grown cool, and some of the others had built a fire on a rise above the small sand beach. Across the lake the block manufactory, out of operation ever since the early fifties, squatted like a desolate Rhenish ruin, specterlike in the chill vapors of the first moonlight. And then you could hear it: the chant or moan or whatever it was coming from where you were not quite sure, from out yonder somewhere beyond the pale blackness, perhaps from the direction of the single far-off light you could see — faintly — from the top of the rise, a sound growing louder all the while — the work of Tombigbee conjure women no doubt, or perhaps only the echo of one of those countless black revivals held everywhere in that country during the late summer and early autumn — conjurer and revivalist alike, and the rest of us too, all held in thrall by the secret emanations of the summer night, the dark enchantments left over from "the year the stars fell."

* * *

Three o'clock. The store had been empty for some time, and Little Brother remained where he had been most of the day, in the two-seated rocker behind the giant coal stove, still with that air of lethargy and faint alarm, holding the newspaper folded in his lap and talking about how sorry he felt for "all the young nigras who had thrown in with King," and what a great disappointment was to be their lot, and why hadn't the world been able to see the extraordinary merit in George Wallace, and what did I think about Queen Esther Bowman, the black Mt. Gizeh schoolteacher who had been to Detroit and had brought back all the alien accents and persnickety ways of the Detroit nigras?

"Yes sir. They all got to show off their dignity now. Of course, she always *was* a right peculiar nigra." His voice ceased, took up again and again ceased, so that at last there was nothing but the silence, the pervasive hum of jarflies, the dustmotes, the fierce glare of the sun outside on the blacktop. And then once more his voice, a more reflective tone in it now, as he recited his favorite verse from the *Rubaiyat*:

For some we loved, the loveliest and the best
That from his vintage rolling time has prest,
Have drunk their cup a round or two before,
And one by one crept silently to rest.

And so it would go now, throughout the bright hot afternoon — more talk about all the "good times before the war," the slaves, the harvest balls, the officers home on leave and all the rest of it, and about the old debt the Yankees still owed....

Debt?

And then, of course, you would remember: the debt still owing to the Holstons and other old planter families for all those slaves the Yankees turned loose. For the second time in less than an hour you would find yourself called upon to contemplate the injustice of it all, to think about how hard his grandfather had worked, "scraping and saving and doing around every way he knew how" in order to acquire those slaves...and then just to have the Yankees come through and turn them all loose like that? Why, he kept asking himself, had George Wallace never seized upon it as a political issue? And Lyndon? He, of all people — himself a Southerner — why had he never stepped in on the side of the South?

A tragic thing it was, the way Lyndon had betrayed his own people. Always smiling so big and scratching himself in all the wrong places and making a constant spectacle of himself on national television. But perhaps there was still hope for the president. Only the week before he had won nomination for a second term at a political convention that left Little Brother more puzzled and bemused than angry. He talked of that now. The Democratic National Convention. Up there in Atlantic City. And a disgusting sight it was too: all those nigra delegates marching around and announcing in the face of all logic that "black is beautiful." Little Brother just couldn't understand that sort of thing. Anyway, it had just gotten so he could pronounce "nigra" correctly when all at once "our brethren of the colored persuasion" decided that they wanted to be called black. He had watched the whole show on television, baffled most of all by the antics of "a certain Mr. Henry," as he called him, leader of the Democratic Freedom Party of Mississippi. "Him and his cohorts all gallivanting around up there insisting on their *rights*. They're always gonna be bound to stand out for their *rights*. They're always gonna have something to say about their *freedom*." What they had stood out for in this instance was the right to unseat Democratic regulars who had come there as Mississippi's duly authorized convention delegation. There had been quite a stir—non-negotiable demands from Mr. Henry, disapproving frowns from Lyndon, howls of derision from Mississippi regulars—and at the end of it all a compromise that mocked all who had been a party to it.

"What do you think of our nigra citizens anyhow? A mighty pathetic lot it seems to me." He emitted a faint guffaw, rueful, uncomprehending. Then: "Must be mighty hard on all those other folks up there. Don't envy them a bit, I sure don't. If I had to sit with nigras all day long, and stand with nigras, and couldn't even go into the bathroom without seeing nigras in all their manifest dignity there, and having nigras tell me that their day is come and mine is gone—and then to be reminded that it was my bounden duty and privilege to assemble with nigras every time matters of high consequence were about to take place...."

But if, perhaps, he had been "privileged" to sit among them, what then? One sensed that he had already thought about that. Even now the scene seemed to assert itself: the crowded caucus rooms, the hotel lobbies aswarm with whores and mountebanks, the sweaty banquet halls rife with cigarette smoke and sordid gales of laughter, and the whole vast horde of pushy nigra delegates all chortling and talking about their rights and how the world belonged to them now...and then Little Brother himself among them, grim and shriveled and maybe even unnoticed at first, elbowing and shoving his way to the head of the table where, perchance, he would come face to face with the arrogant Mr. Henry and all of those other "freedom" delegates who had been in so much evidence on the television screen.

It would have been nothing new to him, to find himself amid so huge a crowd of hostile blacks. I could remember all those times at the Greyhound depot in Atlanta, when he had gone down to catch an early bus back to New Erie and had been forced to fight his way through a mass of black people in order to gain his rightful place at the head of the line. I would see the look of dismay come over him—almost a look of panic—as he edged his way into the crowd and then flung himself boldly, rambunctiously, into the midst of it, and finally to the head of it; him standing there detached and old and quite alone—yet more than a little pleased with himself—amid a crowd of blacks that had been to the city many times and knew city ways and knew, too, about the freedom rides and what King had done to that transit company down in Montgomery and how nigras were no longer obliged to sit at the back of the bus, or stand at the back of the line either, although it would be greatly appreciated if they would....

So maybe it would be the same at the Atlantic City convention hall; the arrogant Mr. Henry and his followers strutting around issuing their preposterous demands and no one but Little Brother to put them in their place, him no match physically for even the least presumptuous and least robust of the black delegates, yet storming his way forthwith into the caucus room and sitting there among them with all the outrageous hauteur appropriate to his kind — almost certainly at the head of the table now, just sitting there amid the cigar smoke and the gusts of tawdry laughter and then lighting up a cigar of his own and pounding on the table for attention, saying, "OK, now, OK." And just why was it that they as good nigra citizens felt that they might have something significant to add to the selection of a presidential candidate anyway?

* * *

Half past four. Out of the molten, almost soundless afternoon, a sudden thump, some shouts. And on the doorstoop a shuffle of footsteps, loud, insistent, menacing. And then the two black girls, no more than nine or ten, standing tentatively just inside the door, each with a fistful of change for Mounds and Dr. Peppers. Startled, the old man watched with growing wariness as they came on up the steps and eased their way in past the last faint reach of sunlight. And then he was in front of them, leading the way back to the drink box and candy counter. He got out the Mounds and cold pop while they stood there staring, silent, looking, holding the money. And then he had it, forty or forty-five cents in dimes, nickles and pennies. He came back around the counter and again watched as they retraced their steps through the dark interior and quickly out into the waiting sun.

"I just never could understand why the North hates the South so," he said as he resumed his seat and took up the paper. "I just never could see the sense in it—why they felt like they were just bound to come in and turn all those slaves loose like that."

But, of course, that was the one part he did understand, perhaps a little better than most. The reason, as he sometimes explained it, was that the South had "so much more culture" than the North and not so many "dagoes and moujiks" to retard the progress of the race. But even that wasn't the whole reason. No, there was something even more basic than that: "It's because they *whupped* us, that's why. It's because we lost. Because if you whup somebody real good you feel obliged to go on whupping him the rest of your life — because you have to go on convincing yourself that he deserved the whupping in the first place."

* * *

"Ain't no use him talking bout no Yankees," the black woman, Eula Sides, told me one afternoon not long after that. "Ain't no Yankees whupping him. God, *He* the one doing the whupping. And God goan keep on whupping him too, cause he gots to *pay* fur the bad way he treat our colored. Lots of times I be's looking at the TV, on the civil rights, and he tell me, 'Whut you get outa that mess? Whut you see in that?' Cause he be's hating King. How he *do* hate Luther King. And I say, 'I see whut anybody else see. That's all I see.' And then he turn to Miss Angie and say, 'Look like *she* want to be the boss around hyar, don't it? Looks like she be's the one that wants to run things. . . .' "

We were in the kitchen at the plantation house, Eula at the sink and me at the small square table, in the oppressive late afternoon heat, with the jarflies going and the mourning doves starting up. A large powerfully built woman who was at least fifty-five and could have been seventy, the maid had just come up from the garden bearing a tub of squash and greens and black-eyed peas. She worked as she talked, busily, scrubbing the greens, her loud voice echoing through the house until, catching herself, she again spoke in something just above a stage whisper, as though all at once conscious that she was in a white man's house, in the captain's house.

". . . God He whupping him good now. . . I alls the time be telling Miss Angie, 'He sho goan pay fur it,' and he paying fur it now, cause God whupping him." A pause; a great splashing and scrubbing of the freshly picked vegetables. "People all changing some now, cause the government say they gots to change. The colored stops now on the time that the white folks stop. Didn't use to be no such as that. Colored use to all work *over* the time that the white folks work. White folks puts down their shovels and the colored go on working. Thar be lots of folks that bring back the slavery if they could. I say to Mis'en Capps down at the Yellow Front, say, ain't my dollar good as yo dollar? My dollar buy whut yo dollar buy. When I goes in the store they don't comes up and say, 'Looka hyar, is this a colored man's dollar?' "

She had grown up on a farm near the community of Vestal, halfway between Mt. Gizeh and New Erie. Like all of her kind, she had worked each day during the growing season "from the time you couldn't see till you couldn't see again." And for two dollars a week at most. "If I don't get thar fore sunup I don't make a day." The memory of all that nagged at her as at so many others. But she was not really an activist, in spite of all the talk going around. She had never tried to vote. She had never taken part in a demonstration or joined a boycott. About her only open form of protest was to visit as often as possible one of those plain whitewashed pine-boarded churches where visiting Negroes — "outside agitators," whites too, sometimes — stood up there in the pulpit and explained in their patient yet frustrated voices what voting was all about, what integration was all about, what the future was all about.

The dusk was on us now, the other voices coming from way up at the front of the house. Some of the kinfolk had come from Farrow Church, and they would go on talking for another hour or so, just talking and rocking until the black woman went to the screen and called them in to supper. In the kitchen, as on the front porch, the talk had turned to George Wallace and his abortive campaign for the presidency. Eula had been talking about how ridiculous it was, the idea of him running for president, and how foolish he looked that day hardly more than a year ago when he stood there at the entrance of the University of Alabama and waved his arms around "like he'uz really goan do something bout keeping the black folks outa dar" and how "he sho ain't goan be the president no kind of way."

"I don't want Wallace. I ain't goan have Wallace. He ain't goan be the president. I sho don't believes that. And another thing: I don't even want Wallace saying nothing on the TV, the bad way he talk about our colored."

Her voice flowed on in that garbled and inimitable patois. She talked again about the old man, how he *did* hate Luther King and favored the 'Piscopals over any other sect, and how God was whupping him, and how he had often refused to let her eat at the dining room table even after the others had left it, and how he had been trying to keep her out of the family bath—even banging on the door after she had gone inside and locked it—hitting and kicking it and shouting that she was supposed to confine herself to the use of the weed-grown privy out at the edge of the barnlot. "I tell him if'n I goan scrub and wash that bowl I sho goan turn my butt to it." And so she had, to such an extent that he had all but given up arguing with her about it and had taken over the old privy for his own use, refusing even to go near the commode as long as the black woman was "turning her butt to it."

And then suddenly she wasn't talking about any of that. Now the talk was of an earlier and much more distant time, tales coming down from her father, from his father, how he—her grandfather—was sold south when he was twelve and served "old marster" until "they freed de worl."

Freed the world?

"The slaves. When they free the slaves." She laughed abruptly, coarsely, her voice growing more decisive now, the sound of it flowing not so much out of the gathering dark as out of time itself. She talked of her grandfather, how he was perched atop the plantation smokehouse on that long-ago April afternoon when the war came to Vestal and Farrow Church, waiting to "tap de bell" and ring the marster and his family out of the woods, where they had gone to escape the detection of Croxton's Raiders. Her grandfather and the other slaves had already burned everything that might have been taken, all the chickens and hogs and every ear of corn on the place. But Croxton got no farther than the Ellison plantation two miles to the north. Some of Forrest's men had come up, together with a detachment of Catalpa County's home guardsmen, and had forced the Yankee general to withdraw from what was actually nothing more than an aimless foraging mission anyway.

"My granddaddy he always say he be's the best off of anybody on the place. He wuz old marster's boy around the house. He bring in the water and stove wood and he be's the one that fan the table while the white folks wuz eating. . . and he wuz the one that greased the others. . . ."

Greased the others?

"The other little chilrun. The other families, their slaves wear different clothes from one week to the next, don't you know, and they treats their colored good. So the marster he have his slaves greased when the company comes so they thinks he be's feeding em good. And my granddaddy he'ud do all the greasing. He take the grease from the fried meat and grease their bosoms and grease their mouths, don't you know, so they say they *feed* em good. So when the peoples come and sit and talk awhile, and maybe get some greens to take home, well, my granddaddy he catch hold of the little ones' hands and bring them to the screen and they looks in whar the white folks wuz setting, and the lady from the other family when she see them she say, 'Look at them little niggers' mouths. Why, I believes them niggers done *et*!' But they might not et *nothing*. They might be all the time hongry back thar, and if old marster's wife see them she'ud say, 'Take those chilrun outa here. Why they got grease all *over* them'. . . ."

And so she talked on, remembering all the old stories, her voice amiable enough yet with a hint of malice too. She talked now about the " 'Piscopals" of antebellum times and how they were always trying to prevent her people from finding out that Jesus "wuz somebody that could holp em." For a long time there was a rule that the slaves were not to pray among themselves or even in their separate cabins — and nowhere else either except discreetly in the balcony of the white church on Sunday morning. But they had a way of getting around that. Each Wednesday evening they would gather secretly at a prearranged spot and "pray wid their haids stuck inside a big old washpot."

"They goes from house to house. . . different houses so

old marster won't find out. . . and sticks their haids inside a big old pot and prays to God! If the marsters finds out they tie em up and whups em good, cause *they* wuz the gods. They had to pray whut *they* said pray." But the whuppings didn't change anything. The next week the slaves would gather at a different cabin, around a different washpot, and pray right on, "cause they'd already found out that God wuz somebody that could *change* things."

Her grandfather, still quite young, had sometimes attended the prayer sessions uninvited. During his early days as houseboy, the slaves gathered each week at a cabin he knew only as "Nigger John's place." As soon as it was good dark, he would leave the big house and make his way through the quarters and climb up on the roof of John's place and listen to the voices through the mud chimney. But later he, too, joined in the big doings around the washpot. "He talk about the other slaves how they all goes to shouting wid their heads inside the pot cause they all be's so happy cause they think Jesus goan come down and holp em."

And then one night the slave named John found another reason to pray. He had used up his weekly supply of hogmeat more quickly than usual and had gone up to ask old marster for extra rations. Old marster doled out an extra slab of fatback but not the ham that John had actually come to get.

"John he jes sot there all evening thinking bout it and thinking bout it—how he'ud sho like to have a piece of that ham. Ain't nothing goan do him but that he get some of that ham. So time come for prayers and he stick his head in the pot and say, 'Ooooooooo Lord, Ooooooooo Lord, O Lord come on down *Jesus*, I wants you to come on down and make old marster give me that ham!. . . Ooooooooo Jesus come on!' And all the others, they doing the same, praying and shouting and knocking that dust all around and some of them praying wid their heads out the pot cause they all wants John to have a big old piece of that ham. And John, he say, 'Ooooooooo Lord come on down here and make old marster *give* me some of that ham cause you know how bad I needs it Lord. . .' "

And then came a knock at the door. And another voice, long and low and mournful: "Ooooooooo John, I is *hyar*. Open the door, John, cause I is ready to go wid you to see old marster and make him *give* you some of that meat!"

A sudden hush as John yanked his head out of the pot and looked around. "Whut dat?" And one of the others:

"Dat's de God." And somebody else: "Yeah, you all hush now, cause dat's de God."

Eula's own voice took on an ominous hush: "They all standing wid their heads out the pot and they shy back a ways and get real quiet cause they thought it wuz the Christ, cause they didn't know, cause they'd all been praying fur God to come. And the voice, it say, 'Ooooooooo John, you comes on out hyar now cause we sho gots to go up yonder and make old marster give you some of that ham.' "

And then the door fell open and God came in. Except it wasn't God. It was old marster. "But they didn't know cause he have on that long sheet and everything and his hair all hanging down and them whiskers all over his face. So they thought it was Christ cause they'd been praying for Him to come and holp John get some of that ham." Only later did they learn what had actually happened: how some "smart" had betrayed the slaves to old marster in the hope that he, rather than John, would get the ham. "Don't make no difference whut you do, some *smart* goan sho tell it. So old marster he come down thar dressed up exactly like he wuz the God." And all the others over in the corner, staring, thinking *Hush we gots to be quiet now cause dat is de God*. "And so old marster he come on inside wid his hair all hanging down and them whiskers all over his face and he say, 'Come on, John, you come wid me now, cause we gots to get on up yonder and tell old marster to gives you some of that meat.' " And the others still huddled in the corner and John looking up with his head barely out of the pot and saying, "Well, Jesus, old marster, he most likely in the bed this time of night and I sho do hates to 'sturb him." But he went on out with him anyway, and the knot of Negroes slowly unraveled, coming out of the corner a little at the time, still silent, moving cautiously to the door and watching the two of them,

John and God, going up to the big house to talk to old marster about the meat—or maybe only to talk about the evils of praying with your head inside a washpot, and John almost certain to get the whuppin that wouldn't stop him from doing it again but only force him and the others once more to find another washpot in a different cabin.

* * *

Evening and another round of spirited talk about the cultured South and the dissolute North—about all the slaves the Yankees turned loose and about the old war debt and the considerable amount of interest that had accrued over the past one hundred years and what a shame it was that Lincoln had died before seeing to it that it was all paid off.

"A mighty pitiful thing," the old man said. "And a mighty sad thing too."

He was at supper now, the dark pushing in on him, replete with a smell of quince and cape jessamine and ripening sloes. He slumped forward slightly, talking to everybody and nobody, the fork poised halfway between the table and his grizzled face.

Behind him, barefooted and perspiring, hovered the lumbering black maid; she was always near at hand, a disquieting and even menacing presence to Little Brother, standing in the door while the others ate, sometimes silent, sometimes not—and sometimes actually drawing up a chair and joining in the meal. No one had ever thought she would last through her first summer. But she had lasted almost a year beyond that and had even, in a sense, come to dominate the house, presiding over it, the old man and his sister both, with a kind of brute efficiency, as though to mock the memory of the captain, whose bearded and humorless face glares ominously down at us from above the parlor mantel.

* * *

He was Virginian, the captain was, lean and implacable, a military man and classical scholar who had studied under Stonewall Jackson at VMI and had stood second in a class of forty-one. A certificate of graduation signed by

Jackson still hangs in a neglected corner of his bedroom. During his later years the captain often remarked upon Jackson's transformation from a bumbling college professor into one of the legendary war heroes of the western world. At such times he would fall into a detached and rueful mood, thinking again of those first exciting days after Fort Sumter and of how he, too, might have been in the group that left VMI that spring and marched away with Jackson to Bull Run, Chancellorsville, and immortality. But he had come instead to Tuscaloosa, as an instructor in infantry and artillery tactics at the University of Alabama, chosen for that task by Jackson himself.

He spent four years there and was among the survivors of Tuscaloosa Bridge, one of the forgotten battles of the war. After the war he stayed on in this lush cotton country to marry a girl of the slaveholding class and to make his mark as a lawyer, newspaper editor, educator, and aspiring planter. By the early 1870s he was already well established as an attorney, sufficiently well known in that line to have won election as Catalpa County's first anti-carpetbag solicitor. But the law must not have interested him greatly, for by the early 1880s we find him dividing most of his time between editorial chores at the *New Erie Whig* and the profession that was to become the ruling passion of his life: education. It was as an educator rather than as a lawyer or newspaperman that he eventually settled in the tiny crossroads community of Mt. Gizeh, fourteen miles west of New Erie and only six miles south of the old Tombigbee river town where the Confederate Belisarius, Nathan Bedford Forrest, had disbanded the last of his storied cavalry command.

The one-room academy of which the captain was headmaster and sole proprietor stands just outside the gates of his plantation home. The house itself, scene of so many of our summer visits, was already more than half a century old when the captain selected it as his future abode, the original section antedating by as much as a decade the building of the great neoclassical "Rosemounts" and "Stanton Halls" that came to exemplify life in the cotton South. Approached by way of a wire fence sagging beneath the inevitable masses of wisteria and across a yard bare of grass and trees, it stands much as the captain left it, a plain white clapboarded dwelling said to be the oldest such structure in the county.

As you move about the place, in the fading light of afternoon, amid a satiny hush of walnut china cabinets and rosewood sideboards, with the gloom of Greek and Latin classics all about, and a shimmer of antique decanters, you can sense anew the captain's attempt to recreate in these remote environs a part of the "aged and mellow world" from which he had come. He brought with him many of the more than eight thousand volumes that line these halls; others he ordered from New York or Richmond, or purchased during his business trips to Mobile and New Orleans. And a mighty company it is indeed: here a worn Dickens, there a supercilious Thackeray, yonder an irascible Twain and, most prominent of all, a proud and lofty Scott, prophet of all who have aspired to greatness in our Black Belt country. Tacitus, too, is prominent, and Xenophon; Thucydides, Ovid, Gibbon, Juvenal, and the Compleat Montaigne: men who long ago passed out of time and into the realm of monuments. Here all sects and schools are alike reconciled, a debauched Burns holding court to a frowning Milton, an abandoned Wilde or a lascivious Hugo now quite at ease in the presence of a conscious-stricken Augustine, choleric German at one with decadent Parisian, imperious Briton and rash Iberian songster, saturnine Scot and ebullient Florentine; the churlish Carlyle on speaking terms at last with the scrofulous Paine, and Paine himself quiescent beneath the strictures of the formidable Burke.

And so the old mood hangs on, the abiding smells of the summer dusk, a scent of old flowers, sweet and oversweet, at once forbidding and seductive. And we hear again the forgotten voices, listening as the captain talks haltingly and a bit wistfully of Chickamauga, Shiloh — and Tuscaloosa Bridge. His wife, of course, had tales of her own, and it was she who had spoken so often, as Little Brother does now, of all those lovely times before the war — of her childhood romps with the nurse Lavinia, of her first trips down to Mobile, of all the times she had stood at dusk on a veranda pungent with the smell of lilac and listened to the "melodious singing of the darkies" as they came in from the fields. Thus did she pass on to a succeeding generation all of those special family legends that are so inextricably a part of the legends of the greater South.

Even as the captain pondered the vanished glories of his wife's antebellum legacy he must have known what neither she nor their children ever quite seemed to understand — that the land to which he had come as a young man could scarcely have attained in less than half a century the grace and maturity of his own fully realized Virginia aristocracy. Indeed, what civilization there was had come into being almost wholly within the lifetime of his wife's father, a Carolinian who had migrated to the Alabama backcountry in the early 1800s, when the land was still a wilderness, and who had lived on into the first years of Reconstruction.

But the captain had put Virginia forever behind him now, and despite the limited financial resources of his middle years he would readily embrace the political concerns and cultural norms of the Black Belt gentry, laying wreaths of tribute at all the old shrines, standing in reverence before the ruined inglorious monuments. In a weekly column he began writing about this time for his old hometown newspaper in the Virginia Tidewater he often bewailed the frenzied commercialism that afflicted the South of his day, mourned the ignorance and culpability of the masses, spoke up "manfully" for President Cleveland's hard-money policies at a time when a populist fever was rocking the nation, and never failed to deplore the declining educational standards of his adopted state. "I have become so hemmed in by these cheap schools as to about break me up, and were it not for the fact that I am obliged to educate my own children, I would abandon the profession in supreme disgust."

In a land that had fallen so far below its best prewar standards, the captain's own reputation as an exacting educator could only prosper. To his Mt. Gizeh academy came many of New Erie's future merchants, lawyers, and men of affairs, to get the education nowhere else available in all of that remote stretch of backcountry. He presided over both the school and the house with a demeanor appropriate to a man of his aspirations; in countless small ways he ushered into his private world all of the customs and ceremonies of Virginia's "golden age." One can imagine him as he sat on the veranda each day at sunset, or before a fire in his study, with the single toddy he allowed himself, a copy of Thucydides open on his lap or perhaps a recent issue of Henry Grady's *Sunday Constitution*. For his children evening meant a return to the regimens of the day: algebra lessons, Latin translations, memory work. "Nothing in the world but foolishness," complained his oldest daughter Nell, in an 1899 letter to her sister Sarah, then dying of tuberculosis in Canon City, Colorado. "It is right disgusting to me. I nearly know this is my last year at school. . . ."

How differently Sarah would feel about all that when, two years later, the captain wrote to her proudly of the disfranchising movement that had recently swept the South. Like others of his class, the captain held that disfranchisement was on the whole a fine thing for the Negro. In earlier years the freedman had been something of a kept voter and, as such, an asset to those who had him in their keeping. But populism was changing all that, awakening the Negro to new possibilities, encouraging him to talk up to his betters. And there were fears now that he would yet join with the hardscrabble "poor white," long a jealous antagonist of the Negro, in a wholesale assault on the privileges of the propertied classes.

The thing to do then was to take away his franchise so that it would no longer be necessary to steal his vote. And if vast numbers of unlettered, nonpropertied whites got caught in the same net? That, too, seemed to the captain an inevitable and necessary step. Nor was he anxious to provide either group with the education that, in time, would have enabled them to join the voting classes.

Was he surprised to learn that Sarah held other views? In one of her last letters from Canon City she admonished her father gently:

> . . . Papa, darling, do you really mean what

> you say in regard to poor peoples' being educated? If you do your little lady is very sorry; for she thinks it is a great boon to *some* poor people. Why, my own darling Papa, listen to me. Last Sunday morning one of our Sunday School teachers came up with a sweet girl, apparently sixteen years of age, and said, "Miss Holston, do you understand Latin?" I answered: "Yes, ma'm, I am thorough in Latin." "Well," she said, "here's a young lady who wishes to be coached during vacation."

A poignant rebuke for the captain in his last years. "I am poor," she wrote, "yes, quite poor as far as wealth, of course, goes, but my mind is not poor, for it craves and loves all that's pure, lofty and noble." He kept the letter with some others at his bedside, its contents never far from his thoughts. But in his own writings he would stand by all of his old convictions. We find him little changed in these years from what he had been all along: stern, dogmatic, capable of humor but never of frivolity, perhaps even more disdainful than before about the presumed rights of the nonvoting classes, never doubting that Alabama and the South had acted correctly though perhaps a bit slowly in establishing the ordinances of white supremacy.

But the South, even in post-Reconstruction years, had not always been so harsh in its treatment of the freedman. The captain himself could remember eating with Negroes in the same hotel dining rooms, riding with them in the same rail coaches, drinking in the same bars. He could remember all that even if his children could not. But the romantic flowering of the Old South legend had snuffed out the frail candles of tolerance.

That legend, like the whole movement to deprive the Negro of the vote, had been largely a product of more recent times, all of it a part of the same dark mood, almost as though the legend makers had first to glorify the white man's heritage in order to diminish the ex-slave and his claim to social and political equality. Now began in earnest the Confederate Memorial Day celebrations, the reunions of aging veterans who would remember Forrest's raid on Memphis or Jackson's Valley campaign, the building of Confederate monuments in a thousand courthouse towns, the writing of stories, books, and verses commemorating "all those good times before the war."

Ah! I forgot thee, father, long and oft
When I was happy, rich, and proud, and free;
But conquered now and crushed, I look aloft
And sorrow leads me, father, back to thee. . . .

Even now the legend clings to us like an old vine. By the time of the captain's death, in 1916, the Jim Crow tradition of which it is so intimately a part had become far more binding than mere law — and his children even more ensnared by it than he. The captain's generation had only disfranchised the Negro; the next learned to hold him in contempt as well. In his youngest son, Little Brother, himself now old, we see the final working out of that tradition; we see myth hardened into law, noblesse oblige into something certainly not much better than contempt if superior to it at all.

How then is Little Brother to cope with the presumptions of a black housekeeper he never even saw until a little more than a year ago? She and the old man often have very little to say to each other and have generally kept to their own affairs, she in the kitchen and he at the store or out roaming the pastures. Yet it is chiefly between them, rather than between her and Miss Angie, that the seeds of enmity have sprung up. Is it true, as she keeps reminding me, that she now does pretty much as she pleases, that she goes and comes by the front door and "turns her butt" to the old man's commode whenever it suits her fancy? And what of the shotgun left standing at the foot of the old man's bed? Does he keep it there solely as a reminder to the black woman — a warning that she had best stay in her place and out of the family bath?

No, the real reason (so Lurellia informs us) is that he

wishes to have it handy for late-night sorties against the foxes that have all but taken over his chicken house. We have heard all about that too: all about the times he has leapt wildly out of bed and rushed out of doors to blast away at noises heard in the night, splintering his hen coops, rousing the countryside, killing more chickens than the foxes had stolen. The foxes eventually got all the others and departed, chortling wildly. But the gun still stands there, a long time after it is no longer needed, taking on a meaning of its own. But it quite obviously has not kept the black woman in her place — *or* out of the family bath.

Different Skins, One Blood, Equal Rights

September 1965

Summer again, more sweltering afternoons in the dim kitchen at the plantation house, Eula talking as she works, her voice ever grim and prophetic and untiring: *it's goan be at the church, it's goan be in the town, it's goan be on the streets and in the alleys–war–and everywhere folks goan be talking bout freedom*... A thousand feet marching, a thousand signs raised in protest: freedom now! And so it had turned out. Even as she spoke it was upon us: the fatal spring of 1965, riot, war, and the coming of sweet chariots. For it was then that the movement finally spilled over into the backcountry. It had come first to Selma, and then to all the other little towns and remote hamlets, to all the forgotten places where old customs had hung on longest and were hardest to dislodge — to Eaton, Little River, Colliersville, and finally to the most insignificant place of all: the Catalpa County village of Town Fork, an old old place and quite forgotten, cradled within the junction of the two great rivers of west Alabama, the Black Warrior and the Tombigbee. The demonstrators had appeared there one Saturday afternoon completely without warning and, everyone said, without provocation, carrying signs left over from other demonstrations in other towns.

Freedom now!
Resist Police Brutality!

And then one day they were in New Erie, the county seat, itself a pleasant old town full of storied monuments, old mansions. "This marching business is getting to be quite serious," Lurellia had written. "Some of the young Negroes are acting as if they really want to take over the county." Not long after came word that Little Brother had been forced to "let Big Mose go." Big Mose had been working in the store for years, a loyal hand; yet he had inexplicably fallen in with the agitators. It wasn't that he had been out marching or carrying signs. What it was mainly was that way he had of swelling himself up so big and calling himself "Mr. Washburn." Lurellia had been seeing that in him for a long time. Big Mose had often visited in her home, particularly during my father-in-law's recent illness, and she had always tried to make him feel welcome. The only trouble was, he no longer conducted himself as in the old days. No. For one thing he always made a point of taking the very best chair, even if nobody had invited him to sit down. O! it was a sight to see — the way he would sit there "smoking all those fine cigars and swelling himself up and crossing his legs just as high and mighty as you please." And then, too, there were some who felt that he habitually addressed the Old Gentleman in a manner that smacked too much of an easy familiarity.

So it had come at last to New Erie and Catalpa County. No one had really expected the New Erie phase of the movement to amount to anything, not even Lurellia, who was quick to remind us how little all the marching and protesting had actually accomplished: "They march around town with their signs, and sing some sort of song, and the whites just get off the streets and let them have it for themselves." It was quite a comedown from the excitement of the early days. As an itinerant sojourner in Southern newsrooms I had covered the movement off and on ever since the days of the freedom rides. I had been in Selma, Birmingham, and dozens of other movement towns. After all that, Catalpa County seemed merely a listless rewriting of all the old scripts, a place to catch up on Macaulay or Baudelaire or just to bask in the plain unadorned quiet of the summer afternoons.

But now it was in Mt. Gizeh too. Little Brother had realized something was amiss when he began hearing about all those suspicious meetings down at the black church. And now it was even in his own house, where Eula not only made constant and unapologetic use of the family bath but also presumed to come uninvited into the presence of the white people and to sit there audaciously working her quilt pieces. Little Brother thought of all that with growing consternation as he took his ease each evening on the veranda of the plantation house, the voices of alarm all about him, the protests, the shouts, the sound of the marching feet....

And it was the same each morning at the store. One morning I found him in his usual spot and in more than his usual amount of gloom. I soon guessed the trouble: it was Lyndon again. Little Brother had become increasingly concerned about the "irresponsible behavior" of the president and hoped that something might soon be done to remind him of where he had come from and who his real supporters were. A year earlier he had still held out a great deal of hope for Lyndon. But now he feared that the president had fallen irrevocably into the hands of Martin Luther King and the SCLC conjurers, and would no long be able to carry out his duties effectively.

The old man had been saying all along that Lyndon had better be careful or King and his boys would sneak up on him and give him "a powerful big bellywhack and throw a half-nelson on him and kick him back and front" till he started popping up and down like a jack-in-the-box, saying, "Yassuh, boss. Yassuh, boss." A slow grin and then an abrupt seizure of laughter as the old man contemplated the possibility. And then again the look of apprehension and faint alarm, the sobering thought that Lyndon — try as he might — would be unable to throw off the conjure spell and become the president so many had thought him capable of becoming.

Yet the old man could not entirely rule out the possibility, even now, that Lyndon would ultimately find it in himself to "do what was right by the South and the nigra race." He confessed indeed to a certain feeling of detachment about it all, explaining that maybe we could "still count on Lyndon" because the president was much too shrewd a fellow to be permanently taken in by the likes of Martin Luther King.

But it wasn't Lyndon, the maid Eula, Martin Luther King, or even the movement itself that had thrown him into such a prolonged fit of agitation that morning. What it was was his cows. And Efren Summers. And the growing suspicion that Summers had been responsible for the recent outbreak of cattle thefts in the community. Little Brother had been the hardest hit, the prize heifers disappearing from his herd so fast that he could scarcely keep count. Would I mind tending the store for a while that afternoon while he went out to work up another inventory? Summers, as everybody knew, had long been the community's best-known cattle rustler. He had even served time for the offense, way back during the early years of World War II. Everybody liked to think he had come back from those two years in prison a changed man. But Little Brother had never believed all that talk. For all he could tell, prison hadn't produced a single mark of change in Summers' character. All it had done was protect him from the draft so that now, at an age when most men began turning to the church, he could resume his thieving ways.

At lunch that day the thought of all those cows Summers might or might not have stolen threw the old man into such a tumult that he was suddenly up and gone without having touched his meal. Miss Angie rose behind him, fumbling with her metal walker and pursuing him into the wide middle hall. "Little Brother, where are you going? You haven't finished your nice dinner." He mumbled something which she took to mean that the urgent business in the lower pasture couldn't wait. "Little Brother," Miss Angie said, "you must be careful now. Don't forget that Sister Beth and Cousin Eugene have promised to make us a nice little visit this afternoon."

Cousin Eugene? All the way up from Selma? Usually he waited till none of the rest of us were about, so that he could rummage at will through the ghostly remains of the captain's library, exhuming a Cicero here, a Horace there. To my way of thinking it was Cousin Eugene, not Efren Summers, who most bore watching. No one would even guess how many first editions had already disappeared into his fine plantation home down in Dallas County. But so far he had not disturbed the Macaulay; perhaps Macaulay was just obscure enough to escape his notice. But what of Plutarch, Euripides, Homer, Seneca, the Elder Pliny? None would long be safe from him if it were true, as Lurellia believed it was, that the "little touch of syphilis" he said he had gotten from sitting on a commode seat down in Mobile had finally gone to his brain. She had told us all about that in one of her recent letters, her prominent well-formed hand collapsing suddenly into an all-but-microscopic script, as though she were whispering on paper. Maybe it was only the syphilis that had brought on his aberrant behavior, or maybe it was as Little Brother had so often said—that Cousin Eugene was just plain "natured" that way. At any rate I would have to place the five volumes of Macaulay where he would not discover them and perchance guess their worth. I had already taken down Volume II with the idea of getting a good ways into it that afternoon while I was tending store and Little Brother was out checking on things in the lower pasture.

But as I was leaving the house Miss Angie caught up with me and allowed as how she also had a little piece of business that wouldn't wait. We sat in the front hall, the bookcases on either side of us, the heat of midday pressing in on us through the front screen, the books themselves crammed sideways, upside down, and in no particular order whatsoever, mingled now with the degenerate literature of our own day—the subscription magazines, Sunday School quarterlies, mail-order catalogs, inspirational tracts. What she wanted to ask was whether I would like to write a "nice little story" about the pearl and gold-embossed locket she wore around her neck. It had been in the family since the time of the first settlers, brought to Catalpa County from Cheraw, South Carolina, by an ancestor—a woman—who had thrown a Tory out of the house during the American Revolution. Miss Angie talked about it each year when we came—the locket or some other priceless artifact she hoped I might write up "in some nice little way" when I got back to Atlanta.

Years later I would look back on all that and find myself

thinking that maybe someday I would return there to hear it all again, even though they would all be gone by then. I would sit there in the front hall or in the parlor while she talked about the locket, or the brass andirons that went all the way back to the reign of William and Mary, or the Haviland china, or the nice little cedar chest in the back bedroom, or maybe about the brocaded antimacasser that had also come there from Cheraw—or the set of Bisque figurines that another ancestor had brought from New Market. Or I would go out to the porch or over to the store and listen as the old man told me again what a terrible shame it was that the Yankees had turned all the slaves loose and how distressing it was that Lyndon hadn't lived up to expectations—or asked me what *I* thought about all the young nigras who were so busy marching and "looking into what society has to recommend for black and white" that they couldn't even take the time to get their cotton into the ground.

"A mighty pathetic lot it seems to me. A mighty pathetic lot."

* * *

Back at the store, I discovered something I had not previously suspected and was very sorry to learn: Macaulay was actually quite dull. My interest lagged completely after the collapse of Monmouth's conspiracy against the throne of James II, and I had already put the book aside when an aging black preacher named Octavious Ponds came in to buy some fatback and a gallon of kerosene. The Reverand Ponds, an ardent follower of Martin Luther King, liked to think of himself as a man with nonviolence in his heart and "a good .38" in his pocket. He kept the gun handy not because he had lost faith in King's ideals "but just in case some kind of different technique is needed." He did not have the gun now. But he always made a practice of keeping it about him when he went into town, wearing it every day in the sun under a hot gabardine coat while he was marching. And if anybody came up to him with a taunt or a threat he would draw himself up and say: "Under whose authority do you presume to confront me in this hyah manner?" He would stand there holding his sign in one hand — "Freedom Now!" — and patting something under his coat with the other. "They ain't goan talk me down from my position," he had told me once, "cause I goan talk right back. They goan tell me what they want, and I goan tell them what *I* want. I look them right in the eye and say: 'I ain't goan change my technique just cause *you* a talking.' "

Everyone who knew Ponds said he had acquired much "dignity" during the civil rights years — a fellow, as Little Brother saw it, whose strut was always trying "to get the best of his swagger." He must have been sixty-five or more. He had grown up in the rich farming country below Ellerbe, on the southern boundary of the county, and through hard work, thrift, and a good instinct for cotton husbandry had escaped from the demeaning crop mortgage and tenantry system that held so many of his kind in perpetual bondage. He had land of his own and a house now as well, and he had been one of the first black men in our part of the county to vote and hold himself equal with his white overlords.

Little Brother and Lurellia could both remember Ponds from the days when he and other black church officials had frequently gathered in Mt. Gizeh for their yearly "association" meetings. At such times he would often come in the store with a group of fellow ministers, or with the deacons from his own church, all of them wearing black gabardine suits, hot black even on the hottest days, with black hats to match, and starched shirts, and ties knotted as though to strangle, their apparel so unvarying that one might have mistaken them for hired gunmen in uniforms. They would come in with their big Havana cigars and gather around the tall rickety unlit coal stove, holding themselves high, disdaining old customs, blowing huge smoke rings, filling the place with loud impudent bursts of laughter; all of them, in short, boasting a certain "dignity" that went well beyond what Little Brother had felt was required for interracial harmony. Yes, yes, yes. You could always tell the ones who felt their importance, who preferred the title of "Mr. So-and-So if you please."

None was more dignified than the Reverend Ponds.

"Likes to think of himself as Mr. So-and-So now," Little Brother always said. "That's right. Mr. So-and-So come to call."

Today was no different. Apparently Mr. So-and-So was again in a mood to trample on old store traditions. This time it was a matter of his situating himself presumptuously in the two-seated rocker that Little Brother had always reserved as his own. I found him there when I came back from drawing the kerosene and wrapping the fatback. "Well, here it is, preacher, all ready to go. That'll be one dollar and fifteen cents." He just sat there. Maybe he hadn't heard me clearly. "All wrapped up and ready to go, preacher." He didn't move. He was talking about the old days in the store, just as Little Brother so often had done from the same seat. He seemed perfectly at ease now, his feet propped on the rim of the coal stove, his voice carrying all before it. He obviously had given no thought at all to the possibility that Little Brother might come in and catch him at his little game. A good thing the old man's other worries had called him away that afternoon. Otherwise there might have been trouble, because the old man had "a good .38" too—and had pulled it on Monk Henry once for nothing more than a little back-talk. In his present state of mind he might be unable to distinguish between the genial presumptions of an Octavious Ponds and the active insolence of a Monk Henry, with unfortunate results for everybody.

"One dollar and fifteen cents," I said, "and you be sure and come back when you can."

Mr. So-and-So just sat there, still very much at home, almost as if he had come there purposely to make a scene. Maybe the SCLC had put him up to it, saying, "Somebody's got to force a showdown with that fellow Holston. How about you, preacher?" And yet for all of his diabolical scheming the old preacher seemed an amiable sort. He was just plain old Octavious that afternoon, no longer wearing his mourning suit, hatless now as well, his faded suspenders drawn tight over a white open-collared dress shirt. Short without being squat, his body still lean and elastic after a lifetime of ceaseless labor, he proceeded to treat me with a courtesy—an openness—that all but belied his secret swagger. He had never been close to Little Brother, but he had been on excellent terms with my father-in-law. Maybe that was his mistake: his assumption that Little Brother would be as tolerant and accommodating as the Old Gentleman had always been. Even Monk Henry wouldn't have made that kind of mistake. The Reverend Ponds remembered the Old Gentleman fondly—one of those rare merchants, he used to say, "that don't frown on the colored."

Ponds had put himself out many a time and risked many a frown in his years of trying to get ahead in the white man's world. He had been all around. He had left home at the age of sixteen to take a job in the Birmingham iron fields and had worked there for almost two years, among men hardened and embittered by the labor strife of the 1890s and early 1900s. One day an old Negro man had taken him aside and explained how he had once struck for higher pay only to find himself supplanted by cheap convict labor leased from the state prison system. Perhaps it was then that Ponds had felt the first stir of passions that one day would carry him into the streets with his freedom signs and his hidden revolver. He talked about all that and about all his other travels as he sat there behind the coal stove, not even thinking about getting up or looking around to see if Little Brother had come in, or jumping up to say, "Well, Missa Frank, how yo is? So sorry I is taking yo seatin." Nothing like that at all. He just kept going on and on about all the dirty double-crossing "advancing" merchants he had known and about the landlord down in Ellerbe who had once tried to run his whole family into the ground.

Ponds had had it relatively easy in his early years. But that was while old man Ernest Leyton was still in charge of plantation affairs. Leyton had operated the plantation store and acted as agent for the landowner, a certain Mrs. Adamsley, who had lived throughout a long life on her family's ancestral slave farm in Virginia. Leyton had often gone out of the way to provide tenants with needed assistance.

But when Ponds returned from his travels he found Leyton dead and the plantation in the hands of a man with a reputation for "frowning on the colored."

That first winter, after the new man, Parsons Frye, failed to make good on a promise to provide each of his tenants with the "rent note" they had come to expect — "Wouldn't have dared put a plow in the ground without my rent note" — Ponds went secretly into New Erie (or so he thought) and struck a bargain with Meads & Co., the largest and most influential of the county's old-line supply houses. "A hard lot, them Meadses is," Ponds's father had told him. "A hard lot." But at least they had agreed to give him a rent note. Ponds would pay two bales of cotton toward the use of a forty-acre tract and take care of his own advancing. In this way he could maintain a certain degree of independence. Before signing the agreement, though, he went back once more to Parsons Frye. "Well, Mr. Frye, the year has done come in and I sho do need my rent note." Frye howled with laughter, explaining that he had heard about the preacher's little adventure and had decided to go ahead and rent out the land he had been saving for him. "Looks like you'll have to find yoself another place, 'preacher.' Har, har, har." There was a sharp exchange, and Ponds retreated amid a flurry of threats and curses, daring the merchant (such was the preacher's story anyway) to step outside without his gun and he would "sho deal with him proper."

* * *

I'm not sure how long we had been sitting there when I realized Little Brother had come in the back way. I could feel his eyes on me even before I turned and saw him standing glaring at us from among the unopened crates of canned goods and dishwashing liquid.

"Well, preacher," I said, "it's been mighty nice talking to you about things. And don't forget to come back when you can!"

He went on talking, unmindful of the eyes, the portents, explaining again how brave he was and how he had stood up to Parsons Frye in that long-ago time and how Frye had refused to step outside and engage him in a "fair fist fight." But why didn't the preacher just take his fatback and kerosene and go on?

"You just be sure and come on back now!"

"Sho now. Yassuh. Yo mighty good and kind." Perhaps I too would soon be counted among those who did not frown on the colored. But mainly what I was thinking about now was Little Brother—the eyes, the implacable stare. He still hadn't moved or shifted his gaze; he stood back there busying himself with nothing in particular, waiting, I assumed, for "his reverence" to abdicate the seat he had so rudely usurped.

And then I remembered the pistol. Maybe at any moment he would move to get it out from under the mail cage—or maybe he already had it, back there amid the shadows and clutter, so that the first shot would come without warning—one shot and then another, blowing us scatterwise out of the place and on out across the burning asphalt, where we would be left for carrion. No one would mind. Except that in a day or two someone would come in the store and say:

"Sho is some kind of powerful stink out there, ain't it?" And the old man:

"What else you expect from a nigra?"

But the preacher hadn't thought about any of that. He just went on talking about his confrontation with the villainous Parsons Frye and how he would sho God have taken him down a notch or two if he had dared step outside the store.

"Nawsuh, I never was afeared of no big rich white man!"

Again I could feel the eyes, blazing away from the back of the store, the old man still motionless, waiting. I sat there thumbing my Macaulay, thinking again about the foolhardiness of Monmouth's mission, about the king's hauteur and all those Tory swells gathered around him with their clanking swords, strutting about with a strut that had long ago gotten the best of their swagger and inviting all the dirty Whigs outside for a "faire fiste fyght."

The old preacher was talking now about his years on the Meads plantation and how he had struck up an uncommon friendship with the plantation "rider," a man named Worth

Cheatham, and — in what was the most improbable tale yet — how he had once been invited to a gala luncheon at Cheatham's home in New Erie.

"All them other folks was around that table, about thirty white folks I reckon, they all looking at me, me looking at them; all them white womens, all kinds of white folks — and nobody but me black! But I satisfied myself. I say, 'Well, maybe it's the will of the Lord.' " He stood praying the long prayer expected of him as "guest of honor," all the while squinting at the platters of chicken and ham and roast beef, at the congealed salads and exotic casseroles, at the watermelon-rind pickles and gooseberry sauce, at a bowl of shiny rice speckled with bits of liver; and all about him a blur of white faces, some in spectacles, some in bas-relief, here and there a lush toupee or blue-rinsed coiffure, fat dowagers, matrons full of years, and him stuck there (so he said) at the head of the table, a black man not yet fifty and looking half that; and then began the gracious stares, the nods, the ingratiating voices as they all sat to eat: "Tell me, preacher, how is life in the cottonfield?" All the best people of New Erie there: garden club members, merchants' wives, organizers of the spring cotillion, officers of the Circle 24 Debating Society, their manners impeccable and they themselves full of the imagined grace of their ancestors. And then more nods, more gracious voices:

"Well, preacher, they tell me cotton's doing mighty well this year."

* * *

Little Brother had not yet gone for the gun. Maybe he had forgotten — or had become distracted. And then all at once I could hear him — a half-crazed laugh — a pained gasp for breath — as he bestirred himself noisily about the fringes of the store, kicking things, dropping other things, rummaging around with a great fury among the cobwebs and shadows, suddenly zealous to shelve goods that had sat unopened and untouched for a month or more: a crash here, a bang and clatter there, a random thudding of heavy wooden crates, bottles and tincans tumbling floorward by the half dozens, by the armfuls—boxes of Rinso and baking soda and whatnot pre-empting shelfspace occupied for many years by forgotten vials of Hoyt's Cologne, bottles of Hadacol and Lydia Pinkham's, dusty cartons of liver regulator and black draught laxative. *The Wine of Cardui.* And again the humorless half-frantic gales of laughter that signaled worse trouble to come. At least that's what Big Mose Washburn had always said: "Ain't nothing to joke about when the colonel gets into one of his laughing fits. That's right. Stay out of his way then cause he sho God mad enough to kill." Perhaps, then, we had had enough talk of equal rights for one afternoon.

"Come back when you can, reverend!"

He just sat there. And then again the laughter, the mad shelving of cans and bottles, the shouted invitations to unseen entities evoked without apology out of the old store's remorseless and unshakable gloom.

"Come on in, Moose! Come on in, Big Buck!"

Ponds merely raised his voice an octave and went on as before, his repertoire inexhaustible, his disdain for perfidious advancing merchants equally so. I had heard a thousand such stories, of tenants too illiterate and tradition-bound to see through the merchant's thieving ways, of other tenants who, even if they had some book learning, would never dare stand up to the merchant and demand a proper accounting.

"But," said Ponds, "I just never was goan let no big-talking white man talk me down from *my* position!"

The eyes again, the blazing malevolent stare, the imminent scramble — perhaps — for the hidden .38. But the preacher paid no mind. He just went on talking in that big way of his, showing off his dignity, his uproarious bursts of laughter not quite filling the void left by the cessation of Little Brother's own tumultuous and uncontrollable glee. Meantime the old man had left off his shelving project and had flung himself into the even more pressing business of sacking up the outgoing mail. Was it possible that he hadn't even been aware of the preacher's usurpation? I thumbed my Macaulay, resolving next to take up Baudelaire. There was very little mail, and the large canvas sack, with its full quota of letters and such, was still almost completely empty. He had gone out to deposit it in the large wooden lockbox when Ponds at last got up to leave. The preacher had let the afternoon quite get away from him. He still had important business facing him before he could get home to his ailing wife. He was even now on his way to minister to a young woman who had fallen under the spell of a Sipsey River conjure woman. Preacher Ponds had been ever an avowed enemy of the "hoodooers," so much so that they had repeatedly tried to hoodoo him into extinction. The last time was on a recent Sunday morning when he had mounted to the pulpit to find half a dozen safety pins linked together and stuck ominously in his Bible. Foolishness, that's all. Just plain foolishness. But was he worried possibly that it was more than that? Perhaps—and then again, perhaps not. . . .

"Takes a lot more than a bunch of little old safety pins to get rid of the preacher!"

Little Brother reappeared in the door just as the Reverend Ponds took up his fatback and kerosene and started out.

"Well, you come back, reverend."

"Grant me good fortune."

"Most happily, reverend. Most happily."

"Good fortune to you also. May de Lawd smile on you."

With many obligatory nods and smiles did Little Brother send him on his way. He was struck by Ponds's sudden show of haste and assumed that "his reverence" was departing on a mission "of some terribly excruciating importance." Would the campaign for equal rights languish in his absence? Would the movement for which he had worked so hard fall into an irreversible decline?

"I just never could understand it," he said. "I just never could understand *why* the North hates the South so. It does so look like they'll do almost anything to make life miserable for the Southern people." But as usual he understood much more than he pretended to understand: "It's because we're more cultured than they are, that's why. It's because they're jealous."

He carefully avoided taking the chair where Ponds had

sat, choosing instead one of the two wicker chairs that had been drawn up to the front of the stove. He had fallen into a near-slumber, quite wrung out by the great debilitating gusts of laughter and by his frantic shelving project. After a brief interval during which neither of us spoke, he looked up at me with a look that had something dark and wild in it, allowing as how it was "fretful hot," and him so awful tired, and his heart palpitant with what surely must be the onset of a fatal illness. Perhaps the time had come for him to pay another visit to the doctor. He had put it off too long already and no doubt would have to continue putting it off until he was past all remedy. It all depended, he said, on when Mrs. Lurellia, or myself, or somebody, could find the time to take the old boy into town for a checkup.

He rose once more to tend the mail before remembering that he had already taken care of that chore. He came back and sat down, in the other chair this time. And again he seemed caught up in a wild fluctuation of moods. One moment he would fall into a profound somnolence, his face grim and whiskery and drained of all color. An instant later he would be full of whimsey, anecdotes, aphorisms, old jokes. "Well, son, it's about time. The time has about come. Yes, my boy, it won't be long now—won't be long till they come and stretch your old uncle out on the cooling board." Even this seemed the cause for some merriment. But the laughter quickly subsided. I had not had a chance to respond when all of a sudden he flung himself violently forward, uttering a profound and improbable groan, after which he slowly looked up to assure me that the time was indeed at hand—the time when all the ones from town would come "to lay him out on the cooling board."

"It will soon be time, my son. The hour comes to us all. 'Man that is born of a woman is of few days and full of trouble.' " He lapsed into another brooding calm, out of which might proceed deeper gloom or yet another round of wholesale merriment. " 'He cometh forth like a flower and is cut down; he fleeth also as a shadow, and continueth not.' Yes, my boy, the hour is near, and the day waiteth not, neither does it tarry. Soon be time for all the good folks to line up and say, 'He was a good old fellow, a mighty good old boy. Don't he look natural?' " And then once more a spasm of laughter that seemed quite out of keeping with the solemnity of his thought and with the hour of approaching dusk.

"Don't he look natural? Yessir, the old boy sho does look the very image of himself, don't he? He sho do look natural. . . ."

* * *

The hour had come and it had not tarried. *Don't he look natural*? I, too, was on the "cooling board," struggling awake in the dim hot front bedroom at the captain's house, hearing the footsteps, the voice: "Macaulay! . . . Hey, Aristotle!. . . Plato, hey!. . . ." It was Calloway, rattling the corner screen and telling me to "hurry up and come on now cause we got lots of fishing to get done." My wife was already at the screen, shushing her old would-be seducer, trying to stop him from waking the house. But he went on in that same fanatical voice—"Hey, Longfellow. . . Hey!"—peering merrily in through the vines, his lean face freshly tanned from a weekend trip to the Gulf. "Come on, honey. Where is he? Where's Macaulay? Come on now. Time's wasting. Got lots of fishing to get done. Gonna bring back all the fish in the pond. Gonna win all the big trophies, the Big Buckle. . . ."

We left the house in the first hush of coming day, the grassless yard lost beneath an overarching tangle of crape myrtle and burgeoning quince. "Come on, Macaulay. Be hot soon." By the time we got to the lake the day had fully come, the land already pallid with haze, the sun a fierce splotched glare that looked squarely down on the ruins of the old block manufactory. The sign that had once said

COMER BROS.
Building Blocks
Sand and Gravel

was no longer there. Behind the plant the land fell away heavily to the water; the place was all wild and desert-blown, full of stunted pines and dingy sand and clumps of purple thistle. Calloway led the way down the slope and ventured on out into the shallows, white slacks rolled to his knees, making his first cast with the fly rod he had bought just yesterday in Tuscaloosa.

I did not know Calloway all that well. I had run with him occasionally during my visits to Mt. Gizeh, but never with the idea that we would become close. He was an important member (as I was not) of the old planter aristocracy, an only son whose whole commitment was to a way of life that even now was falling under the scythe of the civil rights movement. He fit the planter stereotype almost exactly: at thirty-four he had already served two terms in the legislature; he got more federal subsidy money each year for not planting cotton than for planting it; he was ever in marital difficulties and had long been a devout follower of the University of Alabama football team.

He had taken a degree at the university — in exactly what I am not sure —but had never put it to any use. Mostly he spent his time in a ritualistic observance of old Black Belt customs. Each morning at nine or thereabouts he would drive the fourteen miles into New Erie to begin his routine. First there would be coffee at Eddie's Grill with the merchant Farley Meads and other members of the town claque. Calloway's friend Sims Krites would usually be there, and sometimes the wealthy cattle rancher Grady Elmore, who had been a member of the county commissioners court for almost as long as Calloway had been alive; seven or eight men in all, gathered there in the ordinary plastic-and-vinyl cafe to talk about what men always talk about at such times: government programs that reward the idle, chasten the industrious, imperil traditional standards of morality and undermine the beef cattle market. Calloway would often leave before the others and drift over to join the domino game at the sheriff's office, an even more important part of the daily ritual. Nobody could expect to get anywhere politically in New Erie or Catalpa County without an intimate knowledge of dominoes. And Calloway, I understood, had become quite good at the game.

Perhaps it was dominoes that would finally win him the Big Buckle. From the way his luck had been running that morning I was pretty sure it wouldn't be fishing. He had exchanged the new fly rod for one of his older models and was standing now at the end of a narrow crescent-shaped sandspit, making long casts toward a deeper part of the lake, waiting for the catch that would win him a banner headline in next week's *Catalpa County Democrat.* But it was still no good, and soon much too hot to continue. I watched him as he slowly rewound the line and turned to join me in the dissipated shade of a single crabbed persimmon tree that had somehow found its way to these barren banks. "All washed up, Macaulay. That's what all this means. Through — finished — all washed up. Ain't no use trying to make excuses. Ain't no use calling the papers and making a big fuss. . . ."

And so back up the sandy rise past the block manufactory and on out to where the pickup was waiting. The five miles from the lake back to the railroad depot at New Mt. Gizeh was a desolate and almost wholly uninhabited stretch of country, mostly pine barrens and palmetto flats. At the end of it, hard upon the railroad itself, stood the squat brick building that Calloway's old man still operated as a general store. That was where Calloway did a lot of his hard drinking —after hours, with some of the boys. But the biggest parties were at his new home, which stood halfway up the wooded knoll from which Mt. Gizeh took its name. There was nothing of the traditional columned planter's house about it; it was all brick and glass and rock-walled fireplaces and paneled dens so full of hunting trophies that there would be no place for the Big Buckle on the chance it ever became his to display. Janice, his wife, was an important part of those gatherings, a dark nervous willowy girl, full of whimsical bursts of merriment and long swallows of lemon-flavored gin. The community had been disappointed though not too surprised to hear that she and Calloway were having trouble. I assumed it was because of all his other women. Of course, it wasn't really the running around that he cared about. What it was, as he explained it to me, was the "principle of the thing."

"Folks always telling me how they so well cared for at home they don't have to bother messing around. But that's not the point, Macaulay. You know that. It's the principle of the thing. That's all I'm talking about, Macaulay — a matter of principle."

* * *

It was Calloway who brought back to Mt. Gizeh most of the news of what was happening in town. He would come in the store each morning to get his mail and often take time to boast of what he and the other domino players had done to sabotage the New Erie civil rights campaign. Sometimes he would leave Little Brother feeling despondent and uncertain as to where it would all end. But on the whole the old man felt very good about the way things were going, not because Lyndon had done a single blessed thing expected of him, but simply because it now seemed obvious to almost everyone that King and his gang had about played out their hand. He could see so clearly the great evil of Martin Luther King that he felt certain the young nigras would soon begin to see it too — to see how falsely the man had played on their hopes, how he had built them up only to doom them to a big letdown. He couldn't understand exactly what it was King was hoping to accomplish anyway. It always had been something of a mystery to him, right from the beginning. But maybe on the other hand it wasn't so great a mystery after all: King's real aim obviously had been "to puff up the young nigras with more dignity" than they were capable of handling and then let the consequences fall where they may. "A mighty sad and tragic development it seems to me."

What little news we didn't get from Calloway we could glean from my mother-in-law's letters. "I see that the recipient of the peace prize is at his '*peace*!' agitations again," she had written in early March, "and God knows when, where, or *how* it will end." King had traveled all through the backcountry in the days before Selma, preaching revolution in the name of loving kindness, exacting his measure of tribute, striding at will through a countryside already harkening to spring, a land fragrant with jasmine and pink camellias. And then in May had come for the first time to New Erie, gathering the multitudes about him "out beyond the overhead bridge" and telling them that "they could trample all over the white people of Catalpa County."

"A mighty pitiful spectacle," Little Brother had said. "And a mighty sad thing it is to think about all the sorrow he has brought into this old world."

He was just thankful that most of "the good decent nigras" had had the sense to stand up to King and his crowd. There were always people like that, everywhere the civil rights demonstrators had been — black landowners, small businessmen, educators, and a lot of other people who for one reason or the other had a stake in the white man's world. The leader of the black anti-King faction in New Erie was C.M. Putney, a motel operator and merchant whose place of business stood less than a block away from the church that had been the scene of most of the civil rights rallies. I had seen him there once or twice, a man not quite round, glaring out at the marchers from behind the windows of his grocery store. He had already lost all standing in the movement by then. I had been at the church the night he had gone up to make his last appeal for moderation. He had made the speech many times: "We don't need the demonstrations and we don't need the boycott." When the time had come to bring in the federal voting registrars, he had opposed that too: "We don't need them folks in here. We don't need the registrars and we don't need the boycott and we don't need all this marching up and down. All we need is for people to go on down there to the courthouse and register to vote. Those people just sitting down there waiting for you folks to come in." But nobody wanted to hear that kind of talk out of Putney anymore, and suddenly the crowd was shouting him down:

"What you say, Putney? You gone *rashus*, Putney. What you say?"

And then a single voice rising above the others: "Putney gone rashus. We ain't gonna get nothing out of Putney. Let's kick him out!" Putney still had some friends, not many, but as many as he did have, maybe half a dozen in all, had gathered about him in a protective circle as he pled against the commandolike tactics of the SCLC. "What you say, Putney? What you say?" It was the SCLC that had gone rashus now, its leaders crowding in on him, gesticulating, issuing threats. He had come down out of the pulpit and was standing in front of the communion table, short, almost round, and soon invisible inside the gathering knot of "enforcers." And then more jeers and mocking laughter and cries of "Putney gone rashus... Putney sho gone rashus now" as his tormentors bumped him on out into the dark. One morning not long after that Putney woke to find himself and his store the first targets of the boycotters. By eight o'clock the pickets were already marching up and down along the edge of the street. "Black Honkey! Putney Must Go!" He still went back to the church occasionally and attempted to make himself heard, hoping that the assembly would indulge him for the sake of his past contributions or at least not threaten to kick him out again. But mostly all he did was stand there behind the windows of his store, staring out at the hot pavement, the marchers, remembering how it was in the days before the SCLC had come.

Summer found him there, and the August dog days. And it found the movement at the same old stand. At least once each day, and usually more than once, there would be a rally at the old AME Zion Church where Putney had spoken and where he was still chief elder. Sedley Jones, the affable Town Fork preacher who had emerged as leader of the Catalpa County civil rights movement, would be there to talk about the marching and the boycott. "Let the baloney rot," he would say. "Let the cheeses rot. The vegetables and fruits and the big steaks, let all them things rot." Some people, Putney sympathizers mostly, had refused to go along with all that. We had heard those stories too: about the black men and women who, even if they were in the march, would sometimes put down their signs of protest long enough to duck into Meads & Co. or into the Yellow Front and make a furtive purchase; about the black shoppers who found themselves assaulted by their own kind outside the A&P or Foodworld, their groceries emptied on the pavement, their bags of flour and cornmeal split open; about all the others who fought off the "enforcers" with bottles of cold drinks and ax handles.

The chief of the enforcers was an SCLC itinerant named George Sampkins, a humorless young man bitter with the frustrations of countless other civil rights campaigns in towns already half forgotten, the ugly memories stacked up inside him like empty boxes in a cluttered pantry. Was the Putney crowd unable to understand what the boycott was all about? More jobs for blacks — better pay — fairer treatment? Sampkins would provide instruction: "We just kind of tear them up now and then," he told me one evening over beer at the Silver Buckle, the black nightspot where most of the movement leaders hung out. "Of course," he said, "we do it all nonviolently. They know we ain't gonna kill them."

If the enforcers were unable to trap an offender on the street or in an alley somewhere, they would follow him out to his home and "bottle out his windows" or maybe go on inside and scatter the sacks of newly purchased groceries about the kitchen, taking what was edible for their own use and urinating on the rest. Some would still hold to their own inclination, scorning the SCLC edicts, all through that turbulent summer and on into the fall; but others would support the boycott rigorously, driving wherever necessary — the thirty miles into Tuscaloosa or the forty miles into Meridian — to keep from doing business with New Erie merchants. And Sedley Jones would stand up there in the church and say: "Let them things rot. Let them pumps stand full of gas, let them shelves overflow, them stockrooms fill up, them trucks stand unloaded. Let all them things rot."

And often now there was another at his side, the young street marcher Cyrus Blue, himself recently up from the village of Town Fork, lean, angry, well over six feet tall, not yet wearing the Fu Manchu that one day would further distinguish him as a man of vigilance and daring. He too would stand up there in the pulpit, exhorting the angry young, the not-so-angry old: *I believe we can live better in the world. I believe we can have freedom in the world, for God in all generations has raised up men to cast down the evil altars. Are such men among us even now?* As he talked one could feel that it was so: the old AME Zion Church full of men no longer fearful, anxious now to tear down the altars of racism and despair, to root out evil wherever it lurked grinning. I had thought Blue was a man of eloquence. But Calloway explained that he was only a "cotton-patch nigger." And the old man said, "They've got to show off *all* their dignity now." And Blue: *I believe we are made of the same order other men are made by. . . I believe that we can be stronger and better, and the world made stronger and better because we have lived.*

* * *

And always there were marchers in the streets, summer and fall, hot days and cool, shouting and praying and singing, not as in the old days, with their heads inside a washpot, but out in the open now, out in the sunlight, in front of mayors, sheriffs, aldermen, judges, always marching and singing, raising their standards of protest:

> *Freedom now!*
> *Jim Crow Must Go!*
> *I Dreamt I Was Sheriff In This Big Honkey Town!*

At first there were only the young, the outsiders — the ones Eula had called "the hairy faced folk." And they had come only in small raiding parties, eight or ten to a group, looking around for places to get thrown out of—the theater, the hotel coffee shop, the hotel itself, all the places that were now open to black people — supposedly — under the new public accommodation laws.

One morning they had come to the little restaurant where Calloway and his coffee claque gathered for morning political discussions. They appeared there, only six of them this time, just as the claque was getting into some really heavy cursing of all the new federal desegregation laws that had come down. They took seats along the counter, staring at Eddie's tall chrome-plated coffee urn, at the back of Eddie's head, at the jars of nabs and peanuts, at the racks of Chiclets and Lifesavers and breath sweeteners. Calloway rose to greet them with an exaggerated show of politeness while Eddie served them Cokes, Dr. Peppers, and raisin cakes.

"How much?" one of them said.

"Twenty-five cents apiece for the drinks. Twenty cents for the cakes."

The intruders looked at one another, grumbling about the steepness of "the white man's price." But Eddie said,

"It's all on the menu."

They quickly finished the snack and went out. And the claque applauded. But the next day they were back, thinking perhaps that there had been some mistake. Maybe this time Eddie would refuse them service — or maybe smash their glasses after they had finished drinking, the way I had seen it done in New Jersey bars. Something at least so that they could call in the law and then go out to proclaim the dramatic undoing of another grim bastion of racism. But again Calloway greeted them with a beguiling manner and exaggerated show of hospitality — a ruse (he informed us) that had left all their plans in ruins. Again they drank their pop and quickly departed, still lacking a creditable bastion of racism to attack.

But presently they found one: the white swimming pool. Calloway told us about that too — how they had marched on the mayor's office one morning to demand the opening of the white pool to black swimmers. Calloway had been there as a representative of the Town Domino Players. "You all know how the mayor is. He just welcomed them all in and said, 'Well, boys, have a seat, won't you? What can I do for you this fine morning?' And they all said, 'We wants in the white pool.' And the mayor he just laughed. You all know how the mayor is. He said, 'Well, sir, it's mighty hot. A mighty hot morning. Yes, indeed. It sure is a mighty good morning for some swimming. But I'm afraid it's just not in the cards, boys. Afraid not.' You all know how the mayor is."

We knew him well, a great commanding figure of a man, silver-haired, with some humor though not with enough to see the joke of a black agitator in the white pool.

" 'No sir, I'm afraid the council just won't allow it, boys.' That's what the mayor told them. 'Afraid not, boys. And besides, you boys got your own pool now—bigger than the white folks' pool—newer—and it cost a lot more too.' So they all say, 'We ain't negotiating. We *demanding*. This here's a non-ne*go*tiable, demand.' And the mayor, he says, 'I see, boys. I see. Ha, ha, ha. Non-negotiable, eh. Well, I was about to say the same thing. I was about to say that there just ain't nothing to negotiate, because, you see, boys, the council members, they've already made their policy clear, and they gonna stick by it: no nigras in the white pool.' "

And they had stuck by it. They had later closed both pools rather than submit to movement demands. But at least it had given the protestors an issue. It was only after that—after the session in the mayor's office — that the real marching had begun. The non-negotiators had gone straight back to the church with the news:

"Mayor Swint say he ain't gonna open the white pool!"

"Say what?"

"Mayor Swint say he ain't gonna open the white pool!"

Then let his answer be a thousand shouts, a thousand mighty songs, a thousand marching feet!

And so it began at last, in the hot bright sun of the soft spring morning, the line of march forming very quickly in front of the church, the whole student body from nearby Carver High School turning out to join the procession, and more people arriving all the time, the marchers moving out along the highway past Putney's place and old man Sam Underwood's television repair shop and across the viaduct and on around the long uphill curve into town, their standards of protest raised, their mournful songs aloft:

Integrate the Swimming Pool!

When the spirit say move
I gonna move along. . . .

All spring and summer it had been like that, the armies of liberty in the streets, alarm bells in the night, shouts at the gates of the Bastille, the gates themselves down, the fortifications in disarray, the defenders shot from the parapets. . . . And now, in August, there was talk that as many as half a dozen of New Erie's old established commercial houses were about to go under as a result of the boycott. Yet the town had held firm through it all, refusing to open the white pool or change hiring policies, rejecting out of hand all non-negotiable demands. Hence Little Brother's feeling that Lyndon wouldn't have to be called in on the job after all. It seemed to him beyond argument that the movement was already in its last stages, a disgusting conspiracy fomented by dagoes and therefore doomed to early failure, soon to be numbered among all those other nonsensical aberrations out of our national past. Like the Emancipation Proclamation or the Fourteenth Amendment. Let the demonstrators appear at the very door, full of insults and newfound dignity, the rope already in their hands — "All right, old man, let's go" — and I believe he would have felt much the same, no great sense of alarm, no disgust, only a profound regret that so many of the young had been so roundly deceived. Let them present themselves there even in their most rebellious mood and he would simply reason with them in a good fair way, explaining what King had done and what Lyndon had done and what Wallace had done. And then they would say, "Well, Missa Frank, you right. You right, Missa Frank." And then they would all go back to their broken-down front porches, and bend again to the inevitable harvesting of cotton, singing their poignant songs as they came in from the fields at sunset, as they always had in those "good times before the war," all of them embarrassed now to know that they had indeed been hoodwinked, taken in, played upon for no other purpose than to further the ambitions of Martin Luther King.

But not everyone shared his feelings. "People are becoming greatly concerned about all this marching," Lurellia had written. "Judge B. told D. that T.W. had told him that some of the young Negroes had been heard to say that they really *do* want to take over the county."

* * *

Eula, too, had become more active that summer, probably because of her growing friendship with Beatrice Montgomery, a black storekeeper who at one time had represented about all the civil rights movement there was in Mt. Gizeh. One morning I had gone over to her place seeking an interview. Eula had told me how to get there: down the hard surface as far as the old Negro schoolhouse, then up a dirt road that ducked under a patch of low-hanging trees and ran on out toward the black church. Just this side of the church, atop a steep red-clay bank, was the decaying ruin of a building where Beatrice Montgomery kept store. There were steps carved into the bank and more steps leading from the top of the bank to the porch. I had never known the store was there. And I had never even seen Beatrice Montgomery. Eula, fortunately, had phoned her that morning and cleared the way for me. "He from up dar," she had explained, somewhat incorrectly. "From de nawth." That surely was enough to guarantee me a civil reception. Or was it? Mrs. Beatrice sat at the back, almost invisible amid the inevitable clutter, her face slightly concave, her manner unfocused.

"Who dat? What you want hyah?"

She rose as she spoke, wearing an apron larger than her dress, constantly scooping it up to mop away a rash of perspiration. She had a fan too, one of the last of its kind—one of the last, that is, to bear a likeness of Jesus rather than of Martin Luther King. But fan and apron were not enough. The sweat hung on her like a three-day growth of beard. And then I realized I could understand almost nothing of what she was saying. The sentences tumbled out in disarray, a great billowing murk of words, darkly resplendent—words, phrases, whole paragraphs merging without transition or coherence, like James Joyce in Southern patois, yet all of it with an eloquence beyond mere words— a whole history there of street beatings, vicious jailings, despicable "advancement" merchants who made her kind "pay and repay," fat sassy cops, big sheriffs with police dogs held anxiously at the leash, jackbooted Nazis — and, yes, always the barricades — the barricades of Selma and the barricades of a thousand other nameless cities alike indistinguishable. All of it an unfathomable blur, like a newsreel spun wildly out of control: visions of Lester Ritchie, heavyset, bearded, ready for war, of Martin Luther King in the door of a thousand dimly lit churches, talking about "different skins, one blood, equal rights."

And again the clangor in the streets, the barricades by twilight and noonday, the big fat-assed cops with their billy clubs raised, shouting, "You all don't go past hyah! You all go past hyah we gonna kill all of ya!" And the marchers all "holding their nerve" and going on into and around the barricades, and the billy-clubs coming down, and the big cops moving in with tear-gas "towers" on their shoulders, and the gas wafting up violently, nightsticks in a fog of gas. Yes, and the memories — visions — of a thousand unspeakable nights in a thousand stinking oppressive one-horse jailhouses, a thousand marchers crammed a hundred to a room — and most of all the night they had spent at the state patrol camp near Selma, the single large room with a hundred vanquished men to share a single commode, a single spigot, a single drinking cup: the din and clangor of countless demonstrations and countless beatings, stark immutable visions evoked, raging, out of grimmest despair here in a back-country store in a place so remote and forgotten that the post office was still flying a forty-nine-star flag six years after Hawaii had been admitted to the union.

I had said very little and would leave now, calmly, smiling even, quite nonchalantly in fact. She rose again and came toward me, in that same drench of rage, heavily, inexorably, her mien ferociously composed, her billowy apron rising like magic and her body vanishing behind it, hugely, her hands appearing suddenly to renew the violent scrubbing motion. I fell back in some haste, anxious for the sun.

All over Alabama the lamps are out. Yes, it had been very nice talking to her and I would be certain to come back when she had more time and we could talk at more leisure. Shall these bones live? I gained the porch, the steps, and finally those other steps carved directly into the bank. I could hear her coming out behind me, still talking clamorously, violently, in that Joyceanlike patois out of which only one word seemed to emerge with unmistakable clarity:

"Kill!"

* * *

The next time I saw her she was in the march, driving alongside it rather, in her battered Chevy pickup, shouting at the ones standing watching from the sidewalk: "Hey honkey? Hey fat-ass? You happy wid your money?" The truck had become a familiar sight all up and down the back roads of the Mt. Gizeh community as Mrs. Beatrice went about seeking recruits for the movement. We even saw it one afternoon at the captain's house. That was the afternoon Eula was to accompany her on an expedition to the Tombigbee river settlements. Almost as she was leaving she told me:

"You kin go too. I already talk to Mrs. Beatrice. She say, 'Who he?' I say, 'He from up dar.' She say, 'Okay.' "

We set out at a little after three o'clock. The way led down past the old block manufactory and then west on a clay road to an alluvial section of river bottom country known as "the Flats," a mysterious brooding land neither earth nor water—water during much of the year when the river was up, dry land and prolific with cotton and corn and watermelons during the growing season, though not entirely free of water even then. Even in the driest summers and on the hottest days the "slews" stood deep in water—murky stagnant pools choked with the decay of old forests, insect-swarmed, scum-ridden. There was always good hunting down there. The best of it was beyond the Flats in what some called the "Low Flats" and others the "Big Field," a two- or three-hundred acre tract intensely grown over with junglelike thickets, rife with rattlesnake dens and eerie marshes, yet with much open land too—clearings dominated by pine thickets and prickly pear and watermelon patches and small hills of drifted sand.

To this strange netherworld came duck hunters by the score, quail hunters, grouse hunters, deer hunters. The deer hunters came on cold November weekends, to set up their stands along the edge of the river and wait there crouched and still while the hounds gathered themselves for the chase. The tumult would come drifting down out of the distant thickets, random and searching, full of a dim rich lulling clangor. And then you could hear it coming closer, and see it too: the wild vivid chase, hauntingly reminiscent of the painted tableaus in a thousand lamplit taverns — the fleet dusky shape of the running buck, the hounds in full cry now as the first huntsmen took aim; the deer instinctively seeking the safety of the river and then shot over into it, blood streaming the water, antlers sticking above it: again the painted tableau, again the cherished trophy for a paneled den in Homewood or Mountain Brook. In the time of the high water other hunters came, to shoot the small game (and sometimes the large game as well) that had retreated to the few remaining plateaus of high ground; good hunting then for the natives as well as for weekend sportsmen's clubs, squirrel and rabbit for the rustic table, more mementoes for Birmingham trophy rooms.

Beatrice Montgomery had found it good hunting too. The people of the Flats were among the most impoverished in all of the Alabama backcountry, and none were more ignorant of what "society" might be able to recommend for their betterment. Society, however, was no stranger to these parts; in one guise or another it had been finding its way here for many years. First had come the government workers of the thirties, the farm agents and home supervisors, to teach the black people the trick of crop diversification and to instruct them in up-to-date homemaking and canning techniques, to take care of the "advancing" that many merchants were no longer able to supply, to arrange loans so that some of the tenants — the more ambitious and responsible — might acquire land and homes of their own. But in all of that time nothing had really changed. And then years later had come the first of the civil rights workers, anonymous bearded young men who summoned the tenants into churches where blankets hung over the windows and talked long and eloquently about the Supreme Court and Equal Protection and the right of all men to be free. But nothing had changed that time either.

It did not begin to change in any important way until the coming of Beatrice Montgomery. Her visits grew more frequent as the summer of 1965 drifted to a close, and there were few times now when Eula wasn't at her side, ready to climb down from the truck and join her in a perfervid if disjointed discourse that somehow stirred passions left unaroused by all of those anonymous young men who had come there from Atlanta and Birmingham.

And it was always the same discourse, the same murk of words, without beginning or end; Mrs. Beatrice scooping up her billowy skirt to wipe away the beard of sweat and talking frantically about "different skins, one blood, equal rights," telling her listeners — shrunken women in bandanas, old men in underwear shirts — what Lester Ritchie had said in Selma, what King had said, what George Wallace had said. And how all the sassy fat-assed cops had "got their pistols on and got their walking sticks" and their tear-gas "towers" and how they kept on "running around and around and around" and how the blacks kept on running, too, "and getting hit and knocked with the sticks" and fogged with the towers, and how they didn't care because they weren't going to turn around anymore. No, they were going on past the barricades and to jail if necessary. And, of course, it was necessary. It was always necessary, because freedom was waiting for them there inside all the cramped jailhouses of the land. It had even been waiting for them on the night of the big roundup at Camp Selma.

She would never leave out that story: how she and the other marchers had been herded into the place to find George Wallace standing in the door with all his bodyguards, jabbing the air with a stubby finger and saying, "Don't you all let them nigguhs in hyah!" And someone else saying, "It's okay, George. This ain't the university — this here's just the jailhouse." And then him realizing his mistake and falling all over himself just to get out of the way so they could all get inside, a hundred of them to share the single commode, the single spigot, the single naked lightbulb.

All of that and more the two women would explain as they stood there on one of those falling-down front porches with its inevitable Kenmore washing machine or in a hot airless room crowded with worn-out furniture and hung with green shades pricked full of tiny glittering holes. And then Mrs. Beatrice would say:

"You all gots to pray now. You all gots to pray that God'll knock George Wallace in the head."

Eula had prayed the prayer many times: "O, Jesus, you *sho* gots to let that Wallace be hit!" She had talked about the strategy one afternoon at the captain's house. "We say, 'You all *better* pray now, cause we got to get Jesus to hit that Wallace. We sho gots to get him knocked in the head.' " We were in the kitchen again, and dark coming on, and the old man and Miss Angie both in the wide middle hall, waiting for dinner.

"We tell em they got to pray against Wallace *all* the time. That's right. We knock him in the head, we pray."

Knock him in the head first or pray first?

"We pray and then *God* goan knock him in the head. That's whut we tell em—say all us colored got to pray to God so God'll let somebody hit him."

But what about King and nonviolence?

"Ain't none of our colored goan hit him. We ain't praying that. We jes praying that God goan *let* him be hit."

A Little Taste of Dates and Almonds

November 1965

In the autumn there came a lull. But even on the coldest and dreariest days, the movement was never far from the streets of New Erie. It was still there when we went back to Catalpa County for the Thanksgiving holidays. And Little Brother was still wondering, just like always, how long it would be before Lyndon found it in himself to stand up to King and his gang. The real trouble, he felt, now that he'd had time to think about it further, was that the president had lacked the proper training as a youth—no one to sit him down and talk to him straight from the shoulder, saying, "Be a man, son! Be a man!" And now New Erie and Catalpa County were paying for it. "And a mighty pitiful spectacle it is too," Little Brother said. "Mighty sad and tragic."

Business failures had come in bunches that fall. One of the first to feel the impact of the boycotters was the haberdasher, Thomas Empson Lord. Lord's store was in the same block as Mayor Swint's grocery, directly opposite the courthouse, and had been a fixture there since before the turn of the century. Now there was a "for rent" sign in the window. The Yellow Front had closed in early October, and Bill's Dollar Store soon after that. And now there was talk that Porter's Meat Market might go under. Even the prestigious Meads Department Store ("On the Square since 1879") had been struggling to ward off bankruptcy. And still the demonstrators were there, almost every day, with their protests, their signs, their non-negotiable demands, marching up and down the street in the rain, and the lookers looking out from behind their windows.

But there had been no violence to speak of — no barricades or tear-gas canisters to intimidate the marchers, no police dogs held warily at the leash. Maybe New Erie had learned something from all those other places where attempts to thwart the demonstrations had only led to worse trouble. There were a lot of people, though, who thought the town was going about it all wrong. They couldn't understand why Sheriff Fred Cain and the other law enforcement officials had allowed the marchers to take over the streets and why so little had been done to crush the boycott. Calloway, the sheriff's fellow domino player and political confidant, had felt the same way about it at first. But now he had come around to a different way of thinking. "It's just like the sheriff says: You can't stop them nohow. The government's already said you've got to let them march. You can't even give one of these niggers the finger or tell them to kiss your ass or so much as squirt them with a goddamn squirt gun without some fancy-ass federal judge handing down a decree accusing you of violating their constitutional rights."

So mostly the sheriff had just let them march. His no-barricades policy had confused almost everyone, the Wallace people in Montgomery, the town merchants, the state patrol, which had offered to help put up the barricades, and the marchers themselves — perhaps the marchers most of all. Every day they came into town hoping that this would be the day when the sheriff would finally lose his patience and throw up the barricades and come at them with tear gas and police dogs. And then maybe they could get the headlines and the television exposure that they had so far lacked. But it just hadn't worked out that way. And every night Sedley Jones and the others talked about it out at the AME Zion Church: "You gotta march like the spirit say march. You gotta do what the spirit say do. And the spirit say, 'Provoke that mayor to some action. Provoke that sheriff to some brutality.' If you want to be free, you gotta be willing to go to jail, you gotta be willing to suffer, you gotta get some aggravation going. . . ."

And then one day, to break this unseemly calm, a single-engine crop-duster swooped low over the marchers and belched down a lusty spray of cotton pesticide. Some of the town merchants had gathered at the upper end of Taschahatchie Avenue to watch the show. The plane made two passes, leaving an insidious billow of DDT to hang there motionless in the hot still afternoon while the marchers scattered, gasping, for shelter, their nostrils burning, their tongues coated with what Calloway called "a little taste of dates and almonds." It was the first time all summer that the respectable people of the town had found anything to applaud. And it may be that C.M. Putney, the onetime movement leader recently purged by the SCLC, was not entirely displeased as he stood watching it all from the window of his nearby grocery store. Nobody ever found out who the pilot was. But Calloway, I discovered, had been one of the chief instigators of the plot. Not that he meant any real harm: "We wasn't wanting to see anybody get hurt. We just wanted them to get a little taste of how it feels to be on the other side."

* * *

The marchers marched on in spite of the cotton poison, in spite of the heat of the August dog days, in spite of November cold. And then one day my brother-in-law and I drove the fourteen miles into town to see it for ourselves, what the SCLC's crudely lettered handbills had called another "March Against Injustice." The day had been rainy and cold and now a heavy mist hung over the town, with a promise of more rain to come. At three o'clock we could hear the first mournful strains of a freedom song drifting up from the Negro quarter. We walked the half block from Eddie's Grill to the square and stood there amid a white villalike cluster of court buildings—the courthouse itself much the largest — waiting for the climactic appearance of the drums and banners. But there were no drums and banners, only the marchers. They were a bedraggled lot, moving slowly across the railroad viaduct and around the long curve past Mabry's Chevrolet dealership and on up the last rise into town, singing:

Mississippi River
is deep and wide.
Gonna find freedom
on the other side.

And then we could see the others: men inside of stores looking out, faces grim, hands opening and clenching, mouths loud and angry and impotent behind the plate-glass windows: *goddamn niggers out here wasting their time marching all over the goddamn town that goddamn Martin Luther Coon son of a bitch had him in jail once and they let him out, the bastards. Sure just ask any of our decent niggers around town and they'll tell you right quick what those SCLC bastards are saying how they're telling all the niggers they'll lose their welfare if they don't get out and join the goddamn march. Sure by god just ask any of our decent niggers and they'll tell you all about some of the goddamn lies that are being spread....*

The starers — most of them — had congregated in the Western Auto or in Mayor Swint's grocery, the only retail outlets other than Meads Department Store still open on the south side of the square. All over town the impact of the boycott was dramatically evident—a glower of empty stores, shuttered windows, "for rent" signs. And yet the town had changed remarkably little for all that. Time had not changed it in any basic way, except for the paved streets and the parking meters and the three traffic lights; nor had the boycotters. Even in the rain and cold of the November afternoon the town managed to seem as discreetly aristocratic and as smugly content as in the days when it served as hub to the wealthiest cotton-producing region in the state. It had never much held with the conventional ideas of progress even in the great days of the New South boom. When the industrial promoters came, back during the last quarter of the nineteenth century, New Erie turned them away. And it had been doing the same ever since, passing up the material benefits of New South prosperity along with most of its attendant evils. Here one could find no sprawling fortresslike factory complex built by Yankee dollars and begirt by a linked iron fence tall enough to prevent the escape of the tallest and most agile prisoner of a textile loom—no mill village with its long rows of barracklike houses clinging to a red ravine or to a bare spot of ground beneath monotonous stands of scrub pine and blackjack oak. One often thinks of those places, a thousand of them all over the South, the little railroad towns and textile villages, each identical to every other, each inevitably dominated by a company-store mentality and by a plain white clapboarded church where scowling evangelists speak of Judgment Day while overlooking the judgment already at hand....

Mississippi River
is broad and deep,
Gonna find rest
for my aching feet.

The marchers came on up past Meads & Co. and then slowly along Taschahatchie Avenue past the staring men behind windows, still singing, circling around to the west lawn of the courthouse.

Meantime the sheriff had appeared, big, strong, merry. "This ain't nothing today," he told us. "Same old bunch as always. But there've been times that if you coulda been here you coulda really seen a show. Lots of times we've had em in here by the hundreds—enough niggers to fill up the whole town and still a long line of em reaching back out Taschahatchie Avenue. How many are there today? Forty? Fifty?"

He stood there only half alert, yet ever watchful, wearing a scuffed windbreaker, an open-collared shirt, and an old felt hat, carrying a nightstick, no gun. He had been sheriff for more than twenty-five years and before that an all-American tackle at the University of Alabama.

"Naw, this ain't nothing today. But you sure ought to see some of the crowds we get, and hear some of the things they say—vicious things. Like the time one of them niggers looked over here at me and me just minding my own business and said, 'Look at that old sheriff standing over there smoking his big old pipe and grinning. Well, next year, we the ones that's gonna be sitting over there and he gonna be the one that's out here marching.' See what I mean? They can get real vicious sometimes. And them signs — always carrying them signs. Lord knows where they get em. Last time they come up here they had a sign that said, 'Integrate the Bowling Alley.' And we ain't even got a bowling alley. The last bowling alley we had around here closed down during the Depression. So you see? That shows you who's behind this thing. . . ."

Except that this time there were no signs, only the marchers, the songs:

If the spirit say mourn
I gonna mourn, O Lord
I gonna do
what the spirit say do . . .

". . . Keeping the whites off em — that's the main thing. Now it don't matter to me what these niggers say. I just let em talk, cause I'm used to it, and it ain't gonna hurt me none. But some of these whites — you gotta watch em, cause they ain't used to hearing that kind of talk out of niggers. A couple of times we could've had some real trouble around here. But it's like I been saying all along: You might as well let em march, cause you can't stop em nohow. Look what happened to me. One of them comes up to me one afternoon and just kind of walks into my nightstick and falls down, and that night they had me on the Huntley-Brinkley for it."

That's the kind of thing that made Fred Cain mad — all these attempts at provocation — niggers coming up and knocking themselves down with your nightstick, or maybe ramming their legs into the mouths of police dogs, the way they did up there in Birmingham that time, or backing into electric cattle prods, or walking around in a fog of cotton poison. . . .

"But there ain't no use of even trying to stop em. The government's done said you got to let em march. All day and all night, too, if that's what they want."

He watched them now as they gathered at the side of the courthouse, drawn up in a shivering clump, without their signs, singing tranquilly as the young man Cyrus Blue stepped forward to deliver the climactic speech:

"Sometimes when I'm lying in my room at night — sometimes when I'm lying there unable to sleep and all the dreams of my waking hours haunting me — sometimes when I'm lying there and thinking about all the evil in the world, I ask myself, 'When is America gonna change? When is it all gonna change? When is Alabama gonna change? When is Catalpa County gonna change? . . . .' "

"Listen at that," the sheriff said. "You see what I mean? Just plain damn vicious."

Blue stood on a low stoop with his back to the door of the courthouse, a sinewy young man in shirtsleeves, dependably eloquent before crowds if sometimes wary and withdrawn in private interviews. A cold breeze began to stir, bringing intermittent gusts of rain, whipping up a conspiracy of mist and heavy gloom. But Blue's voice triumphed over it all:

". . . I ask myself over and over, 'When is it all gonna change, O Lord? When are New Erie and Catalpa County gonna change? When will all men walk as brothers and raise together a single cry of freedom!' "

"He ain't nothing," the sheriff explained. "Just another field nigger that's got above himself. The SCLC, they took him across the river and taught him how to get past the stoplights and stuff like that. But he ain't nothing, and his folks ain't nothing. He don't know nothing and can't do nothing for nobody and all them niggers out here on a day like this fooling away their time with him. Thinks he's something, though — calls himself *Reverend* Blue now."

Seemed as how the reverend had been going around telling everybody that the sheriff had clubbed him half senseless one afternoon during an SCLC sit-in in the office of Roger Meads, the millionaire lawyer who had served off and on over the years as a deputy district solicitor. Blue's reason for going over there was to seek a warrant for the arrest of one of the city policemen. The way he told it, the sheriff had come in looking for big trouble, laying about him with his nightstick. But maybe there was more to it than that. Maybe Blue just tried to get up in too much of a hurry and bumped into it.

"What else can you expect out of a bastard? I mean, a *literal* bastard. That's what I meant to tell you the first time, how he ain't even got no father or mother either one. Lives down there at Town Fork with his grandfolks. A literal bastard, and the other kind too. But he calls himself the *Reverend* now."

Cain liked to think of himself as "a real kindly easy-going ol sheriff." That's why it hurt him so much to hear all the vicious talk going around. He had learned to expect it by now, though, even from people he was once inclined to trust, like old man Tobe Little, the bootlegger. Everybody knew how tolerant the sheriff had been of Little's illicit distilling operation all these years. When it came to busting up stills—or, rather, not busting them up—the sheriff was just about the most tolerant man around. And he'd never been one to ask for more than his fair share of the take either. But now it turned out that even Tobe Little had thrown in with the SCLC crowd and had been spreading it around how the sheriff liked to rough folks up. It was a mighty big disappointment to know that his old friends were talking about him that way. Anybody could tell you he wasn't the kind of man to go around beating folks up without a good reason. Him? Why, the fact of the business was that he was just about the kindliest and most easy-going sheriff in the whole state of Alabama. Ask anybody. Folks who knew anything about him at all could tell you he'd never hit anybody that didn't need hitting, and Blue he never hit at all, and any son of a bitch that says he did had better bring along a goddamn lawyer goddammit. Why in all the time he'd been the Law he had never even worn a gun. And it was the same with his brother, who had left off being the Law to take a high-paying government job in Montgomery, and with his father, who had been the Law before either of them.

"In forty-four years the people in this town never even

seen a gun, and they ain't hurting nobody but themselves with all these vicious lies they been telling. The Lord knows that Big Fred Cain is the best friend most of these niggers ever had. If they get drunk I don't haul off and throw em in jail, I just send em on home. Or if they get in some kind of trouble I just call em up real friendly like and tell em they'd better come on in and we'll talk it over—and they come in." Cain had even been practicing up on his "soul power" salute and had joined in some of the demonstrations. "Even knelt with them over there at the bridge one time and joined in their prayers. They try every vicious trick they know and they still can't get old Fred's goat, cause Fred he just joins in and does everything they been doing. But nobody ever puts *that* on the Huntley-Brinkley...."

The rain came blowing across the courthouse lawn, driving us onto the porch of a small white stuccoed building where Probate Judge Rufus Honaker had his office. But the demonstrators held fast, Blue there among them, dwarfed between two towering pillars of oleander, his arms going, his voice again triumphing over the gloom:

"...We've come here today to talk about freedom! Is there anybody that don't want to talk about freedom? Is there anybody that don't want to pray for freedom? Is there anybody that don't want to shout for freedom? A man that don't want to be free is less than a man; he ain't no man at all; he ain't nothing worth even calling a man. So we gonna strive for freedom, and talk about freedom, and march for freedom, and shout for freedom until, praise God, we gonna be free at last!..."

If the spirit say shout
I gonna shout, O Lord
I gonna do
what the spirit say do....

"...Free at last! Free at last! O Lord Godalmighty, we gonna be free at last!...."

All the sheriff could do was laugh when he heard Blue

sounding off about freedom. "You mean they ain't free already? That's the first I heard about that. If they ain't free, why we out here putting up with all this foolishness anyway? But it's just like I said before: ain't no use trying to stop em. You might as well just go on and let em march. As long as you can keep em moving, you ain't gonna have too much trouble. Just keep em moving along — that's the main thing. Course now, they're all pretty tame anyway till you get the TV cameras on em — and then, watch out! They can get real vicious then. One of em had a sign one day that said, 'Go on back to your dominoes, Sheriff Cain.' And he's carrying that sign and looking over at me and saying—cause he knows the cameras are on him, you see — just looking over at me and saying, 'Yeah, sheriff, next year you gonna be out here marching and we gonna be over there playing them dominoes.' I'm telling you, some of the things these niggers been doing and saying are just plain vicious. But there ain't no use trying to stop em or saying anything back to em."

If the spirit say march
I gonna march, O Lord
I gonna do
what the spirit say do. . . .

Blue dropped his voice an octave, two octaves: "Sometimes when I'm lying there in my room thinking about all the places I've been, and all the evil I've seen — thinking about the work of our movement — I ask myself over and over, 'When is this old world gonna change, O Lord? When is it all gonna change? When will all men walk in freedom? When will all men treat other men as brothers?. . . .'"

"Naw, he ain't nothing," the sheriff said. "Ain't never been nothing and ain't gonna be. The same literal bastard today he was the day he was born. But he says *he's* gonna be the sheriff now. Reverend Blue, the sheriff."

". . . Sometimes when I look around at the forces of evil in the world, the altars of evil that have been set up, sometimes when I hear the words that are spoken, and the children that cry out in the night, and all the voices that plague this old world—sometimes I say to myself, 'Now this old world don't belong to George Wallace alone. No, brothers, and Catalpa County don't belong to Sheriff Cain. . . .' "

Now, as his voice soared higher, the handful of older participants began to answer him, just as in church, speaker and audience giving and taking inspiration, an unfailing chorus mingled with shouts of "YES sir!" and "That's right!" and the single word "Well!"

". . . I say to myself over and over, 'Catalpa County don't belong to Sheriff Cain, and it don't belong to Mayor Swint!' "

Say on!

". . . It don't belong to Mayor Swint—No sir! I'm telling you right now—and it don't belong to Chief Carruthers!"

No sir! Tell the story, brother!

". . . It don't belong to Chief Carruthers and it don't belong to Judge Honaker, and it don't belong to Lawyer Meads!"

Actually there were a lot of people who felt that it did belong to Lawyer Meads, to him and his brother Farley, that is, both because of the amount of property they owned and because of their standing as the leading social arbiters and dispensers of influence in the town. The lawyer had long been the chief butt of the SCLC's ridicule, ever since the afternoon that Lester Ritchie, the Atlanta organizer, had sneered at him for his mispronunciation of "Negro:"

"Kneegrow, Mr. Meads! KNEE. . . KNEE, Mr. Meads. It's what you Episcopals gets down on when you prays for us nigras. Think of your knee, Mr. Meads. . . ."

If the spirit say pray
I gonna pray, O Lord
I gonna do
what the spirit say do. . .

Blue's voice fell and again rose, all-conquering, indignant. "Yea, brothers! Yea!" Suddenly he was a prophet, an avenger, come to destroy with words alone a white society grown fat on bigotry. "Let justice run down like *water* and righteousness as a *mighty* stream!"

O yassuh!

"...Yea, brethren and sisters, for we must greatly strengthen ourselves today. We must gird ourselves and strengthen ourselves for the mighty task that lies ahead, the great task that will bring equality to all men, freedom to all men, that all men may walk as brothers...."

"Just plain vicious," the sheriff said. "But in my opinion this is just about the last of this sort of thing we're gonna see." He adopted a philosophical and even sympathetic tone. "Their day has come and just about gone. Why, the SCLC is broke. Everybody knows that. Our undercover niggers tell us that the outfit hasn't got a dime. That's why they sacrificed one of their niggers over there in Colliersville a while back. He jumped on a cop over there so he could get himself killed. There wasn't any provocation in it. It was only so the SCLC could get a lot of publicity and money out of it, that was the only reason."

So much then for the young man in Colliersville and all the others who had suffered martyrdom for the cause.

"They needed the money. They figured if they could get a nigger killed they could get a million dollars out of it in donations. But they're still looking up the wrong end of the shit barrel. Leastwise that's what all our undercover niggers been telling us."

If the spirit say move
I gonna move, O Lord
I gonna do
what the spirit say do...

And at last they did move, back across the courthouse lawn and out into the street and back past stores empty even of staring customers.

"That's all it was. They were broke. They needed the money. But the day of the SCLC has come and gone."

But what of the forthcoming primary? What were

Blue's chances of winning the sheriff's office now that the federal registrars had come in and created a black vote more than twice the size of the white electorate?

Nothing to worry about there, the sheriff said. "Nigger don't trust another nigger. You talk to any of the decent niggers around town, and you'll find out they ain't gonna vote to put another nigger in office."

Blue dropped back into the mass of damp tranquil marchers and became invisible. The sheriff crossed toward the courthouse, paused, started off again, and again paused, watching the marchers as they moved along the street past Swint's grocery and the Western Auto. The rain fell more sharply, a stinging cold drizzle, the shadows of dusk already beginning to hover at the early hour of four o'clock.

"Sure, there's no doubt about it," the sheriff said. "There's lots of things the niggers need, but they're just going about it the wrong way — trying to get everything in too much of a hurry." He had told them that himself, most recently during a black and white "summit" meeting at the courthouse. "Naw, you all ain't gonna never get nothing acting this way." That's what he told them. He said, "Until you all stop showing your black asses and stupidity all around town, and in front of all the decent white folks, and start acting the way you were taught to act instead of the way all these outsiders been telling you to act — why, you ain't gonna get *nothing* outa us." But still the marchers came, almost every day, with or without their signs, always singing.

"It just takes time to work these things out — lots of time. That's what you can't make them folks up in Washington understand." He cast a last bemused look at the disappearing marchers. "It's just like I was telling you before: We ain't even had no bowling alley around here since the Depression. And them carrying all them signs that say, 'Integrate the Bowling Alley.' Or: 'Integrate the Poolroom.' Hell, I don't guess we ever had a poolroom in New Erie. Or a skating rink either, although there was a fella that came in here once and talked about putting in one. And, like I say, the last bowling alley we had went out of business along in 1930-1931 — somewhere along in there. Barely remember it myself. Old man Overby down in Taschahatchie City, he's the one that had it. You can go down there and talk to him yourself. . . ."

That Ol' Black Cloud

May 1966

As spring came on we began to hear a lot more of Cyrus Blue and his stirrings about the streets of New Erie. He was suddenly more than just another field nigger who had gone across the river "to find out how to get past the stoplights"; he was now a full-blown dignified unapologetic candidate for sheriff. The SCLC had put up candidates for the school board and commissioners court too. But mainly what was on everybody's mind was Blue's aggressive campaign to oust Fred Cain from the sheriff's office.

Ordinarily no one would have thought much about Blue's running for sheriff, except to stand there and laugh at him while he went around town making a fool of himself. But this time it was different. Thanks to the new federal voting rights law, the black people of Catalpa County had run up such a huge majority of registered voters that no one except Cain himself gave the old order much of a chance of surviving. Everywhere now there were rising fears that the same wind that had brought the primroses and buttercups back to the prairielands of Catalpa County would put a black sheriff in the courthouse — new fears of carpetbag regimes, scalawags, nightriders.

At Eddie's Grill and at Mayor Swint's grocery and at Oscar Odum's two-chair barbershop people talked of very little else except what Blue was doing and what Cain was not doing. Because Cain wasn't doing much of anything. He had scarcely stirred from his office all spring; he was content to preside, as usual, over his inevitable game of dominoes. A lot of people, some of the domino players included, felt that

Cain ought to be out talking to people, shaking hands, explaining how tolerant and understanding he had been all these years and how the "decent nigras" would be the first to suffer if they were to vote a cotton-patch radical like Cyrus Blue into office. But Cain said, "Naw, nigger don't trust another nigger."

By the time primary day came, in early May, Catalpa County and Alabama were big news throughout the country, the first real test of what the 1965 Voting Rights Act, born on the streets of Selma, would mean to Deep South politics. George Wallace, ineligible to succeed himself as governor, had put up his wife as a proxy candidate. And the newly enfranchised blacks had fallen in behind her chief opponent, Attorney General Richmond Flowers, a reformed segregationist who had promised to strike the Confederate flag from the capitol at Montgomery and put it in a museum. But the real hope of the civil rights forces was in local races — in Black Belt counties where they could dominate by sheer numbers. And their best hope of all was Catalpa County, where the black voting majority was now more than two-to-one, heaviest in the state. The SCLC leaders had selected Catalpa as their target county, the one place where they were almost certain of winning big. Most of the state press had already conceded the county to the SCLC ticket.

But the sheriff just laughed and went on back to his domino game, there in the anteroom just outside his office, hunched over the table like a Mexican *hacendado*, under the slow high whirl of the ceiling fan, talking about almost anything except "nigger Blue" and the primary. To those who made it their business to inquire how the campaign was going, he would explain that it was all on schedule —that everything was just as he had been saying it was all along: "You watch what I say now. Ain't nothing to worry about. Most of the niggers around this town, they know who their friends are." Occasionally, when the mood was on him, he would call in the correspondents from the *Washington Post* and the *New York Times* and the *Birmingham News* and the Huntley-Brinkley and go over it all in more detail:

"Now you boys listen to me now, cause what I'm telling

you is a plain fact: Lots of niggers in this town — I mean the good hard-working decent niggers, the ones that want what's best for New Erie and Catalpa County, they ain't gonna vote for a cotton-patch nigger like Cyrus Blue. Why, that man ain't nothing but a literal bastard. A *literal* bastard. That's right. Never knew a daddy. And the other niggers, they all know what he is, and they just as scared as we are of what them radicals might do to this town. They got just as much at stake here as the rest of us."

And so the domino game went on, the players always careful to hide whatever fears they may have had about the primary, lest the sheriff start going around telling everybody that he knew more about the town than they did and why would they get all worked up just because an "out-and-out field nigger and a literal bastard at that" had the gall to think he could get elected to public office. "Nigger don't trust another nigger," he kept saying. And the domino players would all nod and say: "That's right. Nigger don't trust another nigger. You all better listen to the sheriff now, cause there ain't nobody around this town that knows niggers better'n he does."

But the correspondents all nodded among themselves in equally knowing fashion and said, "No, Cain is wrong this time. He's just bluffing. He's scared all right." If not, why had he been practicing so hard on that soul power salute he had learned from Lester Ritchie, the big-name SCLC organizer from Atlanta? And why had he commissioned that citified mulatto — the one that used to scout bunnies for the Los Angeles Playboy Club — to campaign for him? And why, most of all, had he appointed a black man — the big landowner Levi Mumford, one of Putney's friends — to be his chief deputy?

"Don't mean nothing," the domino players said. "The sheriff is just being extra cautious. Besides, it's like he always says: in a county like this one it's time the more responsible niggers were having a little more say in how their government is run. You all just better listen to the sheriff, cause there's a man that sure knows his niggers."

But the correspondents all nodded and said, "No, he's

scared all right. He's gonna lose this time for sure. Wait till the votes start coming in. He'll find out."

* * *

For more than twenty years Lurellia Holston had served as chief clerk and returning officer for the Mt. Gizeh precinct. Sometimes those duties were important enough for her to be relieved of her other duties as a schoolteacher; such was the case in this crucial election year of 1966. But nothing in all of her other experience had prepared her for the reception she got that morning when she went down to open the polls. Almost the whole black population of Mt. Gizeh had been waiting there since before dawn, great masses of "nigras" bunched up around Crawlie Calloway's general store, where the primary was to be held, and around the other old store directly opposite, some of them huddled along the shoulders of the road and all about the adjacent fields and over by the rail siding, or coming walking down the center of the highway in the hot, already molten sun of the May morning, the women in flowery prints or in plain cotton dresses and faded bandanas, the men in Sunday best; some sitting in cars or on the fenders of cars, or lounging in the back of pickup trucks, some even on crutches or in wheelchairs, and at least one voter (an old fellow completely oblivious as to how he had got there or why he had come) on an improvised cot — nigras for a fare thee well! And among them one Aaron Pollard, a lean, bristling young man who did most of his farming on land leased from the Calloways and was therefore risking quite a lot just by being out there.

Pollard came striding rapidly forward as Lurellia got out of the car, hovering over her in all of his glowering intensity and telling her to "hurry up now cause we got to tend to all this voting." She had known him all his life; yet his tone was somehow different that morning—brash, intimidating. He fell in behind her as she went to the door, the others crowding about her too, jostling for position, as she turned to announce "O Yes, O Yes, This Honorable Precinct is Now in Session," wishing above all that she had chosen to remain in the schoolroom that day.

It was the first time the Mt. Gizeh primary had ever been held anywhere except at the Holston store. But Little Brother's health was such that it was necessary to find another location this time. And it was just as well, of course, seeing as how all the old sense of decency and order had been lost. She would always remind us when talking of those other primaries that Negroes had been voting in Mt. Gizeh long before the government came in to conduct its mass registrations. True, she said, there were not so very many of them in those days, five or six at most; but in time perhaps that, too, would have changed. That was the one thing Washington had never been able to understand: that nobody was "trying to keep the nigra down" and that long before all the civil rights agitation had begun — at least as far back as the 1948 presidential election if not before — the "better class of nigra citizens" had participated freely in the Alabama electoral process. Nobody minded that. Everybody trusted everybody in those days. Even as recently as the 1964 general election all the old decorum had prevailed: a fine Indian summer day as she remembered it, the people — nigras included — all coming in to mark their ballots without disruption, and Little Brother obligingly sticking them in his pockets or in the mail cage until the time came to count the vote.

How different and how much less pleasant now that all the young blacks were competing with each other "to see who can make the biggest name for himself." Pollard, an "upstart Negro if there ever was one," was the most conspicuous example, a fellow acutely conscious of his role in history and determined, Lurellia said, that "it be judged favorably." He and Buck Simpson, an older man who still owed the Holstons money, had made it their business to indoctrinate all the inexperienced voters coming into the polls that day. Pollard would wheel out dervishlike from behind his command post — three tables set up under the shed of the abandoned store across the street — and explain to each of the new arrivals how the SCLC felt about the primary and how the Supreme Court felt about it and how Martin Luther King and Lester Ritchie and Sedley Jones and all the others felt about it. To those who could read and write (and there were still a great many who could not) he and Simpson would pass out SCLC-approved candidate lists, with a warning that they "mind them well." Others—the illiterates—would get their instructions directly from the "watchers" inside. "I'm told very reliably," Lurellia wrote, "that several of those who chose to disregard their instructions have been warned in no uncertain terms that they are to have their crops *burned in the field*."

Among those who had gotten the warning was June Washburn, Big Mose's brother and one of Lurellia's most dependable handymen. There had always been a big difference between him and his brother. Big Mose was the one who had begun calling himself "Mr. Washburn" during the early days of the movement and crossing his legs in front of the white folks. But June had always told everybody he was "jes a plain old nigger and not too proud to own it neither." And he had always stood up for his white protectors even during all the agitation about voting rights.

Big Fred Cain, that was June's man. June liked to tell folks about all the times the sheriff had looked after him when he was drinking. Sometimes June would be sitting on the side of the road drunk and Fred Cain would come along in his car and say, "June, you setting out there so drunk you can't find yo ass with a searchlight at high noon. Just don't you be setting there when I come back or we gonna be taking a little trip down to the lockup. Hear?" That's what kind of friends he and Fred Cain were, and now that he had come "into the political" he was sure going to remember it too. In the days before the primary he bragged it all around how he was going to vote for Fred Cain "as sho as there's a sun tomorrow" — big talk that brought the SCLC enforcers knocking at his door on the night before the primary.

That same night June appeared at Lurellia's door, wondering if he couldn't just go ahead and mark "one uv dem little ol ballots" and then she could "take it on down thar and drap it in de box" next morning. But Lurellia told him, "June, what I want you to do is come in that store and hold yourself up just as though you really were somebody. And when I call out Sheriff Cain's name you just speak out in a good loud voice and say, 'I wants to vote for Mr. Cain.' " That was part of her job, to call out the names of the candidates for the benefit of illiterate voters. "Just say it out loud and strong, June." But June had his doubts about that. "Miz Lurellia, they say I don't vote fur nigger Blue and theys goan burn all my crops in the fields." So Lurellia said what he would have to do, then, was come into the polls as quietly and discreetly as he knew how and speak out his choice "in a very low tone." But June wasn't sure about that either. "Miz Lurellia, I jes natural afeard that ain't goan work."

June had tried to solve the problem by not voting at all. But the enforcers were at his house first thing next morning, waiting to drive him to the polls. Wadina Bee, a schoolteacher turned black "watcher," knew about the special relationship between June and Lurellia and would not allow the big fellow to speak his choice in peace. She got up as he came in and followed him back to the voting table; all the other watchers were there too, glaring, silent, waiting, and Big June standing there sweating out of all season as they moved in on him. "Speak up, June," Wadina told him. "We can't hear what you're saying. You can talk louder than that, can't you?" And June: "Wadina Bee, I jes natural can't speak so plain this morning." He stood there in the little circle of watchers, the sweat coming off him, Wadina's schoolteacherish eyes stabbing him like blunt darts, while Lurellia went on reading through the list of candidates. Fred Cain or Cyrus Blue? June stood there, the eyes on him. But at last he drew himself up and said, "I wants to vote for Mr. Fred Cain and the other white gentlemuns."

Wadina blurted out her indignation. "I knew it! She gave that Negro a signal. Admit it, June: she gave you a signal."

"Nawsuh, Wadina Bee, she ain't give me no signal."

"Assuredly not!"

But Wadina was sure it was a trick of some kind. She would refer the case to the authorities and perhaps demand a recount.

"She tricked that Negro. She baffled and humiliated him. More will come from this."

"Nawsuh, Wadina, she ain't done nothing lak you say she done." And Lurellia:

"Wadina, please don't use that tone with me!"

* * *

Big June was one of the few Mt. Gizeh Negroes to vote for a white man that day; the SCLC scored heavily at every turn. Elsewhere the outcome seemed equally certain if longer in doubt. "On election night" (as *Newsweek* informed us) "New Erie's white townsmen crowded into Probate Judge Rufus Honaker's office to sip Pepsi's and bourbon, watch the returns come in—and contemplate the terrifying possibility that a spidery black preacher named Cyrus Blue might succeed Fred Cain as sheriff."

Honaker, the youngish elections chairman, sat at a desk jotting down returns from outlying precincts and relaying the bad news both to bystanders and outside callers: "Well, it's looking real sad, the colored are leading now—and we still got a lot of real woolly bully boxes to come in yet. Looking real sad. Looks like that old black cloud's gonna fall on us for sure."

Prominent among the bystanders was Lawyer Meads, a thin restless man who told *Newsweek* that his wife had just called up "tighter'n hell" and told him to come on home and pack his bags. "She went home just knowing we was gonna wake up tomorrow with a nigger sheriff. Said we was going to have to move somewhere else—she just couldn't face it."

But when the last of the "woolly bully" boxes were in, with some white precincts still to report, the mood abruptly shifted. "Yep, looking lots better now," Honaker was saying. "Looks like Fred could pull it out now. I believe he's gonna do all right."

* * *

So the sheriff was right after all. Nigger don't trust another nigger. He had beaten Blue by almost four hundred votes, no small margin in a county where there were only about six thousand people on the registration rolls and more than three-fourths of them black. The only black candidate to survive the primary was a Taschahatchie City pig farmer named Ezekiel Crune, who won nomination to the school board (though only after a runoff with the white incumbent). But the SCLC could find little consolation in that, because Crune was a Putney man. It was the hour Putney had been waiting for and brooding about all those autumn days behind the windows of his grocery store. Now he was again in a position to assert his authority, to go back into the AME Zion Church and tell everybody that his tactics had paid off while those of the SCLC radicals had failed.

And Blue could only sit there with all the old bitterness festering inside him. Soon after voting day he dropped completely out of sight. The talk was that he had left the county for good. One story was that he had gone to Chicago to take part in the developing demonstrations there. Another that he had gone to California. Still another that he had joined the Black Muslims. Most of the other SCLC workers disappeared about the same time. When all of their big plans for taking over the courthouse collapsed, so did the rest of their equal rights campaign, all at once, like a skirt dropped about the ankles after a night of dancing. It seemed now that the movement was nothing more than what Little Brother had been saying it was all along: a mere transient phenomenon destined almost at any moment simply to vanish — dry up — be forgotten. New Erie was already beginning to lapse into its old ways. The merchants who had been lucky enough to survive the boycott were back in business and more prosperous than ever now that most of their competition had been eliminated, and the black people were again congregating in happy indolence about the square on Saturday afternoons, as they had been doing for as long as anyone could remember.

Phantoms of the Afternoon

August 1966

So they are gone at last, a thousand angry marchers, a thousand cries of protest, all swallowed up in the rank and tumid heat of an Alabama summer afternoon. We are well into August now, the quiet dead time of midsummer when the old store out at Mt. Gizeh seems to fill up with all the vast loneliness and emptiness of the Black Belt countryside. Soon there will be new troubles, up north this time: . . . Chicago . . . Newark . . . Detroit . . . cries of black power— a towering black rage that may one day engulf us all. But here there is only the indolent mood of the August dog days, a curtain of haze and indifference thrown over everything now, the whole land reposing idyllic and unchanging beneath the weight of the summer noon.

In New Erie it is much the same, the town lost in the glare of the afternoon sun, none of the courthouse domino players about, more "for rent" signs in the windows, and almost no one on the streets or in the stores. But along toward mid-August you hear that Blue is back and that he has again taken up his plot against the white man. Perhaps, then, it will soon be like old times: long afternoons of talk at the Silver Buckle, hints of conspiracy and intrigue, fists raised in triumph and anger.

It was like that the last time I saw him there, soon after the spring primary. That was the afternoon I first heard the story of Dr. Wade P. Nance and the big absentee ballot fraud. The rumor was that Nance, a New Erie physician known widely for his crusty ways and penetrating diagnoses, had teamed up with Probate Judge Honaker and gone about the back roads of the county certifying hundreds of trustworthy blacks as shut-ins. Sometimes the sheriff would go along to provide law and order. At each stop the judge would hand the newly declared invalid a ballot and tell him to raise his right hand. And Nance would say, "Now you want Fred Cain here for your sheriff or that field nigger that's running against him?" And the black man: "Why, sho I wants Mr. Cain hyar fo de sheriff. You knows we don't wants no common field nigger fo de law."

As he sat reflecting on all that, Blue had about him the lean somber look of a man suddenly grown wise in the ways of Black Belt politics. There was a tautness about him, a wariness, no glimmer of humor, as he sat there with his string tie unknotted, talking to George Sampkins and two other SCLC "enforcers." Maybe it was all as he said it was; maybe the sheriff really had stolen the primary. But the justice department had found nothing in the tale worthy of investigation. And Lyndon likewise had just sat back and listened and smiled real big and done nothing.

Lyndon? Even the blacks had turned against him now. Suddenly there was a murmuring against him all around the table, an angry show of raised fists. No sir. You just couldn't count on him anymore. You sure couldn't. And a mighty sad and tragic thing it was too.

I took it all down, watching as the night crowd began to sift in and fill the nearby tables. On a low dais across the room a topless mulatto dancer, her body lithe and shimmering in the thin lurid haze, had just gone into her first routine of the evening, to the accompaniment of piped-in sound.

Blue observed her noncommittally. Blue was noncommittal, wary, a bit suspicious, about almost everything in those first days after the primary. Sampkins was just the opposite, always full of big talk and windy threats. He, far more than Blue, understood the unquestioned value of such talk—propaganda talk—in an era when most newsmen were ready to report without verification almost anything that came from movement leaders.

"We gonna be looking at some things," he said mysteriously. "We gonna be going over all kinds of different programs and incentives." I took it all down. "We gonna be looking at this, that and the other, and we gonna be asking a lot of questions — developing a whole new geopolitical configuration. Lots of people been saying there's other alternatives, other ways of accomplishing what we're trying to do."

Blue's face showed nothing even as the dancer dropped the last of her tinsel. Or rather it showed only what it had shown before: disgust over the "tombstone voters" and the failure of the justice department to throw out all the absentee ballots. "Eighty per cent of the county," he was saying. "That's what we are now. Eighty per cent. How can eighty per cent of the population lose an election like that?"

But even he knew he could not blame it all on fraud. He knew that much from what had happened to him in his own campaign. He talked about all that — about how so many of the black people, the new voters, had hidden their apprehension over what the new day was to bring behind a mask of indifference, behind disbelieving sneers, loud guffaws. Like the night he had stopped over at the El Paradiso, another black nightspot, carrying his campaign posters. He accosted the first man at the counter. "Blue's the name. Cyrus Blue. Candidate for sheriff. I need your vote, man. Your vote!" The man had taunted Blue, laughed at him: "You running for sheriff? What you say, man? You running against big Fred Cain? Naw, man. You just talking. Cut out that shit now." And then to all the others: "Hey, you all hear that? Here's a nigger that says he's running for sheriff. Says he gonna be the sheriff and Fred Cain gonna retire out to his farm. Says he gonna wear a big gun and go around locking folks up." Then the whole crowd had joined in, laughing and sneering at him, shouting him down: "Yeah, there's a nigger that says he gonna be the sheriff now." Blue had waded into the crowd, trying to make himself understood and passing around one of his posters. BLACKS FOR BLUE. He had sought the barkeep's approval, asking him how he would feel about putting one of the posters on prominent display, maybe up there in the front window behind the revolving Michelob sign. Nothing doing, the barkeep had told him.

"Hell, boy, you ain't nothing but a field nigger. You ain't gonna be the sheriff. And I got to live in this town."

Blue had tried not to think about any of that. He could not afford to think about it. He went on believing he could win the nomination — had no choice but to believe it. And then it all came crashing in on him — the disgust and bitterness, the memory of all those taunts, the feeling of betrayal, the realization that no matter what he might say publicly, he could no longer blame it all on the tombstone voters and ballot-box stuffers. What more was needed than the matter of Ezekiel Crune, to remind him and the others that a black man could win office in Catalpa County only if he had the support of the Putney crowd?

Still, nobody was ready to concede anything to Putney. At the mention of his name there were more raised fists, more bearded scowls. One could readily sense the evolving mood: disillusionment and bitterness giving over into despair, despair into louder and ever-more-insistent cries of black power.

"We gonna be looking at some things — talking about things," Sampkins said. Nods of approval all around, grunts of dismay at the white man's folly. Here and there, as some of the latecomers joined us, another soul power salute — and then all the fists at once. "Yeah," Sampkins said. "There's got to be other ways — better ways."

Blue was noncommittal. He glanced somberly across Sampkins's shoulder toward where the tinseless dancer was. The Silver Buckle had once been an auto-repair shop and had kept some of its old nuance. One expected to find discarded tools lying about, racy calendars on the wall, tobacco juice stains on the cinder blocks.

"There's a lot of different ideas we're gonna be turning over," Sampkins said, as I strove to get it all down. "We gonna be talking about some answers. And looking at some big questions."

He again raised a fist and glowered menacingly about. As an SCLC enforcer, he had known and practiced violence ever since his first days in the movement. Even so, it was not quite the same kind of violence that Stokely Carmichael and the other black power people had been hinting at; his was merely a tactical violence aimed at timorous blacks who had opposed the SCLC on matters of policy: an occasional beating at the back of a dark alley or alongside a lonely road. But in the early days at least no one ever talked about adopting those techniques as a strategy against the white man. Carmichael had been to New Erie just before the primary, to speak at the AME Zion Church: *White man say he gonna take our arms. We don't need arms. All we need is one little match. All we got to have is that one little match and we burn down the world.*

Blue liked Carmichael — respected him. But he had never endorsed black power even as an abstract principle. I watched him now, wondering how soon he would begin to add his voice to the others and then realizing that he was still unprepared to go quite that far, even though he more than any of his companions had a right to feel angry. For too many months now he had lived with uncertainty and terror. Telephone threats, cross-burnings. And then there was the afternoon he had looked in his rear view mirror to see a fast-moving stripped-down Malibu crowding his bumper, the driver bent fiercely over the wheel, his woman companion shouting curses through the glass; the car still gaining on Blue as his speedometer jumped past ninety-five. He could not make the turn at Old School; he went on through Grand Ridge and Ladd's Crossing, his speedometer hitting a hundred and ten and the Malibu still on him, crowding him ever more closely, then easing up beside him on the long straight stretch north of Taschahatchie City; the woman's face now wrenched violently sideways; the same curses, the same angry shouts. Except he could hear them this time, wind-flung: *O how I hate a liverlip. O how I hate a goddamn nigger bastard*! A woman of moderate good looks, still young. And then he saw the paper bag and guessed what was inside; she held it stiffly out the window — the bag, the gun — and pointed it at him as the two cars plunged ahead side by side down the narrow two-lane highway: *O goddamn you I hate all you goddamn nigger bastards and King will get his too you bastard O yes King is next. . . .*

It was like that all the way into Taschahatchie City, her unable to get the shot she wanted and the Malibu falling back to let traffic clear and then easing up beside him again, and him pushing one hundred and fifteen now as he hurtled past the sign that said: Taschahatchie City Police Jurisdiction. Taschahatchie City was three abandoned stores, a roadside cafe, a Quik-Chek market, an embattled one-pump gas station, and a post office. Blue hurtled on into the decrepit town, meeting more traffic now, watching the Malibu slow for the single traffic light. He finally lost his pursuers on the narrow turns south of town, returning to New Erie by way of a back road and remembering — unaccountably — all the speeches he had made in front of the courthouse there and in all the little black churches: *I know we can live better in the world. I know we can have freedom in the world....*

"We gonna have freedom, we gotta take it," Sampkins said.

The dancer had come back, with her tinsel and spangles on, this time to sing a smoky blues song that somehow called back all the lost wild passions of movement days. Blue watched the drinkers along the counter, wondering aloud now about some of those "other alternatives" Sampkins had talked about.

But maybe it wouldn't come to that. I still felt that there was hope for the town. Were there no white men with whom the streetmarchers could arrange an understanding? What about Roger Meads, the lawyer? And Roger's brother Farley. Good people, the Meadses, despite their longstanding opposition to the protest marches. That's what I'd always heard anyway. So maybe there was still hope — if not in the Meadses, perhaps in some of the other First Families of New Erie.

Suddenly Blue was laughing, the first laugh I had ever seen out of him — a good full laugh that flung his head backward and showed healthy gums above a row of emphatically white teeth. "Worst clubbing I ever got was over there in Roger Meads's office." I had already heard the story — how Blue and some of his followers had gone over there one afternoon to consult Meads, then serving a temporary term as deputy district solicitor, about the need to seek punitive action against Ed Sowers, one of New Erie's policemen. Blue's story was that Sowers had knocked one of the SCLC's female demonstrators to the pavement after he propositioned her and she refused to come across. Blue and the wronged girl and perhaps half a dozen other demonstrators had crowded into Meads' office, singing freedom songs and demanding a warrant for Sowers's arrest. Then Cain came in swinging his nightstick. That was Blue's story anyway: Cain holding the nightstick at just the right angle for the demonstrators to knock themselves down.

But what was Meads doing all this time? He had probably busied himself with some important papers on his desk. Or maybe he had just sat there averting his eyes, looking at the ceiling, over at the door, up the dresses of Blue's female companions.

Surely, though, there must have been some mistake. I had often heard my old friend G. Harold Edisen, the Atlanta-based *Newsweek* correspondent, talking about Roger Meads. They had been classmates at Sewanee and had kept up with each other through the years. It was Edisen who first told me the story about how an earlier generation of Meadses had run the Ku Klux Klan out of town along with the carpetbaggers. It was Roger Meads, Edisen told me, who had hated Andrew Jackson because Jackson hadn't done right by the Cherokees — Meads who had been with the Cherokees in spirit as they plodded forlornly along the Trail of Tears — Meads, too, who had counseled against barricades, police dogs and tear gas during the New Erie civil rights demonstrations — Meads who had vetoed the use of an old anti-boycotting statute that would have (temporarily anyway) put the marchers to rout. Edisen had always thought of Meads as the William Alexander Percy of New Erie, a compassionate upper-class conservative who disdained the single-minded bigotries of the Bilboes and Wallaces. He had even talked about making New Erie and the Meads family the subject of a book. Perhaps a novel. Perhaps even THE novel, the "masterpiece" as he called it. But after hearing Blue's story about the clubbing, he'd had to revise his estimate of his old friend. Not that that would present any special difficulties for him in a literary way; his answer to all that was simply to shrug and relegate Meads to the status of "semi-antihero." He still felt strongly that there was a masterpiece in it somewhere.

Listening to the others, I wasn't so sure. Meads would have a lot of explaining to do if the black power people were ever to take over. He would be lucky to come out of it with even so much as his "semi-antiheroic" status intact.

"Things could get mighty rough around here," Sampkins said, glowering.

"Things *gonna* get rough around here," Blue said, with an unaccustomed show of spirit.

Nods and murmers of assent all around.

"They already getting rough for some of these honkeys, and they gonna get a lot rougher."

Sampkins raised a fist and again dropped hints about "other ways, other alternatives." Somehow I got it all down.

* * *

And so summer again, dreamy afternoons in the old store out at Mt. Gizeh, idle talk behind the coal stove, a heavy mood of Keats and Baudelaire, a Lethelike spell of forgetfulness, indifference, escape, a quaff of nepenthe or a scent of lotus, and always the muted horns of Morpheus, forest-proud... and the old man speaking again of the recent primary, the voting, the foolishness of all the young nigras whose "strut and swagger" spoke no more loudly than their ballots, and the greater foolishness of a government that thought it could destroy all the good work of the South with a few bad laws and illegal court edicts.

"A mighty pitiful thing it seems to me, the way the government's been after all these folks to sign up and go to voting. Don't matter if you can't read or never even saw the inside of a schoolhouse or if you're just plain blubbery-mouthed — nothing will do but that you've got to be hauled out of your house, and knocked all around, and threatened with all sorts of foolishness, just so the government can say it's provided you with a 'lawful' opportunity to exercise your voting franchise. Sure does seem like a right pitiful thing to me."

Yes, it was certainly clear now, to Little Brother anyway, that all "the dignity and pushiness of the young nigras" had availed them nothing. Catalpa County still belonged to Sheriff Cain and Lawyer Meads and Judge Honaker, and Alabama still belonged to George Wallace—or rather to him and his wife Lurleen, whose crushing primary victory as her husband's stand-in had made it possible for Wallace to keep himself solidly enthroned at the top of the Montgomery political heap. A lot of people thought it was asking a lot of Lurleen to run for governor just because Wallace was ineligible to succeed himself. As Lurellia was always reminding us, St. Paul had plainly decreed that no woman was "to usurp authority over a man." But when it came right down to it, what other choice was there? The former governor John Patterson? After the way he had been carrying on with that cheap Montgomery showgirl? Richmond Flowers? After all his promises to desecrate the Confederate flag and "turn the whole state over to the nigra"?

But even Flowers was not the worst. No, Folsom was the worst. Big Jim Folsom, a gigantic ruined shell of a man, wobbly with drink, twice governor and still a candidate, and something of a laughingstock too, even among the Wallaceites who had once been the mainstay of his support. Folsom had always been a man of huge appetites, and a man of many generous impulses as well, with a lot of what the Negro calls "soul." But his long history of whoremongering, boozing, and treating Negroes as equals had violated all the cardinal tenets of Southern fundamentalist society. Everybody thought he was finally finished in 1962, after an election-eve television performance that displayed him at his drunken, bumbling worst. Yet he offered again as one of nine candidates challenging Lurleen in this year's primary. And the odd thing is, he might have actually won, even at this late date, despite all the bad memories, if somehow he could have gotten just a little more support from all those old populist elements that had raised both him and Wallace to power. In his best days Big Jim had inspired a following that even Wallace had never quite matched. His first campaign, way back in 1946, had been an old-fashioned populist whoop and holler, a twang of guitar and banjo, as he and his suds-bucket brigade moved out along the country roads and into the small out-of-the-way courthouse towns, Big Jim standing up there flourishing his cornshuck mop and promising to "scrub out that capitol down thar at Montgomery."

That was the real trouble with Big Jim, Little Brother always said. It wasn't so much his drinking and womanizing. It wasn't even his "cozying up to the nigra element" that mattered so much—not back then, because there really was no such thing as a civil rights issue in those days. What it was was his lack of dignity. That was Big Jim's trouble. He was just too big and clownish and too much of an embarrassment to the state. Nowadays even the young nigras had more dignity than Big Jim had. That was what Little Brother didn't like—that crude country manner of his, the way he would laugh real big and slap everybody on the back and slobber kisses on all the women and then throw up his hands and shout, 'Y'awl come! Y'awl come!"

And then there was that way he had of talking about how if folks would just give him a little more time he would sure figure out a way to get himself elected president—always talking about what a fine thing it would be if he could ever get up there to the White House and resurrect the spirit of Andy Jackson—how he would sure teach the country something about democracy then. He would fill every man's granary with plenty and cover the land with TVAs and startle even the Huey Longs with all his big plans for reshaping the American government.

"Said he'd do all that even if he had to steal the money. Said he'd stole before and he'd steal again. Never could understand why we wanted a man like that for our governor—why he just couldn't seem to conduct himself with the dignity befitting his high station in life. A right pitiful sight, if you ask me, to see a grown man making a plumb fool of himself like that."

Silence. A cluck of hens beyond the doorstep, a drone of jarflies farther out, the heavy silence of afternoon. A casual shuffle of the newspaper that he held inconsequentially on his lap. Immense and imponderable silence. And then:

"Just never could understand it. Never did meet a man who would admit voting for Folsom. Just never could understand *where* all those votes kept coming from."

* * *

There were no customers in the store that afternoon, and the next afternoon only one: the Rev. Octavious Ponds, who had come there to get the credit he could no longer get in New Erie. "No more credit, preacher. Things ain't like they usta." That was the message he had been getting all over town. If things weren't "like they usta," it was because Ponds had taken such an active part in the six-month economic boycott that had driven all but the most soundly based of New Erie's firms into bankruptcy. Among those that had not gone under was the town's largest department store, Meads & Co., where the preacher had been trading for years. That was the first place he had gone after civil rights leaders agreed to an easing of economic sanctions, and there he got the blunt message: "No more credit, preacher. No more credit."

The preacher just hadn't realized it would come to that. It just hadn't occurred to him that men like Farley Meads, whose father, Farley Senior, had helped him through many a difficult strait, would hold it against him merely because he had joined in a plot to drive the New Erie business community to its knees. He just hadn't thought about it like that, that's all. He had been close to the Meadses ever since that day more than thirty-five years ago when a dramatic confrontation with his onetime landlord, Parsons Frye, forced him to take permanent leave of his home community of Ellerbe. From then until the mid-fifties he had lived on land owned by the Meads family, saving every spare penny until at last he had enough money to buy part of that land for himself. During those years he had done most of his trading at Meads & Co. and was quick to avow that he had never been late in settling up a debt. He liked to talk about the time that

Farley Senior's brother, Willis Meads, who forbade the passing of money on Sunday, had broken his own strict rule in order to loan Octavious the fifty dollars he needed to pay his son's college registration fee. "Pay it back when you can, Octavious." That's what "Missa Willis" had told him the Sunday afternoon when he came down to open the store safe and get the money out. "Just pay it back whenever you can."

But now young Farley Meads was saying, "Naw, preacher. Ain't no more credit here." And for no better reason than that Octavious would have driven him into bankruptcy if he could. He just couldn't understand it, that's all. He just didn't know what Farley was thinking about. He thought the Meadses would all be happy to have him back as a regular customer when the boycott was over, and he had gone there thinking he could "make book" as usual. His first purchase was a box of shotgun shells and a hunting jacket.

"How much?" he asked the salesgirl.

"Thirty-five dollars and twenty-three cents. You gonna pay cash?"

"Naw, just go on and put it on the book like usual."

He did not know quite what to make of it when the girl crisply excused herself and plunged off through the thickly hung racks of clothing. Ponds fell in behind her, suspecting trouble, thinking again about the Sunday afternoon that Willis Meads had come down to make him the fifty-dollar loan. *Pay it back when you can, Octavious*. And now Farley Meads Junior, newly emerged from his office at the back of the store, was saying, "No more credit, preacher. No more credit." As Ponds remembered it:

"He tell me, say, 'It's all right, preacher, you can get anything you want, but we can't put it on the book. Ain't no more credit.' I say, 'You mean I can't get nothing without I pay cash for it?' And he say, 'That's right, preacher. Things changed now. Things ain't like they usta.' "

* * *

And so we sat there, caught up in the endless spell of afternoon, Little Brother talking idly on, and almost no one ever coming in to buy a cold drink or postage stamp, and the day gradually sinking away from us, and the old man rising at last to carry out the mail sack and lock the door, and then the two of us — sometimes in the pickup, sometimes on foot — starting back down the dirt lane toward the captain's house, the dusk coming fast, the owls swooping low out of woods already suffused with a lavender gloom. And then we would be on the porch again, in the full dark of the August evening, the old man still talking, idly, inconsequentially, about all the "good times before the war" — how much had been lost, how little gained — and finding what solace he could in the words of a doomed poet:

> *Ay, in the very temple of delight,*
> *Veil'd melancholy has her sovereign shrine....*

And sometimes the black woman would be there, sitting in the rocker and working her quilt pieces, watching us, not speaking. And the old man the same, just sitting there with his back to her and staring out at the dark, thinking about the depravity of the age — or maybe rising frantically to switch out the overhead light, so that anyone driving up out there wouldn't get the idea that the Holstons had nothing better to do with their summer evenings than to sit on the front porch with a black woman in their presence.

And then maybe he would go on inside. And Eula would say, "He always be doing that. I be's in the hall or the kitchen piecing on my quilts and he cut out the light and leave me wid all that stuff in my lap — all my needles and quilt pieces. He go on to bed, and I gots to get up all my things in the dark."

One more grievance to add to all the others that had been piling up. Like all the times she had greeted him with a cheery "good mawning" only to have him "jes sot thar and grunt" or not say anything. Or like the times he had tried every way he knew how to keep her from using the front door. He was ever on the alert to keep her from going out that way or, if she got out, to keep her from coming back in. "I hear him tell Miss Angie, say: 'She ain't got no business coming in that front do'. I goan make her come in the back.'

And he always be taking my eggs from me — say I use too many eggs. . . ."

Eggs?

". . . Too many eggs, too much milks, too many margarines. So he come get my eggs and carry them all to his room." Once he had removed almost the entire contents of the icebox — whole cartons of milk and eggs, packages of bacon and margarine — and placed the lot of it in his room, some of it stacked on the chest of drawers and the rest on a table by his bed. "Practically the whole frigerator in there and all that stuff getting hot and melting. I say, 'Mis'en Frank, don't you wants me to put all that stuff up?' And he say, 'Eula, you use too many eggs, you all the time using too many eggs. You goan use up *all* our stuff.' "

O yes, there was no doubt about it: she had everything her own way now, the choice of where to sit at table, whether to eat with the others or alone, which chair was to be hers when her chores were done, and whether to join them on the front porch or stay inside and turn the television to a channel of her preference. And at least she could sometimes get out the front door even if she couldn't come back in that way. And there was talk now that she had been feeding her own people in the captain's house. Roast beef and mashed potatoes. Chicken and dumplings. Molasses and sauerkraut and fatback. Sometimes it was said that her guests ate better than the old man himself, or his sister. Country ham and apple pie. Corn on the cob. Tomatoes and squash and butter beans fresh from the garden.

But Little Brother's overpowering need at the moment was to keep her from wearing out his one good tub and commode seat. Might as well give up talking about it, though. Might as well give up barring the door, holding the gun on her. None of that had done any good. He himself, of course, had made no use at all of the bathroom since the first summer she had come to the house. It was just too indecent somehow — the idea of him sitting on a commode still warm from the black woman's buttocks or scrubbing himself in a tub where she had sat singing her freedom songs. That was why he kept a basin full of tepid bath water ever at his bedside—and why the path out to the old privy had been worn smooth again, just as it was in the days before indoor plumbing had ever come to Mt. Gizeh, the privy itself sparkling now with a fresh coat of whitewash.

"Yup. She's always gonna have something to say about her 'rights.' I guess that's what they teach them in all those meetings. 'Take the white man's tub. Take his commode. Walk in his front door.' Seems to me that if I'd ever assigned her any rights to that commode I'd be just *bound* to remember it."

There were intervals when he would lose the drift of what he was saying and drop off into a kind of somnolence. But it would be only a moment before he would again turn to me, in a kind of panic, and say, "How do you feel about it? What do you think of King and the way he's been hoodwinking the young nigras?"

I would mutter something unintelligible about the Fourteenth Amendment and equal protection and suggest that in time it would all somehow turn out for the best. And him:

"They've all got to act so dignified now. Nothing will do but that they've got to show off *all* their dignity." And where, he kept asking himself, did Eula and her crowd get the money for all these rallies they had been holding, and for all of their marching and protesting? But he already knew the answer. They had been getting some of it—maybe a lot of it — from the white people themselves, not just "from the cranks and nigra-lovers either," but from the good solid people like himself. He had not been blind to it; he had seen Eula working her shill game. How many times had he watched her come around and solicit "a little something" for her church? He had done what he could to keep her from getting away with it. But it was no use. Little Sister would think nothing of giving her five dollars—ten dollars—whatever she asked—and Mrs. Lurellia, sometimes she'd give her a few dollars too, even though she and Miss Angie both knew where it was going—not to the church at all, but to King and the streetmarchers and the dagoes. And what, he would want to know, was my feeling about the dagoes—or about the wops and moujiks? Had I in all the time I had been working for all those big-city newspapers ever gotten around to examining the immigration problem?

I would draw myself up and offer the hackneyed explanation that the Constitution guaranteed even hated minorities the right peaceably to assemble and petition for a redress of grievances.

"That's right," he would say, avoiding the point. "They're always gonna have something to say about their 'freedom.' They're always gonna figure out some way to make themselves look important. And they're always gonna be waiting for everybody else to throw themselves down and go to bowing and scraping and saying, 'Yassuh, boss. Yassuh, boss. At yo service, Majesty.' "

* * *

The bright yellow sports coupe that I found parked out by the front gate one afternoon was all hubcaps and mirrors and fancy chrome bumpers, as brashly insolent as the young black man who just moments before had left it there. Not only had he entered the house by way of the front door, without so much as a by-your-leave, Mr. White Boss, he had not—as I later got it—even bothered to knock. I found him in the kitchen talking to Eula. He wore patched denims, no shirt, a rope for a belt, and a Gillette blue blade strung menacingly about his neck. I assumed, of course, that he was just one more of the many conspirators who had been gathering there that summer to talk with Eula about the next stage of the civil rights revolution. But Eula said,

"Dis hyah de Young'un. He be's my sister's boy."

He stared at me with heavy dignity, not rising, the razor blade a shimmer of cold blue steel in the premature dusk. Still I would attempt to be civil. I joined him at the small square table and asked about things—the movement—black power—what people were saying in New Erie. He was little help. But from Eula I learned that he had indeed been far and seen much. Most recently he had been a part of the big freedom march that had grown out of James Meredith's one-man "walk against fear." The mention of

Meredith and the shooting that had left the civil rights activist sprawled (though without serious injury) across a blazing strip of Mississippi highway brought "de Young'un" half to his feet; he was already talking about it, staring me down, not as though it were something he had just now thought to relate but as though he had already—countless times—rehearsed the telling of it:

"...Walking down the highway to freedomland. Walking and talking. Out walking for my freedom when the trooper he come up and say, 'Hey, boy, we ain't gonna have none of this walkin' through Mississippi.' He say, 'You think you got a right to do all this walkin' round hyah?'...."

I watched him, the dark gleaming face, the dangling razor blade. "Well," I said. "Well...."

He went on talking, standing half leaning over the table, looking through me and past me to all those other audiences of his imagination.

"...The big bad trooper, he say, 'That's right, boy. We gonna cut all that kind of stuff *out*.' He say, 'How come you out hyah marchin anyway, boy?' I say, 'I marchin for my freedom.' And he say, 'Well, boy, that's what I calls a definite provocation action. You goin to jail, boy.' I say, 'Ain't I done seen all these other black folks using this hyah Mississippi highway?' And he say, 'That's different, boy. They carryin hoes and things; they goin to work; they goin out to dig taters, boy, and hoe cotton. But look at you now. You carryin that fancy sign that say "Freedom!" and you out hyah walkin with that fancy cane and that fancy hat and wearin them fancy satin britches. That's a definite provocative action. We seen enough of yo kind around hyah, boy. You goin to jail. Gimme that sign of your'n, gimme that fancy hat, gimme that cane.' I say, 'Plenty o times I see my people walkin. Plenty o times I see my people walkin down this free Mississippian highway. Plenty o times'...."

"Hush, Young'un," Eula told him. "Hush now. Ain't no use you talking bout all that. You go on and hush."

"...'Plenty o times I see my people walkin. Walkin and talkin. Walkin to freedomland.' And he say, 'I done told you, boy. That ain't the same thing. Them's field nigguhs, boy. They ain't carryin no signs. They ain't wearin no satin britches and silk hats. They ain't goin round hyah talkin bout how they is marchin for their freedom or how they is marchin against fear. Hell, boy, there ain't nothing to be afraid of in Mississippi. You sho goin to jail.' We go down to the jail and he say, 'By God, boy, now I *sho* gonna teach you to come round hyah talkin bout how you walkin for yo freedom.' He throw me in the cell and slam the door. I say, 'Can I walks now?' He say, 'Naw, boy, you goan stop all that walkin. That's a definite provocation action. All you nigguhs — you revolutionaries — out hyah tryin to make it look like folks ain't even free to walk through Mississippi. Hell, boy. Hellfire. By God. . . .' "

"Hush, Young'un," Eula said. "You done say enough now. Ain't I done told you to hush?"

When she gave him the ten dollars he had come to get in the first place, he called a halt to his monologue and started out, with no further explanation and certainly without apology, still walking for freedom, marching against fear. He flung out through the wide middle hall past shelves laden with Thier's *Napoleon*, Gibbon's *Rome*, Tacitus's *Germania* and Macaulay's *England*, past side tables, pier mirrors, whatnots, horsehair sofas, Windsor chairs — and past Little Brother himself. But for some reason the old man seemed hardly to notice the intrusion, scarcely looking up and not even saying, as he almost certainly would have at any other time: "Looks like *he's* the one that wants to be the governor now. . . ."

* * *

There was a whole crowd of them this time, grown bolder with the old man's enfeeblement. They sat around the kitchen table over platters of roast beef and mashed potatoes, bowls of greens and squash, deep-dish cobblers. Eula's cousin from Vestal, Isabel Courtney, and Isabel's husband, Joe Pete, were there, together with "de Young'un" and another couple I did not recognize. They were already getting up to leave when I came in, scraping their chairs noisily across the floor, bumping the walls, laughing, putting their hats on, full of the good dinner.

"Well, goodbye, Eula hon. Goodbye, sugar."

"Goodbye."

"Goodbye."

Then more laughter and talk as they crowded out into the wide middle hall. Goodbye, Eula. Goodbye, sugar. But suppose it didn't end there? Maybe next time they would move right out of the kitchen into the main dining room, and sit around the table that had come with the first settlers from New Market, Eula herself seated in the chair that had once belonged only to the captain.

For many years after the captain's death his place at the head of the table had been left vacant. Only in recent years had Little Brother taken it for his own and assumed the lordly role that went with it, filling the room with dignity and loud prayers and philosophical reflections on "all the good times before the war." But Eula's guests would have none of that. They cared little for Greece or Rome and even less for Virginia, the "aged and mellow world" that had been the captain's first home. They would raise their voices with shouts of "pass this" and "pass that" and with a lot of loud insulting talk about how "the worl' belong to us now." And when the last of the roast was eaten and the last of the tea glasses drained, they would all rise with a final shout of "hallelujah" and go right back out through the front of the house, dusky phantoms of the afternoon, past Little Brother and Little Sister both, in defiance of old customs, or maybe only in ignorance of them.

"How yo is, Miss Angie? How yo is, Missa Frank?"

Miss Angie would just sit there nodding benignly, still holding the cup out of which she had drunk her thin porridge, watching them as they went out past the tottering racks of books and undusted furniture, and on out into the hot bright sun of afternoon. She would speak of the incident, if at all, not as an invasion of unwanted guests or even Negroes; phantoms merely, limp longwaisted stumpy-legged people no different from all the other "visitors" who had intruded somehow into the calm of that old house.

The most troublesome of them came in the evening, to romp about the front hall and to fill the house with harsh conspiratorial laughter, often making such a nuisance of themselves that Miss Angie would finally have to ask them to leave. She would rise with a rare show of impatience and move toward the unseen intruders with a clank-clank-clank of her metal walker, reminding them gently yet firmly that the hour was late and she herself in no condition to receive guests and would it be asking too much for them to come back at a more convenient time? They would leave in a hurry then, not with threats or curses or even with very much noise, but only with a kind of unseen flurry, a sound like the faint rustle of gossomer, "a feeling," as she said, "of them packing their things and going."

The morning, fortunately, would bring more desirable guests. Like the slim golden-haired young women who came often to rearrange her books and flowers, to talk of Mobile in the time of high carnival, to hang wicker baskets full of geraniums and terra cotta pots overflowing with ivy or philodendron. At such times she would think of herself as a kind of adventurer in Arcady: about her, whole forests would spring up, diaphanous curtains of fern and hanging moss, great masses of equatorial vines through which broken shafts of sunlight perpetually shone. There would be a ceaseless gambol of elves and satyrs and dryads, a strumming of lutes, a scent of musk and wild thyme, a splashing of water over mossy rocks — and always the unseen golden-haired girls to please her with their laughter and courteous ways.

"She see all them things cause she already be's on her way over to that other worl'," Eula told me one afternoon. "But our time coming too. The time coming when we goan see all them things."

It was as if the old woman were living again all the poetry she had never been able to get down on paper. It had been a long struggle, all those years in Montgomery, trying to get the words right and never quite succeeding. I knew of no one who could speak more intimately the language of enchanted forests, sylvan groves or rainy mornings in May — but there it all ended. Was it only because she lacked the talent to match her temperament? For years she had filled the mails with her verses — quatrains, sextets, couplets, all written in pale imitation of Horace or Tennyson. And they all came back, even the one of which she was proudest: "The Brave Deed of Anne Haggerty." Anne Haggerty was her great-great-grandmother, a Revolutionary-era heroine who, in family lore, was said to have singlehandedly dispatched a Tory invader:

The seat of his trousers with right hand caught,
Her left in his coat collar. Her muscles taut
With mighty effort, she lifted the man
Whom she whirled through the air in a heap to land.

For that one she had received a note of encouragement from the celebrated poet Marianne Moore, editor of the defunct magazine to which it had been sent. To read these lines, said the poet, "has been a pleasure to me, for I love the South, to read of the oak, the pine, leaves glossy with rain; and to know the story of Anne Haggerty."

Miss Angie had spent most of her adult years in Montgomery. But her only true source of inspiration was the old homeplace to which she returned each spring. Before me is a letter composed during her last years: "Beauty He has given us in abundant measure. Just outside my window — such glory: an azalea of wonderful hue, a lovely 'dump' of flowering almond, and white iris, so fresh and vivid, a purplish red its blossoms. Green grass with sweet woodland violets cover the ground; very small leaf buds which peep from the branches of the fig bushes. 'We are peeping out, to assure you that Spring is truly here even though you may feel much chill in the air.'. . . " There is much more before me, packets of letters, small essays, a mountain of unpublished verse. To a Dandelion. The Flower Wedding. Tis Tulip Time in Montgomery.

Around the fountain in the heart of town,
Their heads with joy they raise
As they sway and play in the gentle breeze;
What a lovely sight for a mortal's gaze!

But it wasn't all nodding primroses and mossy glades. Sometimes it was a paean for her departed mother, whom Miss Angie and her sisters called "Little Darling:"

Once this earth knew my Little Darling,
Fairer than the lilies fair,
Sweeter than the sweetest flower
That ever gave its fragrance to the air.

Yet it was this same Little Darling who had robbed Miss Angie of any chance she might have had to make a life of her own. The pictures of Angie as a young woman show her to have been a striking and fragile beauty who almost certainly could have landed any man of her choice. She wanted only one, a footloose Baptist evangelist who presumed to speak of marriage. The idea scandalized the "Episcopals" and forced Little Darling to act. Even Eula had heard the story of how the old woman so set her face against the match that the timorous Angie never again ventured to broach the subject of matrimony. By the time I knew her, her Montgomery years were long past, and she was again a fixture in the old house where she had grown up, a joyous captive there, caught up in a transport of myth and poetic fancy. Already the forest had closed in, the echoes and voices, the shadows that in time would become actual men and women, with legs shorter than ours, waists much longer, yet in many ways like us, with their own lives, their own aspirations, their own unspeakable terrors.

"Ain't goan be long," Eula said. "Ain't goan be long tills we *all* goan see them things."

From her first days in the captain's house Eula had felt the presence of that "other worl." She could feel it now, all the dark unfathomable mystery of that old house, as she stood cleaning the vegetables and chopping up the meat for supper. And then, in that brief interval between what had been daylight and was not yet dark, I could feel it too: a whole world just beyond seeing or hearing—a faint lonely sobbing, a stir of footsteps along the uncarpeted hall. I could feel the eyes pressing in on me, like eyes beyond fog, the hot wild gaze of Ard the Voodoo king; and again the footsteps, the voices: Little Brother's voice drifting up from the front porch, and all those other voices from another time, and then Eula's voice dominant above them all, evocative of that selfsame spirit that had once stirred the Negroes in their slave cabins or around the washpots where they gathered to pray:

"...Miss Angie, she all the time talking bout getting over thar to that other worl'. She waiting, you see. She waiting fo' the lady that has to come and show her how to get over thar. But we ain't goan see that lady cause our time ain't come...."

Was it possible, as Cousin Eugene had insisted one afternoon, that Eula was herself some sort of "hoodooer?" Had she tried to hex Little Brother (Eugene was certain of it) by stashing conjure balls all around the place — under his bed, in his bureau drawer, even in his back pockets? Maybe the time had come to begin a systematic search. I had read somewhere how it was done:

> Lie flat on your back in contaminated area. Take ten deep breaths. Relax. Wait for evil radiations to begin. Allow evil free reign. Lie quite still until you begin to feel a slight discomfort. Presently the weight of the evil will become intolerable and, in some rare cases, may crush the exorcist's rib cage. Ignore discomfort. Also ignore nausea and disorientation. You should now find it a simple matter to ascertain the direction from which evil emanations are coming. Rise slowly and follow radiations to their source. Remove conjure ball. After carefully wiping off fingerprints, lance ball with silver stake. Proceed to next room and repeat as above.

"... She all the time saying, 'Eula, the lady goan be's hyar in a little while. You wants to bring her some tea?' So I say, 'Yeah, I brings it.' So I takes it and sots it thar on the table whar the lady goan be's sitting, and then I goes on back to the kitchen. And then Miss Angie, she say, 'Eula, would you minds bringing the lady some lemon and a little sugar?'...."

Twilight had caught us there, as it so often did, Eula's voice suddenly quiet, so that for a moment it seemed that only the dusk remained — the two of us sitting there speechless, rigid, abstract, like posed dummies in a wax museum, the dusk itself waxen, filling up all the obscure pores and interstices of the old house; no voices at all now, unless you could count those other voices that drifted back occasionally from the front veranda, where Little Brother and Miss Angie had already begun to wonder no doubt if it was about time to go in to dinner.

"... She be's seeing all her little chil'runs too — all the little ones she wuz s'pposed to have and couldn't, cause her mother tell her not to marry... cause all the 'Piscopals they think it be's a disgrace to marry a Baptist preacher. So she sees them all now, all the little ones. She say, 'Now, my little one, hyar be's a nice place for you to lie down.' Or she bring him to me and say, 'This hyar be's the young marster, Eula. Find him a nice place to rest.' And lots of times she see them out thar playing in the yard and on the porch and all around the house. And she say, 'Eula, let's fix the chil'runs a little something.' And if's I don't do it right away, she come up to me and say, 'The chil'runs, they needs something to eat, Eula. The little ones they needs something to eat.' I say, 'Well, thar be's plenty left from dinner.' So I gets it and fixes them all a place and puts it out on the porch, just like she say do; and then I takes it away and puts their dessert out thar. She say, 'That be's jes fine, Eula. I sho don't wants them to get hongry'...."

And sometimes Little Darling would come to call. Miss Angie always prepared her a special chair and a place at the head of the table. "Lots of times she come bringing me a pillow and say, 'That's Little Darling, Eula. She sleeping so good and nice.' Or she bring her to the table and say, 'She done woke up now, Eula. Can you brings her a little something? I thinks she would like a nice little piece of pie.' So I takes it thar and sets it down in front of the pillow. She say, 'That's nice, Eula.' " But then Little Darling would get up and leave without having touched the pie. "Miss Angie, she call me in and say, 'She gone, Eula. But she say she come back a little later and eat her pie.' "

Again the dusk closed in, unheard voices raging, an effluvium of unspoken terrors, and Eula talking now about the time she'd had to leave Mt. Gizeh for a few days to bury her husband, who had been found dead in a Tuscaloosa alley, and how she had come back to find that a crowd of Egyptians had moved in.

"They be's the ones that's all the time carrying *all* them suitcases. Miss Angie say, 'Eula, you gots to ask them to leave now, cause we can't 'low so many folks in here right at supper time.' So I holps run them off. I say, 'Whar they is, Miss Angie?' And she say, 'They be's right hyar, Eula.' So I jes gets *at* 'em, you know, and say, 'Now you all gots to leave hyar now, cause Miss Angie she got to have her rest fo' supper time'. . . ."

Some Evening Thoughts and a Cold Sign

September 1966

Now, in these last summer days, it is suddenly apparent how much the civil rights movement has cost the people who made it possible. Some five months have passed since we first began to read about all those black tenants and sharecroppers whose participation in the movement had gotten them thrown off the land. The evictions were nothing new. But it was only then, during those first weeks after the spring primary, that most people began to be aware of what was happening.

Land that just a year before had known only the stooped backs and busy hands of seasoned Negro laborers was now alive with the whir and rumble of great cumbersome cotton-harvesting machines, or maybe had been taken out of cotton altogether. And everywhere the white man was explaining that he had no motive in any of it except to find more efficient uses for land that tenants no longer cared to cultivate. He felt betrayed, conspired against, beaten down. What choice, then, did he have? Could one afford to provide keep for men and women who preferred to let the land go and spend all their time marching and carrying freedom signs and seeking by radical and conspiratorial means to undermine the duly constituted processes of government?

If the white man felt himself the victim of a conspiracy, so did the black man, and a much more formidable conspiracy at that: a coordinated attempt (said he) to drive Negroes permanently off the land and into the cities, to sabotage the movement and solidify white rule, to deprive them of gains they hadn't even achieved yet. Whatever it was, Calloway had been a big part of it. So had Jeff Throne and most of the other wealthy landowners in our area.

And it wasn't long before we found out that Eula had been just as active on the other side, walking up and down the back roads, stirring up an insurrectionary spirit among Negro maids and washwomen, saying, "The government say our colored got to stop on the time that the white folks stop. Our colored got to be paid whut the white folks paid." She had had all this from Beatrice Montgomery, who had had it from Martin Luther King, who had had it directly from "society." And as usual, society got its way. Suddenly the whole countryside was full of Negro domestics who no longer even bothered to explain why they weren't reporting for work. "Frances Y. lost her good maid and another who worked one day," Lurellia informed us by mail. "You can't 'tell em off' now. I tried to tell T. that she had better watch, for with all these night meetings they have, her name would be passed around and nobody would work for her."

Almost as she wrote of it, her own turn came. Her longtime maid Vinnie Lott failed to come in one morning and later sent word through Eula (who filtered it out by way of Miss Angie) that she would not return until Lurellia agreed to a raise — how much she wouldn't say — and came personally to ask her back. Lurellia refused to negotiate with Vinnie after learning that the "Great One" had connived in the affair. "I told Sister Angie that if Vinnie came back she would have to work for me, make her arrangements with me and that Miss Big was not to be a party to it in any way."

That was the way matters stood when I set out one morning to try my hand at negotiating a settlement. The way to Vinnie's place lay across a wide pasture back of the captain's house and down through a hollow past clumps of high white sandy hills — limestone outcroppings where one might find reminders of a long-forgotten past: the skeletal remains of tiny antediluvian vertebrates, shark teeth buried in ferocious abstraction, pools of iridescent slime that for all I knew were the slow seeping of vast reservoirs of crude destined one day to dwarf the holdings of the giant international oil cartels. A path led on up through a pocket of dense woods and out onto the high cleared ground where Little Brother had once raised all his corn and now grazed his dwindling herds of cattle. At the "gap" below Sister Evalina's house, a respectable red clay road took up and ran out to join the New West Catalpa highway. Vinnie's house was along that road. But first there was Sister Evalina's house, and Sister Evalina herself waiting to exact her toll. She hollered merrily as I came alongside the gate. "Missa Doololley, give me some money!" She sat on her front porch, a small excessively dark woman, head swathed in a bandana, holding an oversized Bible in her lap and staring out across a bare yard swept as clean as the spotless interior of the house itself. She owned the house and the sixty acres that surrounded it, a bequest from her uncle, an old preacher named Wash Colby, who even in days long gone had managed to save enough from his collection plates and cotton crops to make himself independent of the white man.

Now Evalina had even more independence than Parson Colby had known, enough of it to match the large measure of pride she had come by (Lurellia said) during her years of growing up as a favored servant in the wealthy Kenilworth household. Later she had lived as a tenant on the Holston land, and had spent much time working for the Holstons, both then and after she had gotten her own place, as a field hand and housekeeper. She was too old for that now — though no one knew exactly how old—and anyway she could live passably well off of what she grew in her own garden and the bale of cotton she still produced each year and the money she got from the government. But she was neither independent enough nor proud enough to forget the toll.

"Missa Doololley, you marry my sweet baby?"

"That is so, sister."

"Whar my sweet baby now?"

"At the house, sister. And she'll sure be calling on you soon."

"Give me some money, Missa Whatsit."

"Sister, why do you call me Doololley and Whatsit? It isn't dignified. Besides, I've told you many a time I don't have any money. I work for a newspaper."

"Law! Them newspapering folks. My, you's rich. I knows you's rich. Give me my five dollar."

I gave her two rolled up to feel like a thick five. She didn't look at it. She was happy with it. She knew it was only two. Everybody thought Evalina had been sympathetic with, if not active in, the movement, supporting it with tolls she exacted from the white man. But when it came to talking about all that, she mostly just "disremembered."

"Missa Doololley, I gots all this high blood, and everything jes slip my memory, and I can't think of *nothing* hardly when my blood go to rising."

And was that why she always disremembered my name?

She came merrily on out the gate, holding her Bible carefully inside the protective plastic cover from which it had never yet been removed, saying I had "for sho" hit on the reason that she couldn't hardly ever think of my name and why didn't I tell her just once more and she would be sure and not disremember it this time.

"Adam," I told her. "Adam Doololley."

"O!" she said. "I knowed it. I sho knowed it." More merry squeals and hysterical convulsions as I went on up the road. "O yassuh!" she hollered. "I be sho and not disremember this time. And you brings my sweet baby over hyar to see me, and the rest of my money."

There were no sounds of merriment coming from Vinnie's house. It sat forlornly in the blazing sun, like all the other houses along that road. "Vinnie? Anybody home?" I called a second time, and a third. Nothing. And then a faint stir inside the screen. "Vinnie? May I come in?"

"Yassuh." She held the screen, but wouldn't look at me. She *couldn't* look at me. Her eyes stared out of her head in a pathetic walleyed gaze that marred her otherwise not unpleasant features.

"I be's losing all my health. You kin sot back hyar." I followed her back to a half-room hidden behind faded pink draperies. She had her bed back there and apparently had been lying there all morning. She lay there again as I talked. There was an empty orange crate turned upside down to serve as a nightstand, and on top of it a syrupy glass that had drawn flies.

"Well, Vinnie, you haven't been eating properly. Lurellia gives you two good meals a day and sends a plate for Boomer. And how many good Sunday go-to-meeting skirts and blouses has she given you? It isn't just the money, you know." A very good way of putting it, I would later tell myself, as well as Roger Meads could have done, or his brother Farley—all of it in the very best spirit of William Alexander Percy and *Lanterns on the Levee*.

"There are a lot of other things to think about, Vinnie."

"I knows it."

"How much more money do you want?"

She just lay there, one eye looking ahead to Sunday and the other back to last Wednesday.

"Don't you know how much?"

"Ain't fur me to say."

"Do you want to come back?"

She was close to tears. She sat halfway up and looked dolefully at the opposite walls. She wore a copper bracelet to help her keep her arthritis in check and a tiny conjure pouch about her throat, similar to the one I had seen Eula wearing. I didn't know what was in it—probably a residue of bats' eyes and old dung.

"Is it Eula? What did she tell you? You know ten dollars a week is more than anyone else in Mt. Gizeh pays."

"Yassuh."

"Are you waiting for Eula to say you can come back?"

"Nawsuh."

But I was sure that was it. I wondered if something had been said about putting her under a conjure spell.

"If you get to feeling better, why don't you come on back tomorrow and we'll talk about it?"

"Yassuh."

But she didn't come back, not the next day or the next. I intervened once more, with Eula this time, and she said, "I talk to her. I see." But she still didn't come back. And I wondered again how many times the story had repeated itself: the housewife thrown back on her own resources, the landowner driving out of a morning to round up field hands who are no longer there; shack after shack standing deserted, and at the last shack, on the last road, an old Negro woman who sits looking at the man with the same unyielding gaze that had become so familiar, herself seemingly the lone unbudging survivor of the land.

"Not hyar," she would say. "Ain't nobody hyar today."

And the next day the same. More deserted shacks, another old woman who looks at her questioner unflinchingly from behind her motionless fan.

"Whar Jim and Annie May?" he wants to know.

"Gone to New Erie."

"New Erie?"

But why would they run off like that when his cotton was already past due for harvesting? When would they get back?

"Don't know," she says. "Don't know why they gone or when they coming back."

And so on down the road, another shack, another old woman, who tells much the same story, hiding what is perfectly evident to them both: that Jim and Annie May and Buddy and Eb and all the others have gone into town to a political meeting or to join in the march. And the landowner riding back with his truck empty and the knowledge that the next day or the next year would be no different, cursing King and swearing that by god next year *would* be different too: no more of this "coddling of niggers" whose only interest was in cozying up to "society" and who had kept their place on his land only because of his good heart or because he had promised his good old daddy he wouldn't run them off.

In some such way he reasoned it all out to himself. And it was then that he first began to replace his rebellious tenants with mechanical harvesters or to get out of cotton altogether, bringing in tree farms or selling large hunks of land to big-moneyed speculators who had foreseen and were able to capitalize on a rising market in soybeans.

* * *

And that was where Calloway came in. I had seen nothing of him that summer until the afternoon he came striding across the front yard and said why didn't I give up on Macaulay and come on and take a ride with him down to the bottom where he had most of his cotton planted. All the way down there he talked about it: the means by which the white man had tried to protect himself. A conspiracy? Yes, one might call it that, and he was only sorry to confess that it hadn't really worked out the way he and the other conspirators had planned it. The whole trouble, he said, was that the white man just wouldn't stand up. Many a night he and his associates had gathered down there at the back of his old man's store to plan their strategy. They would sit hunched over a game of poker or pinochle and talk about it all in hearty mocking self-satisfied tones no different from the way they had at other times talked of women or the winning ways of the Alabama football team. And then it had all fallen apart, everything they had worked for. Because they never could really succeed in driving significant numbers of black people out of the county. It was already too late for that; the movement would help the evicted tenants find other homes, other ways of making a living. Sometimes they would move into "propaganda tents," as Calloway called them, or into old swamp houses, and sometimes onto land of their own, newly purchased from well-to-do black men who had not seen fit to throw in with upper-class whites, as Putney and so many others had done.

"The white man just wouldn't stand up, Macaulay—not when it came right down to it. Everybody come just to talking about what the government might do. Afraid the government was gonna take away their cotton payments. Plenty of people, I've heard em say, 'Jack, goddammit, we've got to stick together in this thing.' Sure, plenty of folks was talking like that as long as it was all down there in Montgomery or up in Birmingham. Everybody talking real big until the time came to stand up. And then they all say, 'Well, I don't know, Jack. I just don't know.' God knows we had plenty of time to get ready — plenty of time to see what was happening in all them other places. Yeah, I remember how it was — everybody always saying, 'Hell, Jack, they might get away with that stuff down there in Montgomery, but they ain't gonna get away with it up here. We know how to handle our niggers better'n that.'

"And then it was up in Birmingham, and everybody talking the same way: 'Yeah, they might get away with it up there, but they ain't pulling that stuff down here.'" And then it was in Selma, and everybody still talking about what they would do if the niggers ever started strutting their stuff up here in New Erie and Mt. Gizeh. And then it was in Eaton and Warsaw, Little River—all them other places, and folks still talking that way: 'Naw, it ain't ever gonna be like that up here.' And then the next thing we knew it was up here too, all that mess, bootlegged in here by rapscallion black men on the take, riding around in their goddamn rent cars — and in rented airplanes too — and your tax dollar and mine paying for it all. And nobody anywhere wanting to stand up and do anything about it: 'Hell, Jack, I don't know. I just don't know.'

"And here's another thing, Macaulay: You think it's right for King and his coon squads to be riding around all over Catalpa County — all over Alabama too, by God — in them goddamn rent cars paid for at taxpayer's expense? You know it ain't right. Anybody knows that. But do you think anybody wants to fight it? Well, you see what I'm talking about: when all the cards was on the table, the white man just wouldn't fight. He just wouldn't stand up."

But Calloway had stood up. During the first weeks of the New Erie demonstrations, he had gone to the half-dozen tenant families still on his place and told them that they "didn't have no more land." He hated it for people like old man Mo Jackson, who had been on the place all his life and was left with no choice but to move in with a sister in Birmingham. And he hated it for Aaron Pollard too. He and

Pollard were almost the same age and had often run together as teenagers. But when Calloway found out that his old friend had thrown in with the agitators, there was nothing for it but that he come down on him hard. Pollard was not in the strictest sense a tenant; he had a house and five acres of his own. But he had been renting from Calloway another one hundred acres on which to grow his cotton and grain. So Calloway went to him one night and said, "Aaron, some of these soybean folks, they've offered to buy that tract you been working at a good price. A mighty good price. Looks like I'm gonna have to let em have it, Aaron." Pollard had known what was coming. Or had reason to know it anyway. Calloway had warned him a long time ago to "stay clear of that communist mess, Aaron — stay clear," because, if he got mixed up in it, not even the memory of all the good times they'd had as teenagers—the whiskey they had shared—the hunting trips — could save him from financial ruin.

Pollard had once told me much the same story: "It wasn't no lie. He broke me, Missa Jack did. He sho broke me." Pollard had eventually landed a job with a highway construction crew in Birmingham. But he had never really left Mt. Gizeh; he had managed to hang onto his house and five acres, and was back there every weekend. Big Mose Washburn and I had found him there one Saturday afternoon, out by his pigsty, hosing down a litter of newly born Tamworths.

"Nawsuh, he didn't tell no lie. He sho broke me; he broke me good." We talked for a long while that afternoon. But my first impulse had been to retreat. He stood there banditlike, a handkerchief covering the lower half of his face to help shut out some of the smell, the hose pointing at us like a still-smoking revolver. He flung off the mask and came toward me with a glower that went to the bone. Half of his thin mustache was missing, as though he had ripped that off too. "Yeah," he said, "I played some part in that movement you talking about—some right important part in it too." We dragged up cans of freshly shelled corn and sat talking about his part in it. He spoke bitterly of his experiences with Calloway; yet he had never ceased thinking of him as an old friend. "We come up together, me and Missa Jack did. We come up together."

But the relationship had begun deteriorating even before it came out about Pollard's sympathies with the movement. By the summer of 1965, Calloway had already begun giving him a "cold sign." There had been an argument not so much about politics as about Pollard's duties on the plantation and the inadequate pay he had been receiving. He had been taking more time to do less, quitting earlier, quibbling over terms. That mainly was what had brought on the cold sign. He quickly lost all of his old privileges: the right to drink with Missa Jack and consult with him on a confidential basis, the right to sit in the cab of the pickup on his way to and from the field. Nor was he favored any longer with a ride to the door of his house each evening after work. Now he had to get out on the main road and walk the last half mile or so through a patch of woods.

But in all of that time he had never really been a part of the demonstrations in New Erie. He had stayed out of all that, not for the reason that Abner Lowe and some of the other people he knew had stayed out of it, not because he was opposed to it, but simply and plainly because he wasn't "gonna put up with no hitting and kicking out of all them crackers." He just wasn't nonviolent enough, that's all. He would go to the mass rallies and speak out in behalf of his rights and do what he could to get people to the polls. But mostly he had stayed out of the marches. "Now you always heard em say it was supposed to be a movement of nonviolence. Now you always heard em say that. But I always did say—and I say right today—that if any one of them crackers jump on me and try to kick me or cut me, I gonna fight back. Anybody try to cut me and I gonna kill that honkey."

His speech had become an unrelieved denunciation of just about everything connected with the white man's world. He talked about the Little River loan shark who had started squeezing him for payments on a truck he had just bought and about the Taschahatchie City merchant who told him, "Naw, naw, Pollard, there ain't no more credit here" and about the afternoon the crop duster flew over the AME

Zion Church in New Erie (Yes, he knew all about Calloway's part in it), spraying cotton poison on his wife as well as on his "second woman," both of whom were in the march that day.

He was still talking about all that as we got up to leave, the vestiges of his thin mustache bristling horribly. He followed us out into the sunlight. "Yeah, I sho been playing some part in this movement you talking about. But I always did say if any of them crackers jump on me and start something, I gonna kill them honkey bastards." I walked a little more quickly, Pollard closing in behind me, giving me the cold sign. "Yeah, I gonna kill all them bastards, cause I ain't nonviolent enough. Listen to me now. I gonna kill all them honkey bastards. . . ."

* * *

Calloway swung right onto the New West Catalpa Road and ran alongside the railroad tracks for a mile or more. South of the railroad lay an immense stretch of land that just last year had yielded a bumper crop of cotton—Pollard's cotton—and was now taken up with soybeans. It was the same all along that road: new soybean plantations intermingled with fields of pine seedlings planted by the big paper companies and with other fields that had simply been left to lie fallow—tangible evidence of the white man's "conspiracy"—of what had been happening all over the cotton South for the last year and a half. But even Calloway would insist that there was something more behind it than mere politics. Like other landowners he would lay it mostly to economic realities: tenants unwilling to work except on their own terms, wage rates that were very nearly prohibitive anyway.

So it wasn't just a matter of getting even. It was a matter of protecting himself, of doing what he could to make the land pay. You might even say he had put himself out being tolerant of the darkies—keeping them on the land long after it had become a losing proposition, showing concern for their well-being and loyalty to all the old memories. Yes, he had "sacrificed a lot for the niggers," way too much for his own good. He had known all along that it would be more profitable to engage in other ventures, to plant soybeans or pine seedlings, or to bring in automated cotton harvesting equipment. So maybe there had been too much talk of a conspiracy. Maybe, he kept saying, it was only a matter of his doing what he had to do — what he would eventually have had to do, in all likelihood, even if his tenants hadn't turned on him and started all this marching and voting.

The soybean fields swept past us, fields Calloway had sold, others he had put out on lease, one where his own crop was growing. At a point almost opposite the southern entrance to the Holston plantation, we lurched off onto a narrow paved road that led across land once worked by an old Negro named Buck Simpson and now by Bow Wow McCardle's mechanical harvesters. McCardle was another of Calloway's close friends and fellow conspirators. The strip of asphalt gave way to a sand clay road that led on beyond the McCardle property and off through a wild stretch of bottom country, open land on one side and timber on the other, then timber on both sides — big timber that shut us up abruptly in twilight. Then all of the land opened up and we were out across a wide blazing field set vividly against a fringe of pines — cotton everywhere now, all up and down the bottom, Calloway's cotton, and beyond that — off there beyond the pines — the slow murmur of the river. We got there just as the laborers — the few still needed to operate Calloway's expensive equipment — were beginning to knock off work.

"Evening, Missa Jack."

"Evening, boys. You all have a good day?"

"A right good day, Missa Jack. Mighty preciative of seeing you all out hyar this evening."

"Glad to be here, Elk. How's Moose?"

"Some better, Missa Jack. He getting along."

"Still too poorly to come to the field, though."

"That's whut he say, Missa Jack."

"You boys take it easy now."

"Mighty preciative, Missa Jack. Mighty preciative."

"Them's good niggers," he said as he watched them go on up the rise. "The last of the white man's niggers."

We stood there in what was left of the September afternoon, Calloway and his raised bottle of Jim Beam silhouetted against a melancholy splotch of sunset. Then it was my turn — my bottle, my silhouette.

"Save Krites a drink."

"Krites?"

"He's supposed to meet us here."

Almost as he spoke, Krites appeared, climbing out of his Thunderbird and striding down the rise, a big man with an air of mischievous affability, widely known as a boozer, womanizer, gambler, and all-around dissolute. In less than five years he would be dead by his own hand, one more such death in a county already said to boast the highest suicide rate in Alabama.

"Jack!"

"Krites! How is it, boy?"

"First rate. How's it going?"

He drank the shot that Calloway had saved him and quickly returned to the Thunderbird to get his own bottle. "Here's the real stuff. Ain't no fooling around." So again we stood there, the three of us, the scintillant bottle raised, our silhouettes growing dimmer, Calloway and Krites talking about cotton and the movement and cotton and the lying Birmingham newspapers and cotton and that goddamn Martin Luther Coon and cotton — always cotton, how much of it they had grown that year and how much they had not grown in order to qualify for the government's acreage diversion payments. The new crop program, now in its first year, would net Calloway some fifteen thousand dollars annually and Krites more than twenty thousand dollars. Not bad for once-productive land now devoted to the production of very little except morning glories and buttercups and wiregrass and just plain old weeds. All that land just lying there soaking up warm rain and sunshine and costing the taxpayers even more than that whole fleet of rent cars that Coon and his henchmen had been riding around all over the state of Alabama in. I put forward the Atlanta liberal's point of view, through a fog of drink, arousing only a mild show of curiosity, no scorn as yet, probably because it hadn't registered with them that a man supposedly their friend would up and take the part of the agitators. Or maybe they thought I was only kidding.

"What's he saying, Jack?"

"Beats me."

The last of the sunset splashed feebly down. Behind us there came a sudden flutter of wings, dusk-borne, while off in the pine flats a mourning dove lofted a plaintive cry to warn us, I suppose, of Krites's destined suicide.

"The white man won't stand up," Calloway said. "Damn few of them will."

"That's right," Krites said. "That's right."

"There's no group of white men that's ever gonna stand together like the Jews and the niggers. Now that's a sad commentary on the affairs of our time. But it's the God's truth."

"It's the truth," Krites said. "It's the truth."

Krites wished to know what had ever happened to the real spirit of America. Calloway wasn't sure. He seemed rather mixed up about it all. Only I knew and felt competent to explain, as the bottle again came around. I explained what Kennedy had said. And Thomas Jefferson. "Them bastards," Krites said. "What do them bastards know?" Patience, Krites, patience. The real spirit of America, I told him, and very patiently, too, was Vietnam and racism and the despair of the cities and—get this, Krites—the government's crop control and acreage diversion program. Big subsidies for the wealthy, food stamps for the downtrodden. That's where the real spirit of America was. The pity of it all. The shame. What about it, Krites? Krites doubted the validity of my assumption and railed instead against "the black maw of the octopuslike tentacles of the federal bureaucracy." Calloway nodded. The bottle again came around.

"A goddamn shame," Calloway said. "A goddamn shame that the white man won't stand up."

Krites again wanted to know, and no more nonsense about it, what had happened to individual initiative and free enterprise and all the other things that had made America great. All gone into the soil bank, Krites. Buried there by the same hand that passes out all those cotton subsidies. Yes, it was all quite clear now: the shame and grief and deceit and greed. The sins of the planter aristocracy and the Big Mules and the Wall Street brokerage houses. The robber barons. Vanderbilt. The sordid cartels. The masses too easily led, too easily betrayed. Oh, the pity of it all! The arrogance of the money power! The tyranny of the majority!

But what was all this fol-de-rol? Krites wanted to know. Why didn't we just get down to brass tacks and never mind what Samuel Jefferson and Adam Locke and the Prophet Obadiah had said. Or Macaulay. To hell with all them bastards. The main thing was why a man could no longer do as he pleased with his land, his home, his own soul. A question indeed that had occupied the great thinkers throughout the ages: the uncertain ground between Liberty and Prerogative. I explained what de Toqueville had said, and Mill. But Krites thought Mill a dangerous fanatic. "Them's just the kind of bastards we don't need in this country." Patience, Krites, and bear in mind, please, the three guiding principles of the universe: Change! Action! Progress! Wasn't it Jefferson who said it would be well for the country if we could have a revolution every generation or so?

"What does he know? What do all these fuckers know?"

"Nothing, Krites. Just forget it. Nothing."

"And what does some bastard from Atlanta know?"

"I told you, Krites: nothing. Just forget it."

"All these bastards. All these grand concepts. All these big deals. All these motherfuckers. . . ."

"Here now," Calloway said. "Let's not forget that we're all friends here."

And so we were. Pals. Gathered there like mythical planter heroes in a tremendous rush of sundown, the scintillant bottle raised, our voices growing more clamorous as night grew more insistent; a good feeling about what life had been in the South and what it could be again. If it just wasn't for all them goddamn rent cars. And the International Dago Conspiracy. And the Communist pinko Wall Street money power. And keep the goddamn Harvard pointy-heads out of it too. And all of those federal bureaucrats who couldn't park a bicycle straight and had nothing in their briefcases but peanut butter and jelly sandwiches.

"Amen!"

"Amen!"

* * *

We were in Krites's Thunderbird, the night whirling past, the road coming at us swiftly, unerringly: a rush of pines and moonsilt, undulant sweeps of prairieland, voices indistinguishably mingled with the silken hum of the motor, violent spasms of laughter; and then Krites's voice clearly dominant: ". . . Right along here's where it was that they castrated that nigger that time. Caught him trying to put the make on Miss Minnie Folger. Cut the bastard's nuts out and made conjure dust out of them."

"Conjure dust?"

"Sure, it's an old recipe. You grind them up into a real fine powder and then mix in a little rooster shit and the ground-up eyes of a syphilitic rattlesnake, and then you roll it all up into a conjure ball and stick it in somebody's pocket. Ain't no way they can ever get a hard-on after that."

More spasms of laughter as we rolled into New Erie, the town already dark and quiet at eight o'clock. And then we were beyond the town and out around the long curve toward the railroad viaduct and then across the viaduct too; then down a series of mean streets into the thickets of Purseline, the old Negro slum quarter: a grotesquerie of stilted hovels, miasmic piglots, broken-down fences and rutted alleys, the whole place murmurous with the noises of early evening: people on their porches rocking or out talking by their fences or hosing down shrunken bitter patches of garden. Four more years and it would all give way to an antiseptic government-subsidized housing development. *We shall overcome somedaaayyyyy. . .*

Deep in my heart
I do believe. . . .

Calloway couldn't seem to remember which house he wanted. We plunged frantically about the rutted lanes, like a baffled minotaur on the prowl. "Could have sworn it was right here," Calloway kept saying. "Right down here and turn to your left." But he was hopelessly lost; we all were; we seemed to be always on the same street, at the same dead end, each street identical with every other; houses, storefronts etched sharply against the huge ribcage of night, yet nothing seen clearly. And always the same tawdry play of neon: *Haitian Nights. El Paradiso.* Phantomlike bordellos of the night, to be gone with the first sun. And Calloway saying, "Easy now. Take it easy. Right here. No. Up this way. Could have sworn..." Then he saw it, right where he had thought it was all along: a shotgun shack atop a long flight of rickety steps. And him already out of the car even as Krites screeched to a precarious halt above a steep honeysuckle-choked ravine. We watched him go dimly to the top of the steps and lose himself in the dark of the porch. At last there came a light at the screen, a hand, Calloway himself a mere shadow among shadows, waiting; then again the hand, the bottle, the furtive exchange. And Calloway coming running in three easy strides down the steps and across the street, holding the bottle of cheap Century Club, stooping low to squeeze his long frame hurriedly into the front seat of the Thunderbird.

"Where's Olive? Ain't she coming?"

"Wasn't home. Say they don't know where she is."

Krites scratched off. "You mean I ain't gonna get no nigger nookie tonight?"

"Don't look like it."

Krites cruised the El Paradiso, but she wasn't there either. Or at the other house where Calloway had found her once. Nothing to do but head on back. Getting late anyhow. A lot to answer for when they got home.

Krites somehow found his way quickly and easily back to the hard-surface; and then, inexplicably, we were sitting with motor idling on a graveled lot in front of the old AME Zion Church. Calloway passed the bottle while Krites sang freedom songs. Less than four months earlier the building, dark now, had been the scene of nightly get-out-the-vote meetings and protest rallies, the door always thrown open in those days, the air rife with promise, defiant voices: Sedley Jones always there in the pulpit *let the baloney rot let the big cheeses rot let all them things rot* and, beside him, all the intense young shirtsleeved SCLC organizers from Atlanta; and King himself on rare occasions, all of them standing there talking about "different skins, one blood, equal rights." And among them, without fail, the young man Cyrus Blue, the most persistent of them all, perhaps even the most eloquent, a rival to King himself:

When is America gonna change? When is Alabama gonna change? When is Catalpa County gonna change? O Lord, when is this old world gonna change?

Big Farms and Nice Times

July 1967

"My name's Willie — William, that is — but most folks they call me Buck. Buck Simpson, that's the name I most generally goes by. But old man George Aspers, he give me a new name. He call me 'Bull.' He say, 'Bull, I been watching you real close these last few months, and if you do as well this year as you been doing, and you plowing with nothing but mules, I gonna extend yo lease. I gonna give you a five-year lease."

It was Friday afternoon, the second time in less than a week that Willie had stopped by the store to talk about how well he and old man Aspers had hit it off. "Old man George, he say, 'Yeah, I gonna sho go along with you, Bull, I gonna do something for you I never did do for nobody else, cause I been watching you, Bull, and you works hard.' He say, 'Here you are and you ain't got but one kid left with you now, and you most too old now to farm behind a mule, but you keeps a going. You don't have no Saturday. You works from first thing Monday morning till Saturday night and the sun done *gone*. So I gonna do it, Bull, I gonna gives you that lease you been wantin.' But he say, 'Onliest thing is, Bull — now you know how I likes to go up to the gin at ginning time and see all the boys, and I can't drive no more, and my wife dead, and she can't drive me, and all my kids gone — so Bull, alls I ask is that you let me ride up thar to the gin with you when you goes up thar to gin yo cotton'. . . ."

Willie Simpson, or "Buck" as he says, wouldn't have known anything about the decent white man named George Aspers if he hadn't known Bow Wow McCardle and Jeff

Throne first. They were the ones, he said, who had kicked him off the land he had been farming for almost twenty years. During all of his years there he had gotten on well with the original landowner, old man Dave McCardle. But the old man's death in the summer of 1966 had left Buck at the mercy of the younger McCardle — Bow Wow — and his new partner Jeff Throne. "Said they were going into big farming together, Throne did. He say, 'Yeah, Uncle Buck, we going into big farming — big machines. Ain't goan have no more tenants.' Say: 'Yeah, that's right, Uncle Buck, we goan use all the land you got.' "

It was the old story. "White man allus got some excuse for bringing in them machines. Saying it's good business and all that. But the onliest reason is cause we voted — cause we been up thar marching." Willie had known all along that Bow Wow didn't like him. But he had known, too, that he had nothing to fear as long as Bow Wow's old man was alive. The old man had never much cared whether Willie went into town to catch up on what "society" had to recommend or whether he stayed at home with his cotton and whiskey stills. The way Willie got the story was this: "Bow Wow he allus be going up thar telling old man Dave, say: 'Now that Willie, he done gone up thar to be in the march agin today. Allus up thar in New Erie marching, allus standing up thar in the church saying, 'We wants equal rights. We wants to be free.' But old man Dave, he allus say, 'Well, whut does I care bout all his marching? It's his shoes he wearing out, ain't it? He ain't calling on me to buy his shoes, is he?' But Bow Wow, he say, 'I gonna farm, me and Jeff we gonna farm together, we gonna go into big farming — gonna get rid of all them nigguhs and bring in machinery — big harvesters, big cultivators.' That's the way he talk to his old man, you see. Telling him he wanted all the land for hisself and what a big crop he goan make with all them big machines he and Jeff Throne goan bring in. But old man Dave, he say, 'Naw, naw, naw, Bow Wow, we gots to let Uncle Buck alone. He ain't hurting nothing. Besides, whar is all the poor folk goan go if we kick them off? You gots to let uncle Buck alone now. Ain't none of our affair if he wants to spend his time up thar marching — long as he get his work done. We ain't buying his shoes.' "

In the old days "Uncle Buck" had gotten all of his "advancing" from the Old Gentleman and had been a frequent visitor in the Holston store. But we hadn't been seeing much of him now that Little Brother was in charge. Today he had come in to do some trading in discs and harrows, the first time he had been there at all since leaving the community for a new life on the Aspers place near Vestal. I already knew some of his story, including the part — from Mrs. Lurellia — about how he still owed the Holstons money and how they never really expected to collect it all even if he did get his five-year lease from old man George Aspers. He was past sixty, still lean and vigorous, if slightly arthritic, the hollow of his mouth framed by twin bicuspids and he himself always ready for a good laugh.

There were many like him: old tall thin men from the country, men who had been in the front of the civil rights agitation long before Birmingham or Selma and who had done what they had to do without any prompting from the young SCLC organizers — who had been doing it during all those years before anyone had ever even heard of the SCLC. Buck had grown up on the old Wilkes place across the river and had gotten his first lesson in civil rights from a band of Austrian loggers that had come into the Tombigbee swamps many years ago on a timber-hunting expedition. Big Johann and Little Johann, the leaders of the expedition, had taught him a great deal about the supposed rights of a working man. "First men I ever knowed that'd allus take time out fur their rest break." He was already an experienced lumberjack by that time. During his early years he had worked for a timberman named Hughs McGrady, who thought that "a nigguh wuzn't nothing but a locomotive." Willie, or Buck, talked with amazement of those days, trying to remember how it was, how far he had walked to get to his job, how little he was paid. "Night coming and night going," he said. "Never even see the outside of my house till Sunday morning." Before he was sixteen he was already putting in a twelve-hour day, cutting and stripping timber that lay waist-high in the swamp and then hauling it out in great cartloads to the river, where other men waited with jamb hooks and iron mallets to snare the logs as they tumbled down the high bank and bind them into huge rafts that would make their way untended to the Mobile ports. "Eighteen miles a day — nine miles to the logging camp and nine miles back home. Leaves home walking at three or four in the morning and gets back at ten, eleven, at night. And all that for fifty-five, sixty cents a day."

But that was before the Austrians had come. He would spend five good years — better anyway than anything he had known before — working for the Austrian logging crews, mostly as a hewer of staves for the European barrel-making industry. "Didn't start so early or quit so late — didn't have to walk so fur neither. Finds me an old waste house near the camp and stays thar during the timber-cutting season." And he always got his rest break. That mainly was what he remembered about it — how at nine-thirty or nine-forty-five each morning and again at three in the afternoon Big Johann would fling down his ax and cry out:

Sammer fer juse!

"That was their word fur 'rest break.' Time to set down and eat a little something, talk about things." One of the things they talked about was why the Austrians habitually selected only the prime heartwood from a tree and left the cheap sapwood to rot in the swamp. McGrady had left nothing behind. He had processed it all — the cheap scrap timber along with all the rest — and sold it all for the same premium price. Buck asked about that one day at rest break. "Little Johann, he turn to me real slow and say, 'Willie?' I say, 'Yeah?' He say, 'Willie, Americans cheap beat.' That 'uz his word for it: 'cheap beat.' He say, 'Sap no good, Willie. Sap cheap. Americans cheap. Ha! Americans pay too little. Sell too high. Sell sapwood fur big prices like heartwood. Heartwood last maybe sixty years, but sap rots, no good. Americans no good.' "

Buck had never heard a white man talk that way about other white men. He wondered if there could be some mistake. But apparently not: "Little Johann he say, 'Willie?' I say, 'Yeah?' He say, 'We have got big timber in our country, Willie. Big timber. Old. Big. Not like hyar. We no cut. Americans they cuts their timber. Sell! But we no cut. We save.' He talk about all them big trees they got over thar, trees thicker than I am tall, he use to say, but I threatens to disbelieve him, cause he talking bout all our big timber like it ain't nothing. But I been working in all that timber. I know whut it is. Thar wuz *real* timber in this country then. Big logs, thick logs. Took a nine-foot saw and two men on each side to cut one of them logs in two—and him talking bout it like it ain't nothing but little old scrap timber. So I threatens to disbelieve him. But Little Johann, he come to get right fretted up if you challenges him. He turn loose and say, 'You crazy, Willie. Crazy! Americans crazy. Money, money, money. Hell, you don't know. Americans all *swartsy bastardy*!' That's whut he say: '*Swartsy bastardy*. Americans all *swartsy bastardy*.' I say, 'Well, if you got all that big timber over thar, all that extra No. 1 timber, why you coming over hyar to buy our little old 'scrap' timber? He say, 'Save, Willie. Save. Every two, three, years we go through and pick out bad timber. Timber sick, dying. Sick, sick. Timber goan die...we cut! But we no cut good timber.' You see, we wuzn't looking fur the day when this country would get short of timber. We didn't know that. But in their country they wuz already preparing fur that—and they taking our timber instead. Little Johann he say, 'Willie, one day America...out! No good timber left. We go home. We cuts at home then, and America have to grow its timber all over agin.' "

Buck had lived to see something like the fullfillment of that prophecy. In time—"after the black man come to be a little more in freedom"—he had become an exploiter himself. He got his own logging team and worked as a subcontractor for the B. L. Sams Lumber Co. He had two wagons, a pickup and eight mules, and had once worked as many as eleven men at a time. But by the end of World War II, most of the real timber was gone. He understood then what Little Johann had been talking about during all those rest breaks in the swamp. "Americans no good. Americans cheap." The words would come back many times, in a thousand different ways, as he became more aware of the difference between what the land-of-the-free had promised and what it had been able to deliver. Little Johann had always wanted to know why Buck never insisted on more pay and shorter hours, why he had never taken the rest breaks that were the inalienable right of any working man. Buck didn't know how to answer at first. He had never thought about it like that. He had become confused and had tried to argue with Little Johann, making him "go all fretted." And then Buck had become fretted too, not at Little Johann but at all the things Little Johann had talked about—the injustice and disrespect and inequality.

And he stayed fretted. During his last years on the Wilkes plantation he came to be known as something of a troublemaker. He began talking up to old man Adam Wilkes and was ever making some complaint or other about "advancing" procedures at the plantation store. His days on the place finally ended one winter afternoon when old man Wilkes's son, ridiculed by Buck and some of the others as "John the Third," called the tenants together and announced that he was bringing in a "rider" to oversee production. There was nothing unusual about that; it was a common practice on most of the larger plantations. The difference this time was that the tenants were to pay the man out of the "advancing" money they had been getting from the federal government.

"Fellow by the name of Charlie Ford, he dead now, but he stand up and say, "Missa John, I wishes you to relate this to me agin, cause I believes I done made a mistake in my hearing. Does I understand you to say you is sending in a rider to ride over our farms and give us orders whut to do?' And John the Third he say, 'Yeaaahh.' And Charlie Ford say, 'And does I understand you to say that this man is to be paid $200 a month?' And John the Third say, 'Yeaaaahhh.' And Charlie Ford say, 'And does I understand you to say that it will be so much out of every one of us to pay this man to ride over us?' And little John he say, 'Yeaaaaahhhhhh.' And Charlie Ford say, 'Well, by God, I move.' And we all jumps up and say, 'Yeah, by God, we all move. We all leaves this place.' "

And so they had. By planting season almost the entire black population of the Wilkes place was gone, some seventy or eighty people in all. The exodus brought most of them to Catalpa County, and it eventually brought Buck Simpson and his family (though not before some unsettled years in which he developed a fondness for drink and other women) to the McCardle plantation on the New West Catalpa Road.

Buck had known for a long time before his eviction from the McCardle land that Bow Wow's father was in failing health. Still, he was not quite prepared for the old man's death or for the suddenness with which his heirs moved to take over the land.

"Old man Dave wuz buried on Saturday and they 'uz out riding on Monday. They rode every which a way, all up and down, all over the place, till mine wuz the last house." Buck had waited for them all afternoon. And then at a little after five o'clock he heard the pickup coming. But the man who climbed out of the truck wasn't Bow Wow McCardle; it was Jeff Throne, a lanky West Catalpa farmer who knew all about how to make money out of cotton even if Bow Wow didn't.

"Evenin, Missa Jeff."

"Evenin, Uncle Buck."

Buck had hoped that the two men—or, as it turned out, Throne—would let him keep the house and enough land for a "truck patch" and some sweet potatoes. The tract he had in mind was some two acres of what had once been a densely wooded marsh and was now, thanks to his own enterprise, some of the most productive land on the place. Surely the partners would consent to let him keep that much out of the more than thirty acres he had been farming, seeing as how he had taken it upon himself to reclaim it from the swamp. But Throne said, "Dunno, Uncle Buck. Dunno what Bow Wow might have to say about that." The lanky red-haired gent was amiable enough, as he stood there scratching his head under his lifted cap, but he left the tenant no recourse.

It was all a matter of economics, he explained. What he and his partner would be paying in rent charges — to old man McCardle's widow — would come to more than the worth of Buck's entire cotton crop.

"We gonna need ever hill we can put in, Uncle Buck."

Buck knew it was useless trying to talk about it anymore. He walked off a ways and stood there for quite some time, out at the edge of the yard, looking back at the place that had been his home now for almost twenty years. He had a good house, built of cement block, not like a lot of tenant shacks; a good floor, sound and dry. Later the new partners would lease it out as a nightspot. Maybe they had already signed the contract even before Throne came down there that afternoon. Anyway, Buck knew there was no more to be said. In Bow Wow's mind (and perhaps in Throne's mind too) burned the memory of too many civil rights marches, too many rallies in too many dimly lit churches, too many non-negotiable demands, too many picketers with signs blaring "Freedom Now!" Throne had come there to do what he had to do, to do it as amicably as possible, but to do it in any case. So Buck just wouldn't say any more about it. All he said was:

"Whar Bow Wow?"

"He up at the store."

"Ain't he coming down hyar to talk to me bout this thing?"

"Reckon not, uncle Buck. Reckon he ain't gonna have time to get down here today. Said he had a little business to take care of up at the store."

That was the worst part of all. Not that he cared for Bow Wow any more than Bow Wow cared for him. But it hurt him to think that the young man who had talked so big when his father was alive didn't even have it in him to come down there and face the man he was about to wrong.

"Jes go on and take it all then. Ain't no use talking bout it no more."

Again he walked off from the tall amiable farmer who had come there to do what Bow Wow had been afraid to do. He went around to the side of the house this time and stood gazing out at the two-acre tract he wouldn't even be allowed to grow a crop of sweet potatoes on.

"Naw, it don't matter," he said as he rejoined Throne in the front yard. "Ain't nothing to me no more. Jes go on and take it all."

Throne seemed to be thinking it over as he climbed back in the truck. Then, as he hit the starter, he said, "Tell you what, Uncle Buck. We'll let you keep the house for, say, $15 a month. I believe I can talk Bow Wow into that. We got to have all the land though." To Buck that was the biggest joke of all. "How I goan pay?" he asked the man. "How I goan live? How I goan get that $15 a month if I ain't got no land to farm?"

"Sorry it's got to be like that, Uncle Buck."

"Ain't no help for it."

But Buck was more fortunate than many of his kind in that he had been able to work out a new arrangement — maybe an even more satisfactory arrangement — with old man George Aspers. He could not escape his reputation though; the stories and rumors pursued him even there. This time it was old man George Aspers's nephew, Rich Aspers, who had begun spreading the word about Buck and all his "marching." That, at any rate, was the way Buck had gotten the story: "This young fellow Rich Aspers he go up to old man George and say, 'Doesn't you realize that that's one of them civil rights Negroes?' But Missa George he say, 'Whut does I care bout him and his civil righteousness? We got land to rent. Might as well be him renting it as somebody else.' " For some reason — probably because he was willing to work harder than anyone else on the place — he and the landowner had struck it off right from the beginning. He always invited the old man to go along when he went to gin his cotton, and now he was getting ready to sign a lease that would give him clear and unrestricted use of the land for five years. That was something he had never had, something very few tenants ever got, and in the end it would protect him against the encroachments of a paper company that had brought most of the surrounding land for a tree farm. Old man Aspers would die less than a year after signing the lease, leaving his property to heirs who, like so many others of their generation, would begin to look to tree farms and soybeans for income rather than to tenants and cotton. But Buck would stay on there, for the full five years of his lease, growing his cotton and tending his cows, surrounded by pine seedlings that would be more than half grown before the time came for him to move on. And when that time did come he would have saved enough for a down payment on some land and a house of his own.

But nothing would ever convince him that what had happened to him on the McCardle land was anything but the result of a widespread conspiracy, mysteriously orchestrated by landowners whose motives were more sinister perhaps than they sometimes pretended.

"They always got some slick way of disrecognizing you —telling you you ain't got no more land. But they ain't goan come straight out and tell you it's cause you been in the march. They afeard to do that cause they afeard of what the government might do. They always got to try and disguise it some way. They say, 'We gonna farm, we gonna go into big farming, we gonna farm all the land you got.' But that's just talking. That don't mean nothing. That's just a way they got of disrecognizing you — telling you they ain't got no more room for you cause they done gone out and bought all these hyar big harvesting machines. . . ."

* * *

The man who had taken Willie in was obviously one of those rare fellows who didn't "frown on the colored." But his only brother, Bill Aspers, a much younger man, was part of a different generation and a different way of thinking. It was he who had masterminded what many believed to have been the largest eviction ever to take place in west Alabama. A wealthy landowner in his own right, he was also administrator for the old Pepper Swaim estate, which included among much else an immense stretch of river-bottom country south of Mt. Gizeh. It was there that most of his victims lived.

Nobody knew exactly how many people Aspers had forced out — a hundred and fifty, two hundred, maybe more. The movement—what was left of it—tried to fight back by putting up more "propaganda tents" and by complaining to the newspapers. But the papers couldn't get anything out of Aspers except a lot of talk about the complex economic factors that had entered into his decision to negotiate a sale of the land, and didn't the whole world know how much it grieved him to turn loose "all those good darkies" who had meant so much to him and the Swaim family?

I got the other side of the story from Big Mose Washburn, who came in the store one day, crossed his legs with dignity, and said, "Naw, he jes got mad, Missa Bill did, cause all them folks went out and voted. That's all it wuz. All these hyar paper woods folks they come in making lak the Vanderbilts and telling Missa Bill, 'We wants this hyah land.' But Missa Bill, he didn't have to sell *nothing*. All he have to say is, 'Nawsuh, we ain't selling none of this hyah land.' Stead of that he drap the price way down. That's all it was. He jes got mad cause all them folks went out and started marching and voting."

The "paper woods folks" had acquired some three thousand acres in all, most of it in two large tracts. The one Big Mose and I knew best was the Flats, where Beatrice Montgomery had once spent so many summer afternoons seeking recruits for the movement. The other, lying farther upstream, near the confluence of the Tombigbee and Sipsey rivers, had come down in my wife's family before passing—by what means I was not certain—into the hands of the elder Pepper Swaim, at that time the county's most omnivorous forecloser and advancing merchant, a disturbingly pious man known best for the large rose-colored surveyors' map on which he kept track of his vast holdings. There were three shades of rose: the darkest for land to which he held title, a lighter shade for land to which he held an option or mortgage and would eventually acquire, the lightest of all for those numerous other tracts to which he had no claim but which he planned by whatever means presented itself to make a part of his empire.

One might often have found him at the back of his old store, hunched over a big rolltop desk with the map spread out before him, working frantically, adding new pinks, darkening the old. Death also found him there, one day in the summer of 1941, with his hand still on the crayon, his latest acquisition still only half tinted with its newest shade of rose. His only son, Little Pepper, a close friend of Aspers, did his best to keep up the family tradition. But the spirit of acquisitiveness had died in him somehow. After his father's death the rose-colored map fell into disuse, and the old Swaim store, with its haughty gallery and steeply pitched roof, stood shuttered and empty and choked with vines, as it does to this day, a scarcely noted landmark on the road between New Erie and Mt. Gizeh. It fell out, meanwhile, that Little Pepper had married into wealth almost as great as his own and had retreated across the river to the white-pillared splendor of Oak Grove plantation society, leaving all of his Catalpa County holdings in Bill Aspers keeping.

Aspers had handled all the negotiations for the river property (itself no more than an insignificant portion of the whole estate) and arranged for the removal of the tenants. But it was Swaim who signed the eviction letters, so that Aspers could say: "I could do nothing. It was out of my hands." And it was Swaim who got most of the blame. For a while it was almost like the early days of the movement: tenants meeting again by night in dimly lit country churches, clutching their eviction notices, singing freedom songs, inveighing against a man most of them had never even seen.

Swaim — or Aspers — had given them sixty days to get off the land and find another place, a deadline most of them had been unable to meet. All that spring the river bottoms had been full of the refugees, their mule-drawn wagons loaded with ramshackle bedroom suites, kitchen tables, iceboxes, bulging pasteboard boxes, farm implements, the remains of rotting pigsties and cowsheds to be built back in the same ruinous fashion. By July or August we began to realize what was happening. The whole community of the Flats was busy picking itself up and moving itself in its entirety to a virgin territory some five miles downriver, onto land purchased at $300 an acre from a black man who now lived with a sister in Detroit. The site stood in heavy woods, impassable, or almost so, less than a mile north of the river and almost within view of the old block manufacturing plant that had once been a favorite spot for so many of our midnight carousals and early-morning fishing trips.

For a time the whole land seemed astir: men moving in with axes and swing blades, whacking away at canebrakes and palmetto thickets and second-growth timber; everywhere a sound of land being cleared, a frontier taking shape; an incessant hammering and sawing, a persistent feeling of trees and grubbing up of stumps, great fires in the night; and then one day toward the end of September it was finished, the new village that already seemed quite old from the moment it sprang up there amid the canebrakes and briar thickets, all of it built back as it had been before, with that same air of invincible decay: barns, sheds, hoglots all thrown up in indiscriminate haste and already half falling down, the houses still unpainted, standing on pillars, roofed with the same slabs of rusty tin, covered with the same dreary husks of asphalt siding.

Calloway and I drove through the place one morning on our way down to what was left of the Flats community. Calloway sounded, for him, almost apologetic as he explained how his "good friend Bill" wasn't quite the sordid fellow the SCLC had been saying he was — how he had sold the land only because he had no other choice — because the offer he had gotten was way beyond the going price — because he was acting, after all, as an agent for Swaim, who was said to need the money for the settlement of some of his other affairs.

I had heard it all before and later that morning would hear it from Aspers himself. We ran on him by chance, as he was pacing the rutted byways of the Flats and surveying the work that had won him a headline or two in the *Tuscaloosa News.* He was a big florid tobacco-chewing man at least ten years older than Calloway, with a fleshy and easy manner and a way of stifling his laughter so that it all seemed to well up inside him and ooze out his pores. He stomped about magisterially in his heavy boots, assuring the few remaining tenants that even though they were some two months past the deadline set for their eviction he would not have them think they were under any great pressure to leave. No, he was not at all pleased with the hard task that had been laid before him. He really felt very badly about everything and would try to be as understanding as possible under the circumstances; he was, whatever they might think, a man of heart, and even the government could only drive a man so far.

The government?

Before I got a chance to find out what he meant by "government," Clytie Venable had come out on the porch to besiege Bill Aspers with questions about why he had to go and send her "a ninety-five-cent letter wid all them stamps on it" just to tell her she "didn't have no more land."

Aspers looked at her with a great show of stifled laughter.

"All you and Missa Swaim got to do is tell me to go. So how come you sends me that letter? How come you didn't jes give me that ninety-five cents and I could put a nickel on it and got me a good half-pint of whusky?"

Clytie knew quite a lot about "whusky." She had taken her first drink when she was six years old, too young to go to the field and therefore available to watch over her parents' improvised still. "I learns how to drink it with a teaspoon. It run out the spout; I gets me a teaspoon and drinks it." That had been her job on up until she was old enough to take her place in the field. By the time she was a teenager she already enjoyed a reputation as the most accomplished whiskey-maker in the Flats.

"Oh," she said. "Now I kin tell you something bout the whusky making. O Lawd! Jes clap it on down, cause, God knows, I sho knows something bout that."

She more than filled the ample wooden rocker in which she sat, staring down at us from under a wide-brimmed straw hat that partly obscured her chronically merry face. It was still merry in spite of all the bad news Aspers hated to have to come there and bring.

"Oh, clap it on down! Cause I kin sho tell you something bout that."

She no longer made the stuff. But she still drank it, heavily, monumentally, pausing only long enough to complete a complicated aging process. "Ages it right out the spout into my belly. That's how I ages it." A mighty laugh constricted her great body and flung her half out of the rocker, whereupon she gathered herself up like a bundle of wet crocheting and again railed at Aspers for wasting all those stamps just to send her "a little ol letter" telling her she "gots to move."

We had gone on up to the porch, where, I assumed, Aspers would give her the ninety-five cents she had talked about and maybe the extra nickel to boot. But he just kept surveying the place, looking all around, explaining how difficult it was for him to have to come there like that and ask her to give up the only real home she had ever known. Calloway obligingly joined in the ruse, allowing as how times like this were hard on everybody but that the paper woods folks had been on his good friend Bill something fierce to wrap up this transaction and that he had put it off as long as he could and....

"Whar we goan go, Missa Jack? How we goan do?"

Two years earlier I had seen her on the same porch—the day I had come down there with Eula and Beatrice Montgomery—and she had talked then as she talked now about her life in the Flats and the good times on the river. Even then her husband had been sickly and unable to go to the field. But he had grown much worse after the eviction notice came. "Back and forwards sick fur fourteen years. It ain't never goan be no different. He sick in the bed now. He ain't never goan be no better."

Her two well-wishers nodded sympathetically, Calloway again taking up Aspers' story while Aspers himself rumbled anew with stifled laughter and looked absently off toward the river. Then Clytie was looking at it too, talking about it—all the good times when the water was up and the nights cold and the whiskey clean and wild. Those were good times for all the people of the Flats. We had often watched them at such times, from the river bridge, whole boatloads of them, scurrying about like a breed of bucolic Venetian oarsmen. She talked about all those times, the times they had traveled merrily up and down the river—over to Ellerbe — up to New West Catalpa — to church on Sunday — on shopping trips—or maybe just to visit friends and play a few hands of gin rummy by lanternlight.

"Ever since thar wuz a worl the peoples wuz here," she said.

She remembered from my last visit that I was from "up there" and wanted to know if I was planning to write down all of what she had been telling me and "put it in history."

"Possibly. Yes."

Calloway's only concern was that I put together the kind of history that would exonerate his "good friend Bill here." Neither man, it seemed, could quite find the words that would portray his real feelings.

"Clytie," Aspers said. "You know how I feel about it. You know it's not what I want."

"Yassuh."

"But you understand that I had no choice. I did everything I could."

"Yassuh."

"It's the government, Clytie. The people out of Washington. They're into everything now. Ask Calloway there. A man can't do what he wants with his land anymore. He's got to do what the government says. The government—they're the ones that's running everything now."

The government? There it was again. But surely she would see that it was only their little joke. Calloway said, "It's true, Clytie. Ol Bill here, he did everything he could. Called the people up in Washington, the ones King works for. They wouldn't even listen. Went up to the land office in Birmingham. Same thing there. They just laughed, Clytie. So Bill says to them, says he: 'All those folks down there on the river—where they gonna go? How they gonna do? They don't know nothing but farming, and now you say I got to tell em to get off. . ?"

"Clytie," I said. "It's just his little joke. Clytie?. . ."

". . . Those folks just won't listen to reason," Calloway told her. "You know how the government is, Clytie. They came right out and threatened my good friend here. That's right, Clytie. That government fella stood up behind his desk and told ol Bill just to get on outa there or he'd have him worked over and locked up—called in some of his goons and said, 'Take care of this man. . . .' "

"For sho?"

"For sure, Clytie. Ol Bill here, he says, 'Now ain't this some way to treat a man that only wants to do what he can to keep all those folks down there on the river from losing everything they've been working for all these years?' But all that fella did was look at him and say, 'Take care of this man. . . .' "

"Is the government goan take all this land fur some kind of big farm?"

"I'm afraid so, Clytie. Sure does look like it. But you've got to remember that ol Bill did everything he could. Everything. Those folks just wouldn't listen, Clytie — that's the long and short of it. Ol Bill, he says, 'Now where're all those folks gonna go? How they gonna do? Ever since there was a world the people were there.' "

Ol Bill swore that every word Calloway said was the truth. "And you might as well go ahead and tell her the rest of it, Jack. Tell her I'm gonna let her keep the house—gonna let her and all these other folks take their houses with them. Yes sir, that's right, and anything else they want too."

"That's right, Clytie. That's the news ol Bill came here today to bring. He finally talked the government into letting you folks keep your houses and take them wherever you want. And I tell you what, Clytie: Bill's gonna let you have the house for nothing. That's right. The $200 the government said it had to have — Bill here says he'll pay it himself. The government won't know the difference. All they want is the land and their money, Clytie. They don't care about anything else. Never have, never will. That's why they talk the way they do—all the time talking about equal rights, voting, marching—straw men, Clytie. That ain't nothing but straw men they've been setting up—trying to distract everybody — always talking about what society's gonna do — and then while they're talking and you're all distracted they come in and take the land. And when somebody tries to stand up to em — the way ol Bill here tried to up there in Birmingham that day — they say, 'Take care of this man.' "

* * *

I did not see Clytie again until she had been some two months in her new location. Like the other refugees she had moved herself and all her belongings five miles downriver to the new-old village of McWrenn Quarter, named after the man from whom the building sites had been bought. Her new house, which was also her old house, stood at the head of the village street, just as you came out of the timber. She was quick to greet me when I drove up. She had just come back from her Saturday "lodge" meeting in New West Catalpa and was sitting on the porch with a lap full of unshelled peas. Her husband Will was with her this time, a frail trembly man who seemed incapable of outlasting the summer.

"Back and forwards sick fur fourteen years," she said. "He ain't goan be no better; he done flat gone to dying."

She still had her eviction notice, having placed it for safekeeping in her Bible, the one place "whar you don't have to worry bout folks peeping and prying." Just as she went in to get it, another man, whose name was also Will, came out to join the first, himself frail and unspeaking, each of them staring at me forlornly, emptily, like twin cocoons left vagrant on a roadside at the end of the summer. Clytie came back and handed me the envelope with the ninety-five-cents worth of stamps on it, explaining how she had first thought it was an extra check from the welfare office, a gratuity that would enable her to buy the pop-up toaster she'd been wanting. The message was stark:

> Will:
> You are hereby notified to quit and deliver up the possession of the dwelling house and the land

which you have been occupying and farming by April 1, 1967.

Yours Truly,

I.J. Swaim

That was all. Sixty-four years on the land, man and boy, and no souvenir but this from a man he knew only by reputation. "He dying right now. He ain't never goan get over it." And then she wanted to know why I—we—the government—had wanted to run her off. It was only then that I realized there was more to Calloway's little joke than I had thought: he had somehow managed to convey the impression that I, as an agent for the Great Society, had been responsible for her eviction and that Aspers had only come along to do my bidding.

"Why you tell us we alls got to leave?"

I explained how it really was, that Aspers and Calloway had only been out for a few laughs. But all she said was:

"Missa Jack and Missa Bill, they be's mighty fine and obliging white mens."

And even that wasn't the worst of it. After promising to let her have the house for nothing, Aspers had changed his mind and charged her the entire two hundred dollars. That two hundred, together with the six hundred she'd had to pay to get it moved, had exhausted her life savings and then some. But she would remain philosophical to the end.

"Missa Bill, he couldn't holp it. He have to do whut the government say do."

"No, Clytie. It wasn't the government. It was Aspers. He was agent for that land. He kicked you off. And then sold you a house he would otherwise have had to burn and could've just as easily let you have for nothing."

"O nawsuh. I thinks he done real good to sell me a house—cause I didn't have no house. O yeah, I thinks he done fine, cause that crib out yonder—that corncrib, you see hit?—he lets me have that too. Why, he most gives it to me, you might say, cause, you know, fur a house like this hyar, and that crib around the corner thar, all them planks and tin and everything—why, sho, I thinks he really done me a favor."

It was no good trying to explain any of it. She still had it all mixed up—the paper woods folks, the government, the landowner she had never even seen.

"Why you all make us move? Ever since thar wuz a worl the peoples wuz thar."

Until her eviction she had never left the Flats for anything more than a day or so at the time, except for the two years she had lived with her sister Elvina in Mt. Gizeh. She had gone there after the death of her mother and had come back at sixteen to marry the man who had never been well enough to do his share of the work and who even now, as he sat there at her side, seemed on the verge of dying—or rather not so much dying as actually shrinking up into a kind of cricketlike husk, to be blown away on the first night wind and forgotten.

The sun had gone much lower by the time I rose to leave, and a chill had come up. Clytie was still talking about it, her old life in the Flats—the river—the big whusky-drinking celebrations—and most of all her church, the story of which she hoped I would be able to work into my history. "So many folks say, 'Clytie, that would sho make a fine hist'ry.' " And the river again—always the river—the land and the river—and how lovely it all was in the winter with the water coming out of the banks, and then the wide lovely sheen of it as it spread to the base of the houses and drove the rabbits and quail to the high ground where there would be easy hunting.

I looked back once more and saw her still sitting there holding the ninety-five-cent letter and a lap full of peas—still wondering, I supposed, why the government had told her with one voice to vote and with the other to move. Even the mild good feeling she had about her new status as independent homeowner was not enough to compensate for what she had lost. "Cause down thar in the Flats we all had big farms and nice times. Cause I was born, and raised, and runnin, and jumpin, and happy — all my best days thar. It was all big farms and nice times to me."

YOU CAN COUNT ON LYNDON

June 1968

The old man sits again behind the unlighted coal stove, in the dingy two-seated rocker, the newspapers folded on his lap — not only the copy he has just been reading, but that other more faded copy that says:

**Police Hunt
King's Slayer**

He has saved it as a kind of souvenir from that more troubled time, as another reminder that the civil rights era with all of its delusions and fickle summer madness will soon be at an end. He emits a faint mirthless chuckle and says, "Nothing in his life became him like the leaving of it." He pauses, reflective. Then:

"It does seem like a mighty pitiful thing that a man would have to die in order to make the world so much better for everybody. But all the ways of the Lord are mysterious — and it does so look like folks would just be content to let Him work things out in His own way. They won't do it though. They sure won't. Nothing would do our law enforcement officials but that they had to go out and stir all around and do every which way until they found somebody to blame the shooting on. A mighty pitiful thing it seems to me. You'd think our officials would have the good sense to let the matter drop. I just never did hold all that high an opinion of King's influence on the nigra race." He puts both papers to the side. "But it does help some to know that things are so much more peaceful now — so much more like they used to be."

And indeed, as he speaks of it, it seems true enough. The mood of change, so prominent now in the cities, seems to us as alien and remote as ever. The old man talks of it not with rage or even disdain but only with the plaintive hope that the black people of Alabama, free at last from the malign influences of their martyred leader, will soon regain their lost sense of direction, their abiding sense of decency and humility.

The movement is still there, of course. We can see ample evidence of it in the papers and on television each evening. But it is mostly in the cities now. For more than two years Catalpa County has been spared the marches and protest demonstrations. Once again the land has fallen under the perpetual reign of summer; again a profound calm hangs over the store, over the surrounding community, over all of that vast and desolate countryside. And, best of all, the beleaguered South has an ally where a few short years ago it had none. What else are we to make of the rioting in Northern cities? What of the shouts of "Nigger, go home!. . . Nigger, go home!" on the streets of Chicago? Wasn't it King himself who talked about how the hostility he encountered there was more than equal to anything he had found in the South?

And again the old man, speaking softly, almost philosophically: "It does sorrow me so the way he has hurt our country. But the North. . . the *North,* they're in it too, now." A long pause, no movement, only his shadowy figure behind the coal stove, against a background of dark clutter; and then slowly the head moving, and then. . . what? A laugh?

"Yup," he says. "Yup. They're getting a little taste of it up there now." He rises suddenly and moves to the door. And then just as suddenly he is laughing again, not sardonically or ruefully, but with uncontrollable glee, bent over and holding on to the doorjamb, laughing and saying, "Yup, they're getting a bellyful of it up there now. . . . They're finding out what it's like now. . . what it's like to be told that they can't take a little action without first assembling with the nigras.... Yes sir, it does tickle me good, to think about all those cotton-patch nigras gallivanting around up there in Baltimore and Detroit and telling everybody that 'we wants this' and 'we wants that'... yes, sir, it sure does tickle me good...."

And then no laughter at all. Now he is talking of that other time long ago, before the war, the memory of it hanging over us like the indomitable spell of summer itself: the swirl of crinoline and lace in a thousand lighted ballrooms, the slaves singing in their squalid moonlit huts, the magic of September nights not yet loud with the approach of battle, the haunting sound of flute, clarinet and fiddle: *Going home ... going home ... Past those rolling fields of cotton ... Going home...* All of it flooding back now as it has so many times in the past. And there is talk of that other matter too: the matter of all those slaves the Yankees turned loose on their last march through the dying Confederacy. "They've always been just as resentful as they could be of the superiority of Southern culture, so they felt obliged not only to whup us but rob us too." He speaks of it—the freeing of the slaves—as though it might have occurred in the wake of the Selma demonstrations or during the march on Washington, the memory of it so persistent and clear that surely he—we—all of us—must have seen it on the Huntley-Brinkley or read about it in a recent edition of the *Birmingham News*.

He sits there behind the stove, the sunlight beginning to fade from the doorspace though not yet from the asphalt highway. And as he talks of these things, the slaves, the good times before the war, the old debt still "owing to us," you begin to feel the same regret and bitterness, the same urgency.

There have been times indeed when it began to seem almost plausible that at any moment the government agent himself would appear in the door, sweaty, his shirt pasted to him like damp lettuce, his hat off, a Southerner no doubt, with a soft not unfriendly voice yet with that air of command we have learned to associate with federal bureaucrats.

"Afternoon," he would say. "Name's H. Malachi Brown. With the U.S. Treasury."

The old man would rise hesitantly, clutching his newspapers, and move forward.

"Come on in and sit a spell."

"Got to be moving on, of course. But first I've got a little something for you."

And, of course, it would be the check, made out to Mr. Frank Holston, together with his heirs and assigns. Three hundred thirty-seven thousand, four hundred fifty-two dollars and forty-seven cents. A lot of money even in these inflationary times. And there would be something else too, a note appended to the back almost as an afterthought:

> My dear sir:
>
> Enclosed find check in the amount of $337,452.47, being repayment of the principal and interest on forty (40) slaves freed by the Yankee expeditionary force in the spring of 1865. We at the White House join those at the General Accounting Office in hoping you will forgive this delay. Owing to the chaotic state of public affairs in the first years after the war (not to mention the shoddy paperwork of a fumbling Republican bureaucracy) the innumerable records detailing federal responsibility in this matter only came to light in recent weeks.
>
> Sincerely Yours,
> Lyndon J.

"I suppose you folks just about gave us out," Malachi Brown would say. And by now he would have joined Little Brother in the two-seated rocker, in spite of his protestations of haste, and would sit there fanning himself in the soft dark. "You'll find it all in there, though. Three hundred and thirty-seven thousand, four hundred and fifty-two dollars and some cents. That's in today's currency too. Principal and interest. The government has taken all that into account, including some allowance for inflation. It sure wouldn't amount to a whole helluva lot if we were only going to pay you back in Civil War dollars now, would it?"

Now the agent would be part of the clutter, unstirring, amorphous. "Yes sir, you folks down here in Catalpa County—all over this part of the country in fact—have been mighty patient. It's a shame and a disgrace the way we in the government have let that old debt hang on like that. But that's one thing you can say for Lyndon Johnson: he never does forget a debt. Why one of the first things he did on taking office was call me in and say, 'Malachi, I want you to settle that old war debt.' I said, 'What debt?' And he said, 'Why, you know the debt I'm talking about—the money we owe all those good people down there in the late Confederacy—the money we as good as stole from them when we—or the Yankees rather—turned all those slaves loose during the war.' Yessir. You can trust Lyndon. 'They're good old boys,' he said. 'Yessirreee, there ain't no flies on them boys'...."

The agent would fan himself briskly, both he and the old man in good spirits now, staring out at the empty road, the grassless yard, the sunwasted pine barren.

"...You know how Lyndon is. Maybe he's a little crude sometimes, but...." Malachi would smile ruefully and look at Little Brother. "...I reckon you've heard all them stories they tell about him — how he likes to play pocket pool in front of the ladies and walk around bragging about his privates, and I reckon if he wasn't the president you wouldn't want to invite him to a family reunion or anything like that.... And then there was the one they tell about him and the ambassador's wife...but anyway, what I was about to tell you was...."

"Wait."

"What?"

"What was the one about the ambassador's wife?"

"Well, it ain't the kind of story a federal bureaucrat with a briefcase that ain't got nothing in it but a peanut butter and jelly sandwich ought to be telling out of school...."

The old man would laugh, one of his great debilitating

nerve-destroying laughs, bending over, grabbing himself, because he would almost be able to guess it now. And Malachi would say,

"Well, it was like this... I forget the ambassador's name...."

"That's not important."

"Naw. Don't matter. It could've been any of em. Anyway, Lyndon, he's dancing with her, you see, and everybody else stands back and makes way, giving a little polite applause—you know the way they do at them big society affairs—and all of em nodding at each other and saying, 'My, the president sho does dance divinely, don't he?'..." With that Malachi would rise and promenade the coal stove, holding it by its single gaunt pipe and moving it gingerly off its footing. "...They were dancing like this here, you see, and Lyndon he was holding her real close like, and she says, 'Why, Mr. President, you sho do dance divinely....' "

"And Lyndon, what did he say?"

"Why he says, 'Feel that thing down there, baby.' And she says, 'What's that, Mr. President?' And he says, '*That*!' And she says, 'O *that*!' And he says, 'That's a flashlight, baby. That ain't no candle.' "

Then laughter indescribable from both the old man and the bureaucrat, both of them standing gripping the flanges of the coal stove, and the whole thing about to come down now, tottering and shaking, and most of the store with it, as though the stove pipe had been all that was holding it up the entire time.

"Lyndon says, 'Feel that flashlight, baby!' And she says, 'O, Mr. President, I *do*!' And he says, 'That's a *real* flashlight. That ain't no candle.' "

Then more laughter as the stove again heaved off its moorings. From high above, a great tearing sound as the flue wrenched loose from the ceiling.

"...A flashlight...ha ha ha..."

"...No candle..."

"...ha ha ha..."

"...A flashlight..."

"...No candle...ha ha ha...."

Then they would be sitting again, talking about it quite seriously, the laughter all dried up and the bureaucrat saying it was like that with all the women in Washington, all of them trying to figure out some way to get in the White House and make the President, because of all the honors available in a country like America that was just about the highest.

"If you was a woman, wouldn't you like to be able to tell your grandchildren that you'd had it off the president of the good old U. S. of A.?... But anyway, what I was about to tell you is that, deep down, Lyndon's a pretty decent sort of fellow, and wants to do what's right by you folks down here in the South. Let's face it: the way the niggers are getting everything handed to em these days, it ain't no more than fitting that we do something about taking care of all the old slave-holding families too. That's Lyndon's philosophy. He's a good square shooter any way you want to look at it, even if he does have a way of feeling up every woman he runs into....and then there's the story about how anytime he's got to take a leak he always makes it a point to do it in one of them Republican sinks up there on Capitol Hill....But anyway, that wasn't what I came here to tell you...."

"Wait."

"What?"

"What was the one about Lyndon relieving himself in all of those various and sundry sinks?"

"Yup — Ev's sink, that's the main one they talk about. Sen. Dirksen, that is, the minority leader. Seems like he had one of them real fancy jobs up there in his office...color of pigeon-egg blue with all them fancy curlicues and gold watchamacallits all over it. Heard tell it cost the government about $75,000 to put that sink in — and you ought to have seen the door on his office, with all them gold letters on it. Heard tell that that one door cost upwards of $150,000 — that is, if you count all the gold lettering. Now a lot of folks might complain about a thing like that — putting all them expensive sinks and doors in those offices up there at the Capitol. But now you know it ain't befitting a high officer of the land to have just an ordinary sink in his office or one of them doors with nothing but plain white lettering on it — even if he ain't nothing but a Republican... Anyway...."

"What about Lyndon? Tell about Lyndon and the sink."

"I was just a-coming to that. Seems like he and Ev — they was good buddies, you know, even if they was in different parties — used to always get together after a hard day up at the Hill, and they'd open up a couple fifths of liquor and bring in some women and talk about what they could do to screw this fella or that fella — you know how all them politicians talk...."

"What about Lyndon and the sink?"

"Well, like I was about to say, Lyndon he comes just to grabbing himself all of a sudden and saying, 'I swear, Dirk, I got to *go*!' So Dirk, he says, 'Fine, LBJ, right back this way.' But Lyndon, he says, 'Naw, Ev, I can't wait no longer, boy.' So he whips out all his plumbing and, the way I heard it, just about knocks all that other plumbing right outa Ev's nice big fancy sink. Naturally, there was some that didn't know what to make of it, and everybody was just sort of standing around not saying very much, and then this nice little switchy-tail that Lyndon was particularly interested in, she kind of sidles up to him and says, 'Why, Lyndon, honey, that sho is something *else*.' "

Then laughter again as the old man and the bureaucrat stood gripping the now precariously leaning coal stove, shaking the flues.

"And the president, what did he say?"

"Why he says, 'That's a flashlight, baby. That's a *real* flashlight. That ain't no candle...' "

" ...A flashlight...ha ha ha...no candle..."

"...A regular flashlight, baby..."

"...Ain't just some little ol candle...ha ha ha..."

"...A flashlight..."

"...ha ha ha..."

"...no candle...."

Then Little Brother would catch himself and suddenly regret his show of mirth over a matter so vulgar as Lyndon's flashlight. He would grow somber and say, "Well, I still believe we can count on Lyndon." And the bureaucrat, taking his cue of sobriety from the old man, would say, "That's right. You can sure count on him. That's just what I was trying to say. He's a good square shooter, Lyndon is, in spite of some of the things you might have heard about him, and there's nothing that pleases him more than to be able to do a good turn for his fellow man. Maybe you read that article one of these big writing fellas wrote about Lyndon—fella by the name of Steinbeck—John Steinbeck—a big Nobel Prize winner, so he ought to know—Luther Coon won one of them prizes too — You remember that? — the Nobel *peace* ha-ha-ha prize. Anyway, this fella Steinbeck sure told the truth about Lyndon if there was ever a man that told it—wrote this big article talking about how Lyndon would do just about anything in the world to help a man down on his luck. Reckon he deserved that Nobel Prize, if what he said about Lyndon is any sample of what's in all them books he wrote. Because it's just like I was telling you before: the very last thing Lyndon did before announcing he wasn't going to run again, he called me in his office and said, 'Malachi, there's one thing I want to do for all those folks in the South before I lay down the high honor that the people of this country have bestowed on me.' I said, 'What's that, Mr. President?' And he said, 'Malachi, I want to reimburse them for all those slaves the Yankees turned loose.' That was quite a gesture on Lyndon's part. A lot of folks they've been saying Lyndon wasn't going to do anything for the South — that he had turned his back on all the home folks—that he was too busy giving the niggers what they wanted... But Lyndon's got a good sense of fair play about him, and I know for a fact that that thing had been preying on him for a long time... a long time... I expect in years to come, after people have forgotten all about Vietnam and the niggers and the Great Society, they'll still be talking about how Lyndon took it on himself to pay the South back for all those slaves them Radical Republicans turned loose back there after the War between the States...."

Then Malachi Brown would slap his thighs and half rise out of the rocker, his face sweaty and his nice bureaucratic suit speckled with ashes and soot. Then he would get all the way up and move toward the door, the old man following him on out into the fading sunlight of the August day.

"Yes sir," the agent would say. "I know how you folks might feel. There was a time there, a couple years back, when it looked as if Lyndon was just plain turning his back on the South. But you don't have to worry about Lyndon. The only thing is, I never could understand why he would let the likes of Luther Coon and all those Black Power boys tell him where to head in."

"Well, that sure is the truth," Little Brother would say. "A mighty sad and tragic thing it was. But I sure want you to know how much we appreciate you folks getting everything straightened out."

"That's the least we could do. But like I said before, the less we talk it around the better it's gonna be for all of us. This fella Rap Brown and the rest of those Black Power boys —well, you can imagine how it might look if they ever got hold of it."

"You can count on me. Not a word."

"That's real good. We'll see you later now."

The agent would stride off across the yard, pause momentarily beside the melting asphalt road, and then go over and climb in his white vinyl-topped Cadillac and throw up his hand.

"Now don't you go and forget what I said now. You can sure count on Lyndon. He's never forgotten that old debt for a single minute."

* * *

No one — not even Eula herself — knew for certain whether it was Efren Summers or somebody else who first asked Little Brother to donate a cow to the George Wallace presidential campaign. All we knew was that there had been a lot of talk about the matter and that Summers, as chairman of the local Beef-for-Ballots committee, had been behind most of it.

Everybody said there wasn't the slightest chance that Little Brother would give a notorious cattle rustler like Efren Summers one of his beef cows. But we couldn't be sure. With the big Catalpa County Wallace Rally coming up, the old man would find it difficult to hold out against the overwhelming sentiment of the community. And the sentiment had been running heavily against those who would refuse to do their duty by George Wallace and the American way.

The cows were to be sold at the New Erie cattle market and the proceeds donated to Wallace on the day of the big rally. For weeks the *Catalpa County Democrat* had been headlining the event: **"George Wallace Brings Presidential Campaign to West Alabama. Catalpa Countians Prepare for Big Day!"** The rally was almost wholly the work of Grady Elmore, a Snopeslike entrepreneur whose hunting lodge on the Westphalia Highway was to be the scene of the festivities. Elmore, a member of the Catalpa County Commissioners Court and the area's best-known Wallaceite, had long been charting the strategy which he hoped would win him a high diplomatic post in the next administration (the Wallace administration, that is) or maybe even a seat in the Cabinet. Was Grady Elmore on the point of winning nomination as secretary of Health, Education and Welfare? Possibly, if what one read about him in the *Democrat* were true. "When Grady Elmore gets behind something you can bet your last nickel it's going to be a success," the paper assured its readers. "So stand up for Wallace. Stand up for Grady Elmore. Feast on good west Alabama barbecue. Shake hands with the next President. Hear the Kennedyites being put to rout."

Efren Summers had already been by the house once to talk about Wallace's need for "a big fat cow." Little Brother had been out counting his own cows at the time, but Summers found a willing audience in Miss Angie. It was Eula who told us about that visit: "He say, 'Well, Miss Angie, you know we got this big rally coming up, and we gotta be raising lots of money, cause George Wallace he sho goan be the next president; he got the sense, Miss Angie, he got plenty of sense, and so we all goan donate a cow to him. Mrs. Moseley, she's got a big fat cow she goan give, and I got a big fat un, and we all goan donate these cows and bring George Wallace lots of money.' "

Summers obviously had reason to know what he was talking about, seeing as how he was by far the community's most accomplished rustler. People still talked about the time he had wound up in jail for stealing two of Mr. Worsham's finest Angus steers. Little Brother, of course, had long believed that many of his own cows had found their way into the chairman's hands, to be sped away in the dead of night and sold in towns far from the local cattle markets. But Summers had outlived his unsavory reputation to become one of Mt. Gizeh's leading citizens, not only chairman of the local Wallace committee but also one of a group that almost three years earlier had helped conceive an abortive plot to attack New Erie's civil rights marchers with clubs and power saws.

On the afternoon he had first spoken with Miss Angie he had gotten so carried away with the importance of his role in the community that he decided on the spot to give George Wallace two cows. "Two cows, Miss Angie, that's what I say I'm willing to do, cause we want George Wallace to know that the community of Mt. Gizeh is behind him one hundred per cent. I know for a fact that Mr. Doc Forbisher —and everybody knows how tight he is—is gonna give a big fat cow. And Mrs. Kenilworth, Mrs. Moseley, everybody I've talked to about this thing, they all say they gonna give George Wallace a cow, and that's gonna bring Wallace lots of money, Miss Angie, and we sho gonna make him the president, cause cows is bringing good money right now."

Having gotten nothing but polite conversation out of Miss Angie, Summers promised to come back another time, when the chances of catching Little Brother at home were more favorable. The day appointed for his return visit had now come, and along toward the middle of the afternoon we heard his knock at the door. From her seat in the front hall Miss Angie rose to answer it, moving hesitantly behind the slow clank of her walker. Summers had brought with him the four women who made up the bulk of his ad hoc Wallace committee. The delegation included none of the "better sort," none, that is, except Mrs. Amy Childress, and even she had long been suspected of indiscriminate adultery. They sat in the front hall, amid towering columns of books and great stacks of *Life* magazine, with here and there a litter of Biblical tracts and piles of unopened junk mail, and about them a mute ghostly effluvium that was perhaps the most palpable presence of all.

The chairman was the last to enter, a large square-jawed man stooped with what appeared to be more than his fifty-odd years, his mouth a confusion of gold fillings and decaying shards of enamel. He talked about the weather, the crops, Miss Patricia Farmer's recent bridal soiree. And then the talk turned solemn. Cows, that's what he had come to talk about. George Wallace's cows. And he was in hopes that Little Brother might join them so that he would have a better understanding of the critical issues at stake. But again there was only Miss Angie to hear him out, to nod approvingly and promise nothing. Eula had not presumed to make her presence known either, as I had thought she probably would; she was in her room ironing clothes, though within easy earshot of all that was being said. And Little Brother? Out counting his cows, of course, but not with any idea of making George Wallace a present of one. In recent days he seemed very definitely to have made up his mind about that, despite the large number of times he had described Wallace as a "man of sense" and the young black people as a pathetic lot who had nobody but King and the Humphreyites to thank for their impending disgrace.

Summers, visibly hiding his impatience at Little Brother's failure to appear for the conference, once more set about trying to convince Miss Angie of the surpassing importance of the community's beef-for-ballots project. As he did so he whacked himself soundly and often with a rolled-up copy of the *Birmingham News*. "Two cows, Miss Angie. I'm gonna give George Wallace two cows." Whack! "And Mr. Burt Moseley, he says he gonna give two, and we want it to be one hundred per cent in our community, Miss Angie. One hundred per cent. If they can do it up at Vestal

—get everybody up thar to give at least one cow—I know we can do it in Mt. Gizeh. One hundred per cent—that's what we're aiming for, and we're gonna let all them eggheads and fancy-pants liberals know that they ain't got the good decent right-thinking citizens of Alabama to kick around anymore."

Whack!

The thighwhacker, a common enough bird. I had seen his kind often: an executive new-risen from the ranks, sitting in his paneled Atlanta office, with a two-day-old copy of the *Journal* or *Constitution* folded just so, driving home every point with a lusty whack. "Free enterprise is the salvation of the country, boy. You agree with that?" Yassuh, yassuh. "Wallace? Why he ain't nothing but a socialist, boy. He ain't nothing but a socialist." Whack! "Naw, he ain't nothing. Goldwater, boy. Goldwater! He's the man for this country right now." Whack! "Free enterprise, private initiative, the profit motive—what about those things, boy?" Yassuh, yassuh. "And something else you can say about Goldwater, boy: he sho don't talk so very good about our colored. . . ."

Whack!

So it was with Summers, as he talked on and on about the cows, waiting for Little Brother to come in and not at all sure but what he hadn't wasted another trip. "Lots of folks saying George Wallace can't be the president, Miss Angie. Ain't so. Folks all over the country been looking for somebody to talk up to the federal government, and let me tell you something: Thar ain't no man that can do that job like George Wallace. Even if he don't win he gonna get enough votes to keep that Nixon crowd and all them Humphreyites outa thar; they gonna have to look to Wallace first, and that's when he gonna make all them liberals sit up and take notice, Miss Angie. That's when the whole country is gonna sit up and take notice of the kind of power George Wallace has got."

It may be that the thighwhacker had inferred more than he should have from Miss Angie's affable manner. The vigorous nod with which she answered each gesture, each whack, was in truth no more than the involuntary tic of age; and the smile that seemed ever-present only a gracious reflex bespeaking the good manners of her plantation heritage. But to the thighwhacker, who knew nothing of such things, they seemed a clear signal that his remarks had struck home. But what of Little Brother? Had he not once agreed, at least in principle, to the idea of donating a cow to the Wallace campaign? And why did he not come on in from the fields and join them? All of that—and more—the chairman must have been thinking. He bided his time, whacking himself and going through it all again, his mouth sparkling with decay, his voice carrying all before it. He talked about Wallace's recent campaign in California and Ohio and Wisconsin — states where "all the big race-mixers" had mistakenly assumed he had no support—and how he had surprised everybody by establishing himself once and for all as a formidable force in American politics. One could not really find much to say against all that. Few of those who had kept closely informed about the campaign — liberals, pointyheads, big-city editors—had foreseen the growing popularity of Wallace's bucolic outpourings and cranky obstreperous posturings. And it had begun to seem possible, if not likely, that his third-party candidacy would so snarl the November election that the U.S. House of Representatives would have to choose the next president. That's mainly what he had wanted anyway, to throw the election into the House, where each state would have an equal voice in determining the outcome and where he could set himself up as chief powerbroker, transferring his bloc of electoral votes to the candidate who best learned to say "yassuh" with a straight face.

The thighwhacker leaned forward, quite beside himself now, sped along by the ever-increasing vigor, the rapidity, of Miss Angie's tics and nods. There was new hope in his voice as he talked again about how Wallace had put it to all the Northern liberals and how he had gone all across the country boasting about the moral superiority of Alabama's rednecks—"The reason their necks is red is cause they don't mind getting out in the hot sun and working for a living!"—and how he had stood up and told the whole world something that a lot of people didn't understand: that the editors of the *Washington Post* and *Baltimore Sun* put on their britches just like everybody else. And all those Washington bureaucrats — the curse of the country! "Always holding themselves so high, Miss Angie. Always telling the good decent people in this country when to get up and when to lie down and when to come to dinner. . . ."

Whack!

". . . So we got to get all these cows together, Miss Angie. We want it to be one hundred per cent, right down the line. Like I was saying before, if they can do it up thar in Vestal and over at Ladd's Crossing, we can sho do it down here in Mt. Gizeh. So that's all we're asking, Miss Angie — that you and Mr. Frank will consent to let us have just one nice fat cow for this big cattle auction we got coming up. . . ."

It was then perhaps that he first became aware of an alien force. I felt it myself: the black woman planted squarely astride the opening between the two sections of the upper hall.

"Cow? Whut cow?"

Another good lusty whack from our chairman. Yet the abruptness of Eula's appearance had momentarily thrown him out of countenance.

"Whut cow?" she said. "We ain't giving George Wallace no cow."

"What? What?"

"You thinks we goan give George Wallace a cow after the way he talk bout our colored? Why, he say if'n they lays down in front of *his* car he run over them. I don't wants Wallace. And I don't wants him on the TV saying *nothing* bout our colored. We's all praying Wallace won't get up thar. We's praying that somebody goan knock him in the head."

"By God! . . ."

Whack!

The black woman smote her thigh too, open-handed, a lively blow almost rivaling the thighwhacker's own.

Whack!

Whack!

The woman suspected of adultery explained very emphatically that Wallace had never actually been her first choice for anything. She had much preferred DeGraffenried and had felt "plumb sorry" when she heard he had been killed in "that old plane crash."

"Miss Angie," the black woman said. "If'n you gives George Wallace a cow I *leaves* hyar. I packs my things and leave."

The chairman sat stunned beneath the cascade of big talk. He half leaned forward and leaned back again, half rose and then dropped to his seat, and had almost begun to speak when his mouth fell shut, his face a mass of purplish ganglia and unkneaded dough.

"By God, I don't allow. . . ."

"I don't wants Wallace," Eula said. "I ain't goan have Wallace. He say all the time he goan run *over* our colored. And you think a man like that fit to be the president? The president, he be's a honorable man."

Vigorous assent from Miss Angie.

"George Wallace is the smartest man in the country," Summers explained.

Vigorous assent!

"Ain't no man in the country can tell the government whar to head in like George Wallace. I'm gonna give him *three* cows!"

"Miss Angie," Eula said, "why you letting him talk you into giving George Wallace a cow? You ought to be shamed of yoself. You ain't give me no cow and I out thar milking them."

Laughter, but no assent from Miss Angie. The other women, all but Mrs. Childress, had already risen to leave, muttering their goodbyes almost as an afterthought and then turning away in such haste that Mrs. Yeager's heels caught in what was probably only a crack in the floor and flung her into Mrs. Swink and both of them into Mrs. Tesh who had been the first out the door; all of them scurrying across the porch and gathering in the bare front yard, to look back once more at the house, their faces a mingled tableau of white voiceless rage, their last shriek of horror and defiance as yet unuttered:. . . *a nigger so full of herself she'd dare come in there sticking her nose in our business and did you hear the way she talked to Miss Angie? Why my God in heaven that's a crime in itself Can't anybody do anything with her Can't somebody at least call the sheriff?....*

The chairman squirmed in his seat, horribly, immensely wrathful, his face still bloated and purplish, like a *fasching* mask left out in the rain too long. And then he too was out the door and gone, saying he would "have that goddamn cow and no goddamn biggety nigger goan stand in the way of it either." His departure left only Mrs. Childress to sit with Miss Angie. She talked again of DeGraffenried. "He was always such a favorite of mine. I was sure sorry to see him get killed in that old plane." Miss Angie nodded her vigorous assent.

* * *

Summers never did get the cow. All he got was a broken-down cream separator left over from the days when dairying had been a big part of the Holstons' farming operation. The cream separator and hundreds of other objects donated by white people either too poor or too niggardly to give the governor a cow would be auctioned off on the eve of the big rally, together with more than a thousand head of cattle, and the money presented to Wallace's aides in a rousing ceremony at the county courthouse.

Little Brother's worsening health had not permitted him to be a part of the "big day." But maybe he wouldn't have been a part of it anyway. Although he had often spoken up for Wallace, he could never feel at ease with the likes of Grady Elmore and Efren Summers and Doc Forbisher. They were all of them old Folsomites who had turned against their man not because he had "stolen once and would steal again," as Little Brother always said, or because he was a sot and a loudmouth and an embarrassment to the state, but only because he had openly sought the Negro vote. That was reason enough to be against him, of course, but not reason enough to betray him if one had supported all his other "malicious and unseemly acts." Little Brother's distaste for the Wallaceites, if not for Wallace himself, did not entirely escape Eula's notice: "I have to say that much fur him: he never did club up with them Wallace folks; he never did get in the band wid them." But God was still "whuppin" him, she explained, "cause he still got to pay for all the wrong he done."

God whupped him almost every day now. He was able to keep the store open only part of each morning, and he had already given up his job as postmaster. People had felt badly about that, even if they hadn't been doing much business with him lately, because without the post office the community had lost its last reason for existence. Mt. Gizeh was just another name on the RFD route now. There was no longer much reason for the store's existence either, and soon the old man would give that up too. After that there would be very little for him to do except sit out on the porch or at the back of the hall or in front of the television soap operas and take his whuppings like a man. "Cause God sho goan whup you fur every single thing you does." But he would still find excuses for an occasional afternoon ramble about the farm. There was always a section of fence to repair or a drainage ditch to unclog. And it was more important than ever now to keep a close eye on the cattle, what with the likelihood that Summers would yet find a way to get the cow he wanted — and maybe a lot more than just that one.

Sometimes in those aimless rambles he would get as far as Sister Evalina's house. She would always be sitting there by the door, holding her Bible carefully inside its plastic cover and waiting for him to reach the top of the rise before leaping up to begin her ceaseless barrage of mingled praise and condemnation. If he was of a mind to return the tribute, he would inevitably get all the worst of it. She would confront him at the edge of the porch or out by the gate and berate him for grievances — most of which he had forgotten — that went all the way back to her days as a tenant on the Holston plantation.

She had left the place one morning in thirty-six after a horrible wrangle over the size of her "furnish bill." No one could say after all this time exactly how big a debt she had owed. But it must have been a lot more than the three dollars she said it was (such was the feeling anyway) or she wouldn't have been in such haste to quit the premises. By the time Little Brother got over there to lay a claim on her corn, there was nothing left but a crib full of shucks. She and her three children had left before daylight, with two whole wagonloads full of corn — "a one-horse load and a two-horse load" — and not only with the corn but with all her "vegetubbles" and "syrups" and "lards" and even with the mule she believed was hers but wasn't.

She still believed it and would often revile the old man with jeers and laughter for trying to get that mule back when she had already "cleared the law" and why did he want to treat her so hard and take all her stuff "jes over them little old three dollar."

"Now, sister, you know it was a lot more than just three dollars."

"Wuzn't!"

"Sho it was, Sister Evalina."

"Wuzn't!"

"Was, sister."

"Wuzn't!"

"Was."

"Wuzn't!"

The old man would be laughing now. But he could no longer hold up his end of those arguments the way he had in other years. He was whupped down now; he was whupped bad. On our last visit to her house I watched how sadly he came into the yard, how wistful he looked as he sat at the edge of the porch and gazed back toward the slope of prairieland across which we had just come.

Evalina was severe. "Missen Frank, why you wants to treat us so hard? Why you wants to take Old Rose from me? Why, I'd done paid fur that mule twice — might as well say three times. But you goan take her back and all my other stuff too jes for them little old three dollar."

"O sister, it was a lot more than three dollars."

"Wuzn't!"

"Was."

"Wuzn't!"

Whether it was or wuzn't, Evalina got everything and the old man nothing. She took all the corn and vegetubbles and lards and syrups and even Old Rose the mule, but no lasting enmity. She had gone on working for the Holstons long years after she left the place, though never again as hard as in the early days.

She had been the lead chopper during her first years on the plantation and had prided herself on being able to chop faster "than a big man could walk."

"Child, I chopped *some.* Up at four and be's all day in the field. And Missen Frank, he work us so hard. I falls down many a day down there in that bottom and gets right back up and takes hold of that hoe and goes to chopping. Ain't it so, Missen Frank?"

"It sho is a fact, Sister Evalina. I sho do believe it for a fair."

"Sun to sun we be's in the field. Sun be rising and I already have my breakfast and be on the way walking wid my hoe. You acknowledge it, Missen Frank."

"I acknowledge it, Sister Evalina. I'm duly bound to acknowledge it."

But he still wouldn't pay the toll. After he had gone I slipped her my usual two and hurried off to assist him through the fence gap. She watched us as we went back down the rise. When I looked back from where the path turned into the trees she was still standing there in front of her porch, holding the Bible beside her like a carefully preserved artifact. It was almost dark before we got back to the house and Eula had just set out looking for us. We met her as she was coming down the path alongside the garden fence. Miss Angie was there too, way back up at the head of the path, holding on to her walker, saying, "Little Brother, you must be more careful now. We must remember that it is not wise to overdo." She already had his toddy waiting. He downed it in a single gulp and retired to his room, inviting me to join him for another; we drank it after the manner of schoolboys, straight from the bottle of Jim Crow he kept under his bed. When I left him he was already drifting off, wondering half aloud why even the well-meaning darkies like Sister Evalina had to work themselves up into such a lather trying to impress folks with their "dignity" and why she and the Yankees both didn't just go on and pay him all the money he had coming. Evalina sure had some strange ideas about that old debt. Anybody knew it was a lot more than three measly little old dollars.

* * *

Evening, a long ride into town for another bottle of whiskey and back with some of it still left; the old man asleep in his room and his sister alone on the veranda, the metal walker by her chair, and the black woman hurrying now to get supper on the table, talking again about the days when the slaves had prayed with their heads inside the washpot and how the Episcopals had sent spies out to catch them at it and how even in our own time the Episcopals thought that they "wuz de gods." Even as she spoke of all that, the revival chants began drifting down from the old Negro church behind Beatrice Montgomery's store. For more than a week now the spell of the revival had hung over the land, the chanting and singing, a mood of the lingering dusk itself; a summer evocation of magic and ancient tribal ritual, something that the Episcopals in their fine churches knew nothing about. Here there was no hush of mighty organs, no decorous placating of the gods, no crosses of silver or elaborate candelabras or monks in vestments. The Episcopals knew nothing of "striking a moan," as Eula called it — nothing about falling "all out in the spurit."

She herself had been caught up in that mood no longer ago than yesterday — or was it the day before — as she was putting away the breakfast dishes. All at once it had come over her, a vision of ritual fires and beaded dancers, and she too had fallen "all out in the spurit." Little Brother had come in from the barnlot about that time, to be met by a hail of flung missiles: dishes, cake pans, tableware, a cabbage grater that sailed past his ear, a sodden dishrag that struck him full in the face.

He fell back to the porch and finally made it into the house by another door. He had the shotgun now, just in case, and had taken cover behind the hall wardrobe, peering warily out from behind it like a jungle hunter looking out from behind a curtain of bamboo. Miss Angie had come haltingly in, from the parlor, disturbed by the ruckus and certain that the Egyptians had struck again. But Little Brother knew it was only the footwashers.

"He all the time talk ugly bout the footwashers," Eula told me, as we sat there over my dwindling fifth of whiskey. "He say, 'Eula, you be's a damn crazy woman.' But I say we alls got to be crazy fo we die, and we alls got to be whupped if we goan see God. He say folks ain't got no business going to church to get their feets washed; he say they sposed to wash their feets fo they leaves home. But I say the Lord teach us to wash feets fo he go away from hyar; he left it fur a power. But Missen Frank he think the Piscopals too good to wash feets; he say thar ain't no other church like the Piscopals. But the Bible ain't said nothing bout no Piscopals and it ain't said nothing bout no Baptists. All it say is, 'Come my little ones, come unto me'. . . ."

* * *

His drinking was suddenly much worse. He had begun enjoying a noontime toddy, if not more than one, to supplement the four or five with which he dosed himself each evening. Perhaps, said Eula, it was the whuppings that had driven him more heavily to drink. Others would ascribe it to his age or to his high blood pressure and weak heart or to his fear of dying. But no, Eula said, it was only the whuppings. "He drinking too much cause he done been whupped." A drink or two beyond the single toddy prescribed by Dr. Nance would generally be enough to send Little Brother off on another of his aimless afternoon rambles. And when he wasn't out looking for cows, he would sometimes appear unexpectedly at Lurellia's house, to inquire after the Old Gentleman (who was also in his last days) or to ask his sister-in-law's help with one of his perpetually snarled financial transactions.

Once he found his grandniece and her two brothers there and was thoughtful enough to offer each of them a shot of his ninety-proof bourbon. "A fine thing it was to watch Little Angie as she practically gagged to death," Lurellia had written. "Mr. F. was most amused. . . ."

But his mood would grow somber when he went back to look in on the Old Gentleman. Often he would spend whole afternoons back there talking about his days at the university or how if circumstances had been more favorable he could have made a fortune practicing law in Birmingham. Other times he would leap up and go to jerking violently at the covers, wanting to know why his brother just didn't "go on and get out of that bed and dance the light fantastic."

"Go on, brother Anse! Go on and get up and let's dance a little jig!"

Lurellia, quite put out by such doings, would come in to explain in that patiently martyred way of hers that her husband had lost a leg (lest Little Brother had forgotten) and was now completely blind and that it was most depressing for him to be always reminded of "things he can never again do in life." But Little Brother didn't understand that kind of attitude. Why, Anson still had some good years left. He ought to be up and around and stop feeling sorry for himself. He ought to get out of the house and wheel himself about the drive and up and down the yard and take an interest in things. Why, other people had lost their legs without letting it get them down. He himself was in much worse shape than the Old Gentleman, much worse, so much on him these days, what with all the cows getting out and the fences falling down, and Summers always on the prowl. But he hadn't let any of that get *him* down. "Be a man, Anse! Get up and be a man!" And again he would go to yanking at the covers and telling his brother to get out of that bed and "dance a little jig" and why didn't he stop dwelling on his misfortunes and start thinking about all the good times he had to look forward to.

It went on like that all summer. But there were days and sometimes whole weeks when he didn't stir from the house at all. He would just sit there on an old couch at the back of the hall, worrying about the erratic beating of his heart. And there were times now when everybody assumed that the end was already upon him. Like the morning Eula had found him lying half-conscious in the tall weeds out by the old privy. He had been going out there regularly now for almost four years, leaving Eula to preside without interruption over the indoor toilet since there was nothing he could do to keep her out of it anyway. One morning she had watched him visit the outhouse as usual, not realizing until after she began spreading the noon meal that he hadn't come back. Then she saw something stirring out there in the weeds, a limp arm raised. In only a little more time than it took her to rush out and fling him over her shoulder and bring him to the house, Miss Angie was able to prepare him a "very nice little toddy" — but too late, it seemed. Everybody was thinking, "Well, it's over now. He's gone. Don't he look natural?" Eula, of course, knew better. No, it was not over and perhaps would not be over for some time, because "he ain't sorry yet. Cause he still got to be sorry fur all them things he done."

The affliction passed. He sat up again and was soon back on his feet, and out of the house too, just like old times, off looking for cows or stopping at Negro shacks to be asked for money. Miss Angie would always be outside waiting for him when he got back. She would be standing there by the wellhouse calling to him with weak tremulous shouts as he climbed through the fence gap way down at the end of the garden: "Little Brother, it is not well for you to overdo. You must look after yourself, Little Brother."

And then one day he did not come back at all. It was already growing dark when Eula set out on the run, calling as she went. Miss Angie watched her as she set out down the garden path, moving clumsily and heavily through the tall weeds yet with a speed and agility that seemed to contravene all known laws of physics. She got all the way over to the big prairie that gave onto Sister Evalina's sixty acres before turning down a path that took her around by a sterile expanse of limestone hills and on over into a dense pine forest where for the past week the sawmill people had been working. She already knew where he would be; she did not even need what little was left of daylight to find him. He sat on a stump in the middle of the wide field, pale and grizzled, his mind completely gone, cursing the foresters who had cut more than their quota of trees and had left uncut the ones he had expressly marked. "You been whupped," Eula told him. "You sho been whupped good." But perhaps not good enough, because "he still wuzn't sorry."

She went back with him flung over her shoulder like a sack of flour already half empty and the rest of the contents rapidly draining out. And so at last up the steep path past the garden, the wellhouse, and Miss Angie, whose alarmed face greeted them from behind the porch lattice, and on through the wide middle hall and at last into the dingy bedroom, Eula telling him he had been "whupped fur a-fair" and "jes rest easy now." She let him down gently. He lay there grizzled and still pale and breathing heavily and threatening even now to get up and have at the sawmill people for cutting all the wrong trees, raising and lowering his head in sharp jerks while the black woman dialed Dr. Nance and told him to come quick because Little Brother was dying this time "fo sho," knowing even as she said it, however, that it was really not true, because "he still got to be sorry first."

* * *

The last time I saw him on his feet was the afternoon we drove up to his ancestral homeplace at Farrow Church. The house stood on a forgotten road some twenty miles northwest of New Erie, overlooking the Tombigbee and Sipsey river bottoms, its curtainless windows staring blindly out through thorn and cedar thickets. It had once been quite a place, built very much in the grand manner, with columns, porticoes, and intricate entablatures, though on a scale far more modest than most of the finer antebellum plantation houses. In the beginning it had not been a planter's house at all. A gambler from one of the Tombigbee steamers had built it as a rustic gaming palace. There were rooms for dice and cards, pits for fighting cocks, and a racetrack still visible amid the cane and birch saplings.

For many years after the war it had been the home of Little Brother's Uncle Benjamin, an unredeemed Confederate who had been with Forrest at the surrender and who till the end of his life retained a fondness for ribald doggerel and homemade whiskey. After his death the place stood empty until sometime in the late forties, when the family finally began leasing it out. The first tenant had been run off for cutting down two of the main columns for firewood. The columns were still missing, so that the front portico seemed to gape at us like a mouth without its bicuspids. Only recently another tenant had moved in, a mangy character known as "the judge"; everyone roundly disdained the fellow, but so far he had paid his rent on time. He was watching us (I soon realized) as we came up the overgrown path that had once been a circular brick walkway. We heard him shouting at us as we emerged from the cedars:

"Who's that a comin up the walk out thar! Who's that out thar under the cedars! Who is it, I say!"

Little Brother joined eagerly in the merriment: "Who is that a yellin! Who is that in that house up there that's wantin to know all these things!"

"It's the judge a yellin! It's the judge that's a setting up hyar and wantin to know all them things!"

The judge's clamorous voice beckoned us up the steps past the stubs of the missing pillars and into a dark smelly room where the rich men of the surrounding country had once gathered to talk about the price of slaves and to drink fine imported brandy — and where the young woman who was one day to be the captain's wife had often sat playing the piano for her gentlemen callers.

Now about all that was left to remind us of those days was the single frayed Chippendale rocker where the judge sat having his lunch, the cats and flies both helping him at it. Almost as we came in the judge's wife appeared, sweeping the cats smartly out the front screen and then turning to reenter the kitchen, leaving us to our business, whatever it was. The judge went back to his meal with only the flies about him now and tobacco juice all over him and his hair like Toscanini's. He had once been a justice of the peace.

"Glad you dropped by, Frank. I been aimin to ask you if you'd consider giving my boy a job."

"Where is he now, Judge?"

"Tuscaloosa. Been workin up thar at the paper plant. But they's gonna start layin off come September."

"Isn't much work around now, Judge. Sho couldn't give him much in the way of wages."

The judge seemed satisfied with the old man's response and soon went on to more serious topics of conversation. He had much to say against Rap Brown, Stokely Carmichael, the Kennedys, the lying Birmingham newspapers (which had generally opposed Wallace), the NAACP, Martin Luther Coon, and a whole host of nameless agitators who were always sticking their legs in the mouths of police dogs and killing off their own kind for the publicity that was in it and knocking themselves out with police billy clubs. Damn them. Goddamn their souls. And he hadn't even gotten around to Lyndon yet.

He fell in behind us as we left the house to take a look around back. More than ever now he seemed an incarnation of a bucolic Toscanini, his hair going wild and his arms even wilder, much as though he had assembled about him the ghosts of a forgotten philharmonic.

And he had finally gotten around to Lyndon. "Hit's a shame in the world, Frank, what them fancy-pants coons has done to this country. And I blame the president fer it. Always have, Frank. Always have. And I say he's got to pay fer it. Yessir. Sho as thar's a God in heaven that big old redneck has got to pay. . . ."

"Well, it does seem like right much of a shame," Little Brother said.

"Now you know as well as I do, Frank, that a man like that ain't got no business being president. Sho is good news to hear he ain't goan run agin. But now we got this Humphrey. . . ."

"Yup. It sho is right much of a shame. Right much of a disappointment to all of us in the South. Always used to feel that we could count on Lyndon."

We followed a barely visible flagstone walk through ragweed up to the remains of an enclosed gallery where the children of the house — among them "little Miss Martha

Anne," the captain's future wife — had once listened to the singing of the darkies as they came in from the fields each day at sunset. We stood there for a while looking around, not knowing what to say, thinking about things, wondering how it was back in the "good times before the war," hearing the judge rail on about the sad decline of decency and honor in the country.

"Used to be said that this was a free country, Frank — a white man's country. Used to allus be hearin folks talk about that. 'Goddammit, this here is a free country.' That's whut they used to say. But no more, Frank. No sir. Hain't nothin about it free now. Hit's the niggers' country now. Might as well just go on and give em the deed, Frank, cause they got it all now — all the big jobs, all the big TV ads. They the ones gittin all the new buildings and superhighways named after em. No sir, Frank. Don't let nobody ever kid you into thinkin it's a free country. No more it ain't. No sir. Hit's the land of the coon and the home of the wop. And somebody's got to pay fer it, Frank. Somebody's got to pay. . . ."

We had gone on back to the truck, and none too soon either, because the old man was now quite plainly exhausted. His breath came in short erratic gasps as I helped him into the passenger seat. The judge was still there, hanging on us. He had almost forgetten about his boy needing that job. But now he remembered.

"What cha think, Frank? Think you kin find something fer that boy of mine?"

Little Brother looked at him without seeming to have heard him at all.

"Sure does seem like right much of a shame," he said. "It sure does. All the young black folks wanting to act so dignified now. A mighty pitiful thing to behold, and a little sad too. . . ."

"Sho would be mighty obliged if'n you could find him a little something, Frank. He's a good boy. A real hard worker. Don't make no difference if'n you can't pay no big wages. . . ."

". . . A mighty disturbing thing to think about all the heartache that has befallen this old world. But here's what

I've found: a man that's always got to be strutting around and showing how much dignity he's got hasn't got any. You mark it down now..."

"...He's a real good boy, Frank. Sho would be beholden to you if'n you could just holp him out a little..."

"...I've always found it so. I sho as cotton have. First and last, all up and down through life: a man that goes strutting around with a feather in his tail is just begging to have it shot off..."

"...A mighty good worker, Frank..."

"...Mighty sad and tragic..."

"...Sho would be mighty obliged, Frank. I'll send him right on over thar come the first of the week...."

At Jericho's Walls

June and July 1969

A little before seven o'clock on the evening of 12 June 1969—prayer meeting night—a black man wearing a dark suit and no hat got off a Greyhound bus at the corner of Main and Forbis streets and walked quickly through the lingering dusk to the New Erie Baptist Church. Some of the teenagers lounging about Forbisher's drugstore were the first to see him: a man of more than medium height, thin, wasted, with a look of nervous desperation about him, carrying an attache case that identified him (so it began to seem) as an official emissary for the SCLC — or maybe as a professional troublemaker for the Great Society.

The way we heard it, he had gone directly to the front of the church and demanded entrance, only to be turned away by the chief deacon, old man Everett Willoughby, who had arrived late for the service and was waiting out Preacher Gilchrist's long prayer.

Willoughby may have thought he had gotten rid of the man for good. But later that evening Mr. Jeffrey Owens, manager of the local power company, had seen the same fellow lurking about the shrubbery beneath the pastor's study. And so did most of the others, the ones leaving church, their headlamps spraying past him as they moved down Palmyra Street and on out into the black night of the county.

And there may even have been some who saw what happened next—how Preacher Gilchrist came stealthily to the back door, after the traffic had cleared, and motioned the man inside.

Or was it, rather, that he had forced his way in at the point of a gun?

No one knew just what had happened next—whether it was Gilchrist or someone else who had finally gotten the drop on him. All anyone knew for certain was that at nine o'clock or shortly thereafter Willoughby and two of the other deacons had come past the drugstore walking the man hurriedly down to the city jail.

But the town knew that wasn't the last of it. He would soon be back, and all the others with him, all the "biggety niggers" from the city, the women in Afros, the men in long beards and double-breasted suits. The congregation would look up one morning to see them striding boisterously to the front of the sanctuary, carrying their attache cases and shouting their righteous songs of protest:

Yassuh!
O yassuh!
Amen! Amen!
Well?

* * *

The Reverend Gilchrist was on the phone till after midnight and most of the next day, trying to dispel the many rumors that had circulated through the New Erie community on that warm spring evening. The man, as Gilchrist kept explaining it, had not come there to integrate the church. He was unarmed and harmless, a working-class individual who had spent most of his adult life in Indianapolis and had been on his way home to Meridian, Mississippi, where he had the promise of a job in the town's largest drycleaning establishment. But he had gotten only as far as New Erie before running out of money. Would the Baptist church help? Naturally the pastor and his deacons were willing to do what they could. A matter of fundamental Christian charity. Besides, the man had given every assurance that he was good for the debt. It might also be said to his credit that he had made no fuss at all when Deacon Willoughby explained that his presence might alarm the congregation unnecessarily, and would it be asking too much for him to please wait outside—and well out of sight—until the service was over? The jail? Easily enough explained. Where else was the man to stay? There would be no more buses running till morning. And he had no money other than what the church had donated toward his fare. Under such circumstances it was only natural that someone—Gilchrist perhaps—would think of the jail. It was clean enough there, very quiet, and Chief Carruthers would have the man up and fed in plenty of time for him to catch his bus. The pastor explained all that in the soft calm reassuring voice that he had brought with him from Tupelo, Mississippi, in 1948, hoping (as he said) that the congregation would help him put an end to the rumors that had thrown the town into such an unseasonable turmoil.

But the next day the stories were still rampant—talk of how the Baptist church had been integrated at gunpoint by a mindless drug addict from Cincinnati. So Gilchrist was again hard at it to explain that the black laundryman was not one of the undesirable "outsiders," no terrorist or drug addict or SCLC militant. He hadn't come there to force his way into the congregation or to threaten anybody—and he had nothing to do with the election....

* * *

The election. That was the big talk of the summer—the special election ordered by the United States Supreme Court in the wake of a 1968 ballot controversy. At the center of the controversy was the Catalpa County probate judge and elections board chairman, Rufus Honaker, a genial sort who, as Fred Cain explained it, had unexpectedly decided to get tough with "all those big federal judges up there in Washington."

The trouble had begun one February afternoon when six black men who Cain had always thought were "good honest niggers" came into the elections office to announce that they "wuz takin' over the Democratic party." Their more immediate objective was to enter their names in the spring primary—four of them to seek nomination to the commissioners court, the others to the school board. They did so poorly in that primary that, by Cain's account, their own people almost laughed them out of town. But before the week was out they were back clamoring for another chance; this time they would run as independent candidates in the general election. The same thing was happening all over the state, black men joining up in something called the National Democratic Party of Alabama and trying to force their way onto the November ballot. It looked bad for a while. But fortunately there was a way out. Everywhere the candidates went they got the same story: "Looks like you fellows didn't quite make the qualifying deadline... Yessir... It's all right here in the book... Something a little funny about the way you boys got yourselves nominated too... Looks like you didn't follow the law exactly...."

The law was plain. Nothing to do then but to "disrecognize" the NDPA candidates and deny them ballot position. An old story, it seemed, the sort of dispute that was always winding up in the courts, as this one inevitably did.

Of the three federal judges empaneled to hear the case, only the hated Frank Johnson would take issue with the local registrars. In a dissenting opinion that would provide the basis for an appeal to the Supreme Court he argued that the various statutes cited to keep the NDPA candidates off the ballot had been applied with an "evil eye" and an "unequal hand" by men anxious to frustrate the ambitions of "a small, new and almost surely impecunious group of candidates seeking to form a new party in Alabama."

It was all very predictable, of course, all very like Johnson, who was always on the lookout for ways, Sheriff Cain said, to "put through" the Black Belt gentry and whose reputation as a "race-mixin fanatic" reached far beyond the bounds of his judicial district. No other judge of his era had become more famous for sweeping aside old laws and traditions in defense of minority rights. As a native of the "Free State of Winston," the mountain county that had once declared itself independent of secessionist-minded Alabama, Johnson had his own traditions to uphold. He and his brash populist-style liberalism had found favor with George Wallace when Wallace was in his early Folsomite phase. But after the future governor discovered the Negro question, Johnson became more useful as a propaganda target: "A low-down carpetbaggin, scalawaggin, race-mixin liar." Like most crusading jurists, Johnson had made a practice of looking beyond confining legal precedents to the higher ground of the Fourteenth Amendment and its equal protection clause. A settled matter of law? For Johnson there was no such thing — not when it stood in the way of a basic constitutional guarantee.

So it was in the present instance. It was no big surprise when the Supreme Court stood by Johnson and ordered the disqualified candidates back on the ballot. But it came as a shock to learn some months later that Rufus Honaker, alone among the nine probate judges named as defendants in the NDPA suit and one of New Erie's most reputable citizens, had scorned the court order and was soon to appear before Judge Frank Johnson to answer charges of criminal contempt.

* * *

And what of the special election that was to give the Catalpa County NDPA a second chance? That was doubtless the worst news of all. During all of those weeks leading up to the election, the SCLC kept up an intense vigil outside the squarish white stuccoed building where the defiant probate judge kept his office. "Honaker Must Go! Integrate the Bowling Alley!" The times I saw him he seemed very much untroubled by this great swirl of events and anything but defiant — only a little surprised at all the fuss being made over something that was really nothing more than an unfortunate oversight.

Sure, he knew it looked bad. He knew what everybody was saying. He had heard all that talk about how he had defied the court. But the plain truth was there just wasn't anything to all those rumors; it was just that he had never heard anything from the federal authorities to suggest that "something had to be done about all those NDPA fellows."

Such was the story that would see him through to the

end. But no one other than his closest associates would ever fully believe him. People just kept nodding and saying, "O yeah, he knew about it all right. Good old Rufus. Never realized he had it in him. It's time somebody was standing up to those judges. . . ."

But maybe it was all true—maybe he really didn't have it in him. Somehow it was hard to imagine Honaker standing up to the court like that. His predecessor, old man Buford Story — yes, something of the kind might have been expected of him. An estimable and sometimes high-handed fellow Story was, unlike Honaker, whose ways were cautious and bland. Not that the younger man lacked power; it was just that he chose to exercise it more sparingly than had most of his predecessors. He was a little of everything: trial judge, chairman of the county commissioners court, processor of wills, elections supervisor, county treasurer and purchasing agent, registrar of deeds, and the man most responsible for maintaining close and productive ties with the political power brokers in Montgomery.

But it was characteristic of Honaker that he had drifted into the job almost casually. At the time of Story's death he was the town's chief dry goods merchant. He had a law degree from the University of Alabama (though he had never practiced) and had gotten his first taste of politics during the 1958 governors race, campaigning for the segregationist John Patterson rather than for the young George Wallace, who was still trying to shake his reputation as a down-home Folsom liberal. When the probate judgeship fell vacant for the second time in a little more than a year, Honaker moved quickly into contention as an interim appointee. To men like Roger Meads and Fred Cain, each of whom feared the rise of another political boss in the mold of Judge Story, Honaker seemed the ideal choice, even though he too had paid his dues to the old Story machine. They liked and trusted the young dry goods merchant, and Honaker would not disappoint them. He would display so few of the considerable powers of his office that the uninformed might almost have assumed that they did not exist.

Was this, then, the man who supposedly had stood up to the Federal courts and refused to sanction their "sordid processes"?

Or was it rather more likely, as he kept insisting, that his problems were really the result of official negligence somewhere up the line? What he remembered most about that fatal summer and autumn of 1968 was the great confusion of court orders that had come down — "some to put the candidates on the ballot and some to leave them off." The only trouble was he'd never heard anything directly, or said he hadn't, about putting them on there to stay. O yes, he knew there had been a big court suit, an appeal filed, hearings held, a verdict rendered. But for all he knew personally of any court order it might as well have been floated out to sea in a cork bottle.

Summer was soon gone and almost before he knew it he was into October — and still no word from the court. "Already had the ballots ready to go by then. Kept telling myself, well, it's quite likely I'll be hearing something in a day or two and then I'll have to redo all the ballots. But we — none of us here in the office — ever heard anything. So there was never a time when I could look around and say, well, today's the day I've got to do something about straightening out this situation. . . ."

The way he told it, it sounded reasonable enough. Maybe it just hadn't occurred to him, in spite of the newspaper stories and television reports, that the directive had anything to do with Catalpa County. Maybe (as he thought at the time) it was only meant for "the big boys — all those fellows running for Congress and the big state offices." But was it possible that no one — not even his own lawyers — had ever alerted him to the implications of the court decree? And why was he the only defendant, out of all those mentioned in the suit, who had failed to heed the government's wishes?

Maybe what it really was was some kind of big frame-up. Or what was even more plausible, maybe he had been acting as a front for someone else. Roger Meads, perhaps. Everybody said Meads was the real boss of the town. Maybe he was the one who had persuaded the judge just to forget all about that little ol court order. Honaker himself seemed an improbable martyr, an unlikely villain—hardly the sort who would choose on his own to stand up to the likes of a Frank Johnson. So it must have been someone else, Meads and Cain and the domino players, who had pressured him into the single great defiant act of his life.

Throughout the town one heard the talk, just as in the days of the evictions, talk of a conspiracy, of Honaker himself as scapegoat, a mere pawn to further the aspirations of other men. But the judge just laughed and dismissed all the talk with a casual indifference, not even bothering to seem exasperated by it — not much changed, in fact, from the freshly scrubbed young man who had won his high school declamation contest back in 1948. Yes, it was perfectly true: he had never gone to the best parties (his father was nothing more than a moderately well-to-do sawmill operator), or been chairman of the 24 Circle Debating Society, or built a palatial home on Meads Hill. But he was his own man nevertheless, a proud man, and he would willingly accept whatever blame —or credit — might come from his decision to "disrecognize" the NDPA candidates.

But everybody else just kept nodding and saying, "Yeah, Roger Meads. It was his idea. Rufus was just doing what he was told. . . ."

And now, after all the talk and rumors, there was the terrible realization that Honaker would eventually have to face the scowling Judge Johnson in person. And it was even beginning to look as if he might go to jail.

* * *

But first there was the election. It would be the toughest yet for the white people of New Erie and Catalpa County. They had won by comfortable margins in 1966 and 1968, but to protect those victories they would now have to stave off the combined force of the U.S. Department of Justice, the American Civil Liberties Union, the Supreme Court — and a whole phalanx of big-name civil rights workers. Hence the seeming hopelessness of the white man's task as June wedged its way ominously into July. "Many people fear that the Negroes are going to really take over the county," Lurellia had written. The mood lay heavily on the town, a hush galvanic, brooding, monumental.

At Meads and Co., shoppers poked about noncommittally through racks of clothing or about shelves stacked with goods they were not sure they had actually come to buy. Elsewhere about the square, the shopkeepers and store-owners stood looking out at the street, saying nothing, their hands clasped behind them or propped on the window sills, their curses and angry shouts all dried up into harsh brittle ashes of bitterness and contempt. The people on the street looked back at them, nodding, and passed on to wherever it was they had not fully intended to go. And everywhere now, in their homes and in the stores and at quiet summer parties, the residents of the town talked calmly — almost too calmly — of the fearful and uncertain days that lay ahead.

Only the sheriff managed to keep matters in focus. As usual, he had adopted a philosophical attitude about it all. He just sat there in his office, slumped over his domino game. This was not his year to seek reelection, but even if it had been it seems inconceivable that he would have found time to do much campaigning. What was the use in it? "Nigger don't trust another nigger. You go out and talk to any of the good decent niggers around town and you'll find out they just ain't gonna vote to put another nigger into a white man's office."

* * *

But the county was in real trouble this time. Even the domino players must have known that. Lurellia had it on good authority "that the value of property has decreased at least fifty per cent already." So far there had been no panic auction sales, no mass exodus of old white families to other parts of the state. But there had been talk of that too, even in her own case. Her sister Thelma had recently written of a small house that had become available on the street where they had grown up. Why not sell her place in Mt. Gizeh and move back to her hometown, where there was not so much talk about politics and civil rights?

> I can't think of doing that. Frankly, I think we should try to be calm and accept what we can't change. I've told two or three Negroes that I wish the six men well and hope they will do their very best to do a *good* job—that I have nothing against any person holding an office who is qualified and who can and will do the very best possible job while he holds the office. Some seem quite surprised that *any white* person could feel that way....

But the courthouse was only the beginning. Next would come the white pool, the country club, even the churches. The churches and then the bedrooms of the town, in that order. Today New Erie. Tomorrow the world. That was the schedule. Almost every day now the Reverend Gilchrist heard the rumors. Sometimes the Methodist or Presbyterian minister would call up to say: "I hear you're going to be integrated Sunday." Sunday would come, and still no black faces. But there was always the next Sunday, and the next: *Word's out preacher everybody saying there's gonna be niggers at church Sunday what're we gonna do preacher what're we gonna do*?...And the minister responding in that same patient reassuring voice that had become such a comfort to the town.

Gilchrist's connection with the New Erie church went back more than twenty years, but he had been away for all but about five of those years. He had first come there in the spring of 1948, newly married and fresh out of the seminary. Almost from the start he had taken a charitable attitude toward blacks. During that first autumn after settling into the life of the town, he had organized an extension school for young black men aspiring to enter the ministry, the first such program in Alabama, holding classes in an abandoned church near Taschahatchie City. The whole thing was a magnificent success, and he looked back on it fondly, remembering every detail, even the special taste of the lemonade and fried chicken that had been served on commencement day. But when his deacons found out how much time he was spending down there working with black people, he was soon spending it all somewhere else — at a remote Baptist outpost in the Florida panhandle, the first stop in his fifteen-year exile.

Then in 1966 he was back. Most of the marching had ceased, but the rumors, the phone calls, were now a part of the daily routine. *It's all over town preacher niggers gonna be in the church tomorrow niggers gonna take over the church.* Gilchrist spoke calmly and reassuringly, offering to buy land from those who had become frightened and wanted to move away, encouraging his wife to stay on as a teacher in the public schools even after most of the white students had fled to a private academy.

Once he had gone down to the Town Fork community to visit Sedley Jones, then completing his first year as leader of the Catalpa County civil rights movement. Jones had been one of Gilchrist's first students at the extension school. The two men embraced warmly and talked for a long time — but not about civil rights. Or so Gilchrist remembered it. It was sort of an unwritten agreement between them, he explained later, no bringing up of controversial subjects at a time when all that was wanted was a renewal of old friendships. "When we talked he said, 'There are some things I'm sure you do not understand, and some things we do not want to discuss because we are friends,' and he was very wise. So we did not discuss it."

But Jones would remember it a little differently: "I said, 'Brother Gilchrist, as ministers of the gospel we need to join hands now and lead forth in this movement.' He said, 'Well, I don't know, maybe it ain't time yet.' I said, 'Well, the church ought to be the one to stand up for that which is right.' But he said, 'I just don't know, Sedley. Maybe the time ain't ripe. . . .' " They had met often since then, on the street or at the courthouse, to talk about how the black man felt and how the white man felt. But Gilchrist could not always talk easily. He felt that something had changed—that somehow Jones had thrown up a wall between them. At first the wall was higher than either man's head. Little by little Gilchrist chiseled away at it until he could see over the top. Finally he could rest his arms on the coping and talk comfortably with his old friend.

But that too was a little different from the way Jones remembered it. For him there had never been a wall. "Not from my side. Never. You can't pay me to hate a man." Whoever built it, it would become, finally, not much of a barrier at all except when the talk turned to the possibility of integrating the white church. It would be Gilchrist's turn to build the wall then—to explain in his patient unassuming voice that it was quite out of the question for the black man to worship at the white church. Because the "decent nigras" didn't want that anyway. That was all a political plot hatched by SCLC "mercenaries." All of the more "reliable" black ministers had told him that. "White folks don't worship like we do," they told him. "White folks say, 'We can't be waiting around on the Spirit. We got to be getting home to Sunday dinner.' White folks always watching the clock, but the Spirit don't go by the clock." It was clear, then, that the decent black man would never feel at home in the white church. He would much prefer his own church, where he was free to "strike a moan" or to sit and await the pleasure of the Holy Spirit without having to worry about getting home in time for the big Sunday meal. So the wall went up, higher and thicker than ever, shutting out the clamor of protesting voices though not yet the rumors: *Niggers gonna take over the church preacher where we gonna go what we gonna do?*

* * *

And so the matter stood, "dubious, fateful, in the sultry days of July." The SCLC had sent in a sixteen-member task force, a college-age crowd mostly, all business, clad in checkered jumpsuit uniforms, sporting militant beards and Afros. A lot of the big names too: Ralph Abernathy. Lester Ritchie. The old block church out at the east end of town, devoid of major civil rights activity for more than three years, was suddenly alive with mass meetings, speeches, songs. It was like that all day long, seven days a week, as the election drew near. Abernathy — or maybe Cyrus Blue — would rouse the faithful with a stirring reminder of what it meant to live in these apocalyptic times, and the Southland Rhythm Boys, or some other string band brought in for the occasion, would send them away humming joyous songs of conquest. After the main event there would be further meetings: late-night strategy sessions at the Silver Buckle or at Miss Cora Watkin's house on Roosevelt Avenue or — perhaps most often — at Alvis Childers's little place over on Constantinople Street.

Constantinople Street was a rutted byway that ran down past C.M. Putney's motel and groceteria. Alvis had lived there since 1950. But before that he had lived in Mt. Gizeh and had been close to the Holston family. He still went back for the weekly church service, as well as for all the revival meetings, and I had occasionally seen him there, chief deacon and most vocal occupant of the Amen Corner, a short man with a tie tied too long and his gabardine coat always gaping open. I had first gotten to know him during one of his not infrequent visits at my father-in-law's. He had been coming there much more often now that the old man was near the end, to hold long talks with him about his soul, hoping to convert him from Episcopalianism to Baptist fundamentalism. Alvis knew all about the Old Gentleman's obliging attitude and his "accommodations" at the store, because he had often benefitted from them himself. But none of that would be enough to pave his way into Glory. Until then I had not realized he was in any real danger of damnation. But the worried look on Alvis's face told everything. And so I was not surprised to come in one summer afternoon and find him praying over the old man in the dark bedroom at the back of the house, his voice almost though not quite lost in the hoarse whine of the air-conditioning unit: *Ignore him not O Jesus lay yo hand on this old man relieve him of his great thirst O Lord and yes quench his thirst wid yo blood O my Jesus rebuke him not in this the hour of his need and relieve his great sin. . . .*

The next time I saw him he was at his house in town. I knew he had become active in the movement, but I did not know how active until I went by his place one day and found that he had been doing something most black people were unwilling to do, which was to provide regular lodging and occasional entertainment for both the white girls who had come to take part in the political campaign and their black male companions.

"What's it all about, Alvis?"

His explanation was simple: Don't ever refuse anyone a place to stay lest it turn out to be Jesus.

"God forbids that I turn you away from my house," he said, as he welcomed me into a dirt yard grown up in random corn stalks and sweetpea vines. We went up to the porch. "God forbids me to turn you away from here if you is hongry and wanting a place to stay. It don't matter yo color. How does I know you ain't Christ? Maybe that's the way Christ comes back — all raggedy and dirty and hair all over him." He looked at me. "God forbids it. If you been reading yo Bible, you know it's dangerous fur me to turn you away from here, and you ain't got nowhere else to stay."

He had not been blind to the more immediate dangers either, for as he went on to say, "Yassuh, it's true, I all but lose face wid some of my white inhabitants hyar." He was no longer welcome in stores where he had once gotten credit, and his ailing wife had found it difficult to get the medical attention she needed. One of the two physicians in town had refused to see her at all. The other, crusty Dr. Nance, had been a bit more considerate, though not without telling her, as Alvis recalled it, "Goddammit, Belle, get them stinking white folks outcha house."

One of his female lodgers came by that afternoon while we were talking: a white Agnes Scott sophomore who had grown up in one of the nearby plantation towns and who had signed up to work in the Catalpa County election campaign without her parents' knowledge. She was quite pretty, in that severe and challenging way of the sixties, and she had come there apparently for a rendezvous with a black youth named Cletus Park, who appeared shortly thereafter and made himself at home with her in Alvis's empty house. It was getting dark when they came back out and started up the rutted road toward the church. Alvis watched them, nodding with the air of one who suddenly realizes he has achieved all he ever hoped for in life.

"If she had him, I delight in it," he said. "I honor her fur it."

He confessed that he too had had an opportunity to make time with some of the white girls. They had come by his house one morning, a carload of them, and explained that they wanted him to accompany them on an "orientation" trip about the county. "Somebody had told them, 'Now, if you wants to find out something bout Catalpa County, you go see Alvis Childers, cause he can tell you more about it than anybody.'" But Alvis felt obliged to turn down the invitation. "They wuz young and pretty and mighty tender," he said, "but they wuz going right up through town and all down through the county and I could most hear whut some of my white inhabitants be saying: 'Look at that old black man. He most *glad* to be setting around up thar wid all them white girls.' " Alvis's way out of it was to send his wife instead. "I got to be truthful now: one thing I never did, I never did get fresh wid no white ladies."

Yet there had been many a time when he'd felt he was skimping on his duty for not doing so.

"Son," said he, "you may not know this, but thar's many a white lady that likes a black man."

"Yes, I've heard as much."

"And you know how we at one time been treated?"

That too, yes.

"The white man, he like my black sister, but he say I can't have his white sister."

Alvis's former landlord, old man Walt Mattison, the big Ellerbe cotton planter, had been one of the more notorious fornicators of black women. The story Alvis told was this: the call had come one day for him to go down and visit his landlord, down there in the big house on the river. But the why of it all he didn't know until after he got there. He rapped uneasily at the back door and heard the old man bellow from deep inside: "Who that out thar!"

"Ain't nobody. Jes me. Alvis." He had been on the point of turning away, remembering what some of the other tenants had told him—how the old man sometimes without the slightest provocation would "come jes to fret and rile up." He was already on his way off the patio when he heard the voice a second time:

"Come on in, Alvis."

The door swung open and a tall Negro in a white coat led him back to a small, crowded den. Mattison was at his bath, in a room two doors down the hall, getting himself dried off and sprinkled with powder. "Them nigguhs wuz all mighty good to him—cleaning him up and making him smell real nice." The old man came into the den wearing a loose satiny robe that flapped about obscenely as he walked. "Sot right thar, Alvis. You sot thar and I'll sot over hyar." Alvis "sot" where Mattison directed and a moment later realized that the old man was about to "drap off" to sleep. That was all the cue Alvis needed; he was immediately up and out the door. But the voice jerked him back. "Sot right thar, Alvis. Sot right thar." He did as he was told and this time tried to make conversation, asking Mattison about his churchgoing habits (for even then, apparently, Alvis had developed a profound interest in such matters) and whether he counted himself among the "Episcopals" or Presbyterians.

"O he pure rile up then for sho. Cause he don't belong to no church and he want to turn it around and blame it on his wife. He say, 'Naw, goddammit, you can't belongs to no church around hyah!' and then he come just to cussing and storming tills I all but hated I brung it up. He say, 'That old woman of mine keeps me perplexed to hell, goddammit! Ain't no use talking no church talk around hyah!" Alvis hated more and more that he had brought it up, and again got up to leave. "Sot right thar, Alvis!" He had just sot back down when the old man's invalid wife appeared, rolling herself to the door in her wheelchair. "She come just cussing worse'n he was. She say, 'Why you goddammed big-bellied son of a bitch, you better be trying to seek yo God! You talking like you can't do nothing towards the Lord. You talking like I the one keeping you from yo duty. Why goddamn yo soul!' . . ." She wheeled herself into the den and yanked furiously at the satin robe until she had it mostly off of him, and him yanking back at it with lurid curses, and her whirling at him and pounding him with her feeble fists, and whirling again to wheel herself right back out the way she had come, leaving him half stripped of his robe and thrown open to all the world, like an obscene hunk of flounder or liverwurst, and him scrambling to make himself decent as she disappeared into another part of the house, the curses and insults trailing behind her: "You goddamn big-bellied son of a bitch. You *better* be thinking how you can come to your God."

Alvis got up to go.

"Naw, Alvis. Sot back down. Sot right over thar, Alvis."

Alvis, returning to his seat, began to believe that the old man had taken a liking to him. "He ask me if I want a little something to eat. He say, 'We got some real good meat, Alvis. You wants some?' Well, I likes meat, any kind of meat, I tell anybody that. But I say, 'Nawsuh, I ain't hongry.' "

The big-bellied son of a bitch leaned forward. Maybe he was getting to it at last, whatever it was that Alvis had come for.

"Well, Alvis," he said at length. "The time has come that I'm gonna die."

Then he proceeded to tell the story that Alvis and the other people on Mattison's place had already told among themselves a thousand times: how he had seduced the wife of one of his tenants, dressed her in silk and jewels, and paved the way for further seductions by putting her husband in charge of a river ferry, a good job that would keep him away from home much of the time.

"Alvis, if it hadn't been fur me, Hoss and Lottie would've been together right today."

For the first time Alvis felt no sense of uneasiness in Mattison's presence, because he knew now why he had been sent for — because even Mattison had heard about Alvis's reputation for "knowing the Bible" and what better way to find salvation than from someone who had already saved many a soul and who furthermore had been a close friend of the man the landowner had wronged? Alvis would remember later how he had talked right up to the white man, or at least he would tell it that way: "I say, 'I knowed it. I sho knowed it. You took yo stuff and yo money and you took advantage of that nigguh.' 'I know it, Alvis.' 'God forbids,' I say. 'God forbids me jes cause I got more riches than the next man to go in thar shaking my dollars around and taking that man's woman.' 'I know it, Alvis; I know it's a great wrong I done.' " But Alvis offered him a way out. "That nigguh is still down thar right today. You go down thar whar he is and humble yoself and talk wid him bout whut you done, and then you kin go to God." Alvis saw what he was thinking: maybe he could just go to God first and avoid a confrontation with the man he had wronged. "Ain't no use you thinking bout that," Alvis told him. "Ain't no use you thinking bout trying to bypass that boy and going to God first. God ain't studying you. You go to that boy and get his forgiveness and then you kin go to yo God."

Dubious theology perhaps, but how was Mattison to know? "You big-bellied son of a bitch," his wife yelled, "you better be thinking about some way you can come to your God! You better be thinking about how you're gonna make that shiny ass of yours presentable to your maker!"

But it was all too much for old man Mattison. He again "drap off" while Alvis was sitting there. And a week later he was dead.

Alvis had not attended the last rites. He was stacking hay on the Holston farm the morning that one of the other Mattison tenants had come to advise him about the burial plans. "I wuz goan be stacking hay all that day and the next. Now thar's an art in stacking hay—a way you kin stack it jes like it's a house wid a top on it. I wuz known as 'the good old haystacker.' Folks use to come from all over that country to get me to stack their hay, cause I knew how to stack it up so nothing but the top would ruin." So he hadn't gone to the funeral. "You can't help dead folks. Anyhow, the rest of us got to live on."

Alvis reminded me again of the "rule" that the white man had, Mattison and all the others. "If I comes to yo house and you ain't thar, or you busy somehow, yo wife goan be damned if she do anything but come to the door and say, 'He ain't hyar' or 'He taking a nap.' And then she go on back in the house. She ain't studying me, or thinking bout letting me *git* her. That wuz jes a rule the white man had. But that same man, he come on to my house and he be looking to stay all day. If he have any dominion over me, he'll send me on to the field, or to the mill or whutever, cause he thinking bout *having* that black woman; man, you thinking bout *gittin* her. That wuz the rule the white man had. Why, we come up spotted to death wid yo class of folks."

He dropped off into a kind of detachment, looking out at the sweetpea vines and the sagging fence. He rose and went to the edge of the porch without seeming to increase his height by more than half a foot.

"But the fear of the white man's done gone out of the nigguh," he said. "Now I don't mean me. We old folks, we always goan gives you due respect. But we got some terrible young colored boys coming along, and they goan run *bully.* They goan be taking these little white girls and using them, and the white man, if he swell up and go to talking big, they goan kill him."

Maybe the time was already upon us when the black man would demand all that as his inalienable right. Perhaps that would prove to be the most non-negotiable of all his non-negotiable demands, the one right above all others he would claim as an outgrowth of Equal Protection. And, of course, that had been the white man's biggest fear all along. Not the fear so much of what the black man might demand as of what the white woman might be willing to provide. Maybe there was a little bit of Desdemona in them all. And soon it would all be out in the open, the black man's insistence on the fulfillment of all his Fourteenth Amendment rights, the white man's bitterness and recrimination. Even now it was written on every face, communed from the skies. In times past every drummer who had entered the old store out at Mt. Gizeh had been full of it, the rumors, the talk, the savage invective: *goddamn white bitches screwin those goddamn niggers look at what happened on the Selma march O goddamn those bitches every campground a stinking cesspool a mire of filth O goddamn that Martin Luther Coon had the bastard in jail but they let him out O goddamn them bastards....*

"It's coming," Alvis said. "The day's coming when my sister kin be black as night and you goan come over hyar and go wid her—and I kin go on over thar and go wid your sister. They gonna get jes that loving."

But none of the movement leaders talked about any of that, not yet, not openly, because they realized that that would be too much even for their white supporters. The great fear was that they would end up by driving away all the liberal political backing that had been so crucial to the movement's success. So not only did they not talk about it, they were quick to discipline those who did, removing them from positions of influence even if they couldn't drive them out of the movement altogether.

"But it's coming," Alvis said. "I can feel it. You watch em — these young colored boys, they goan sho run bully...Ain't no covenant up thar bout a black man and a white lady nohow—nothing cept whut the white man *say* is up thar."

So it was all inside him too, all the old hatred and bitterness, the memory of all the lynchings and castrations and midnight whippings, his disgust with the "rule" the white man had. It was a rule that had shaped most of the stock themes of Southern history and literature, the one imperishable totem by which Southern society must, the white man felt, at last assert and maintain itself. But maybe Alvis was right; maybe all of that was about to be thrown over. Maybe any day now a promulgation to that effect would come down from Judge Johnson's court: "I do hereby order and decree, and it is hereby ordered and decreed, that every man of color and each of them shall have for his use, enjoyment, and constant moral edification a certain portion of nubile white maidens, which portion shall be determined on the basis of quotas hereinafter specified...."

Alvis went on talking about all the suffering that had come about because of the white man's rule and about how he had tried to do what little he could to correct the situation by promoting liaisons between the white girls and black boys who lodged at his house. For some reason he had taken a particular interest in the relationship between Cletus Park and Agnes Scott. "Who is she anyway, Alvis?" He looked at me as though he had just remembered something he had been meaning to tell me all along. "Ain't I done told you that? Why that girl thar — that's old man Walt Mattison's granddaughter!"

I said, "What?" And he said,

"Old man Walt Mattison's granddaughter. The day she come here, she don't know me, but I knowed her the minute she tell me her name." And that's when he had begun looking around for someone to throw her with, thinking it would be a fine joke to play on the dead landowner. And it had all worked out so well he was still congratulating himself. "Nature is jes nature," he said, "and if the young folks gets a chance to do, they'll do. And not jes the young ones either — the old ones too, till they is almost dead." He was still standing, not tall, looking at me. And then he looked back along the rutted remains of Constantinople Street and on up toward the main highway and the church. The nightly rally had already begun and I had promised myself to attend. Alvis, however, would not be going; he had done quite enough for the movement already.

"Yassuh, if she had him I delight in it. I honor her and hold her in high regard."

* * *

The talk at Alvis's house sometimes went on until three or four in the morning. But no matter what the hour everyone would be up again by six and over to Miss Cora Watkins's house for doughnuts and coffee —and more talk of what it would be like when the white man was cast down and the black man lifted up. And then on out to the main business of the day. Occasionally we could see them as they scattered about the countryside, the small anxious brigades of uniformed blacks, moving from village to village, from shack to shack, sometimes on foot and sometimes in rented Chevys and Pontiacs, talking, cajoling, exhorting, circulating leaflets that said:

Martin Luther King
Died To Make Us Free!

And always there was Putney, C.M. Putney, the discredited NAACP leader, to stand there glaring at them from behind the plate-glass window of his grocery store, as though in perpetual reminder that their real enemy was not the white man, not Honaker or Sheriff Cain or Lawyer Meads, but Putney himself and all the other black people who felt as he did, the educators and landowners and small businessmen who abhorred the uncompromising ways of the SCLC crowd.

Some of Putney's followers, and even Putney himself, might admire King after a fashion, but they would stubbornly reject his revolutionary doctrines as an affront to the memory of Booker T. Washington, the turn-of-the-century black leader who taught the Negro to embrace the virtues of "nonassertiveness" and to make his way by conciliation and compromise. There were still a great many Catalpa County blacks who felt that way, probably up to a quarter of all those who had been voting in recent elections, and no faction could hope to gain control of the courthouse without their support — or some of it anyway. The white man had been forced to rely heavily on their votes in 1966 and 1968 and had not been disappointed. The question was, could he do so again? Or had the SCLC "mercenaries" slowly and imperceptibly begun to chip away at the base of Putney's support?

At the Silver Buckle and at Alvis Childers's house, leaders of the task force pondered the issue. It was a fearsome thought — the possibility that they might actually lose another election in a county where they held a solid two-to-one edge in voting strength. Another loss and even the Supreme Court would be unable to redeem their cause. Probably never again would circumstances be so favorable for a black takeover of the county government. Nor was Putney the only concern. What about the white man — what new mischief was he plotting? Would he again resort to that Reconstruction-era trick of forcing his black laborers and tenants to spend election day working on plantations in other counties, where they would be unable to cast their ballots? Lester Ritchie expressed the fear publicly, forgetting perhaps that after the wholesale evictions of the mid-sixties and the impact of technological change the white man no longer controlled vast numbers of obedient tenants. But the task force feared the worst, seeing Putney's influence everywhere. Meantime, over at the AME Zion Church, Ritchie strode about in his checkered jumpsuit and tugged militantly at his thick dark beard, his voice raised in merry song:

We're all gonna place an X
under the eagle...

But the festival atmosphere of those days could not dispel the disquieting thought that the fat man behind the grocery store window—Putney—was still in command. The campaign workers asked themselves the same thing over and over again: What about the Putney crowd? Would enough of the Toms rally behind the NDPA eagle to make a difference, or would they go on marking their ballots under the rooster, the traditional emblem of the Alabama Democratic Party? If anything, the philosophical barriers separating the two factions had grown even more pronounced during a summer of hard campaigning. And as election day approached, a headline in the *Tuscaloosa News* raised the specter anew:

NEGROES FEAR
CATALPA DEFEAT

* * *

But what were Putney's feelings about all this? One

morning I decided to look in on him and find out. His place of business, a square brick building with a grocery outlet on the street level and six motel rooms upstairs, sat less than half a block east of the AME Zion Church, where on a summer night some four years earlier I had watched him brave the angry taunts of the SCLC crowd. He still served the church as chief fundraiser and chairman of its board of elders, but that was nothing much to boast about now that he'd had to give up the more important role of political boss. I found him at the back of his dimly lit store, barely discernible amid the sacks of flour and corn meal and Purina hog chow. "Yes?" he said. "Yes?" He had just sat down to breakfast, a big Saturday morning breakfast of country ham and three eggs fried sunnyside up and half a loaf of raisin bread. He did not offer to get up or shake hands. He just sat there with a huge bib draped down his shirt front like an exotic vestment, smiling a smile that invited me to state my business quickly and be gone.

I had heard it said, though not by the most believable of sources, that Putney had already begun looking for ways to claw his way back into favor with movement leaders, hoping to hedge his bets. Did he wish to comment on those reports? He shook his head enigmatically, ponderously. No, he had nothing to say about that, thank you. What of himself — all those old feelings of betrayal and bitterness? Was he now resigned to the power-grabbing ways of the SCLC? A difficult question, best left unanswered. Best not to say anything about that at all. Would he care, then to speculate on the probable outcome of the election? No, no, that was quite impossible. Nothing to be gained by that. There were other reports that, given a black victory, his large experience in the business affairs of the town might compel his participation in the new government regardless of how he might fit in politically. Would he care to elaborate? No, no, nothing to be said on that score either. The truth was that he had very little time to lavish on such questions that morning. Perhaps, then, another time? No, no. By no means, no. Quite out of the question. So much on his mind at present — business matters to tend to, church meetings, the PTA, civic responsibilities. He was really very sorry and hoped I might understand, but he had nothing at all to say with respect to the marching and voting. Nothing. Mum's the word. His breakfast over, he gathered himself for a concentrated effort that would bring him heavily and unsteadily to his feet. He worked his way past me, not unkindly, moving toward the door and smiling the smile that would send me quickly on my way. But as I went out he did confess, in strictest confidence naturally, that he had begun work on a definitive history of the civil rights movement in Catalpa County. It would also be something of an autobiography. I pressed for details. What kind of history? An expose of the SCLC? How far along was he? When did he hope to bring it out? All I got for my trouble was that same knowing and secret smile. The title then — did he have a title?

He nodded. Yes, he had chosen the title.

What then?

"Uncle Tom Speaks Out!"

* * *

What dat white lady doin? Whar she goin wid de ballot box?

Lurellia had thought nothing of the taunts at first. It had been like that ever since she had come down early that morning to open the polls — taunts, threats, insults, disorder rampant, all "dignity" forgotten, a kind of midsummer saturnalia with Aaron Pollard as the lord of misrule. It was, as she later wrote, 1966 and 1968 all over again: great clusters of black people backed up along both sides of the road and waited clamorously for her to get the door open so they could "tend to all this voting." Pollard, whose political activities had predictably cost him his leasing rights on the Calloway land, was again the most active of the SCLC "intimidators." But Buck Simpson was there too, with all those memories of his own hard eviction, of the Austrian loggers who way back in 1923 or 1924 had encouraged him to strike out against his white overlords. As in all the primaries and general elections of the past three years, the two men had fought to prevent all who would attempt it from "voting their own conscience." They and all the other "watchers" had fought their way into the polls despite Crawlie Calloway's attempt to keep order, Wadina Bee among them, and Queen Esther Bowman, and the redoubtable Beatrice Montgomery, each of them standing over the voters as they attempted to make their choices and saying, "No, don't mark dat one. Here de one to mark."

> The "Watchers" grew quite noisy when informed that only one was allowed to stay inside and watch. The people in New Erie had signed their papers for them to watch, and they had a paper which they called "The Law" that they tried to read to us. It is one grand mess, if you ask me.

Pollard had vanished in mid-afternoon, carrying his copy of "The Law" with him. He and Crawlie Calloway had come near blows half a dozen times that day. Crawlie had ignored "The Law," announcing that he was "still the boss here" and laying it down that Pollard and his fellow intimidators were in gross violation of the Alabama election code. Didn't they know that it was against the rule for any "marker" to mark ballots for more than ten persons in a given election? A fabrication, of course. "But he was only trying to restore order, and was not to be blamed." The two federal men who had come to oversee the election had refused to intervene, explaining that their task was only to observe the affair and report their findings to the Justice Department. So Pollard had left to seek help elsewhere, apparently with some success. For it was only a short while afterward that probate judge Honaker had called to say . . . well, she wasn't exactly sure what he had said . . . but whatever it was, it had left the storeowner with no alternative but to propound a revised rule. The essence of the new rule, as I later pieced it together, was somewhat as follows: "Just let the niggers go ahead and mark their goddamn ballots as they goddamn well please, cause we can't stop em nohow now that the government's got into it."

I could imagine him standing there, a monstrous Buddhalike apparition swaying about uneasily in his tight-fitting store khakis, looking like what he had been for a good portion of his married life: the community's best-known cuckhold. He would not live long after that. And when he was gone everyone would say: "It was that election that did it. He'd be alive right today if it hadn't been for that election."

* * *

How come she takin de ballot box? What she doin?

As Lurellia emerged from the polls that evening, the watchers again closed in on her. They had responded sullenly to the news that the black ticket had carried the Mt. Gizeh beat by a margin of almost five to one. They knew from what had happened in previous elections that the Mt. Gizeh totals meant little; they had carried the beat by an identical margin in 1966 only to discover later that the white man still had control of the courthouse. Maybe it would be the same this time. So they waited, not cheerfully, as Efren Summers and two other men locked the ballot box in the trunk of Lurellia's car.

Whar she goin wid de ballot box? Whut she doin?

She would leave it in the trunk overnight, as she had done after every election for the past twenty years or more, and return it to the courthouse early the next morning. In all her years as returning officer, this was the first time anyone had ever suspected her of wanting to tamper with the ballots. Maybe it was only to be expected, given the large amount of wildly exaggerated talk that had afflicted the community in recent weeks. Still, she was quite surprised that so many of the black people who had traded with the Holstons and knew their reputation for fair dealing would join in the mischief.

She goin. She leavin. She taking de ballot box.

She knew even as she got in the car that she could not escape them simply by driving away. As she crossed the railroad tracks she looked back and saw them behind her — a whole string of vehicles in close pursuit, Pollard leading the way in his new pickup. It was then that her thoughts flew back to another piece of news she had heard that evening —

something about Mr. Julius Greene, the Ellerbe grocer, being robbed of a month's proceeds as he was preparing to lock up for the day. But wasn't Ellerbe where Pollard had gone to phone in his complaint? Was it possible that there was some connection? It was certain that he answered the description of the robber. A tall, slim man —or so the radio had described him. With a mask and gun. And it would have been so like him too: to borrow Mr. Greene's phone and then turn on his benefactor and rob him of his last cent. Perhaps he still had the money stuffed in his pockets, the mask too, the gun... Yes, it all added up now... Pollard, the phone call, his long absence from the polls. And she knew what he was after this time: the ballot box.

She watched as the caravan pursued her bumper-to-bumper to the top of the long uphill grade, forcing her to speed up more than she thought wise on that "quite dangerous little stretch of highway." But even after all that, she was not prepared for what happened next. As she turned into her drive, one of the cars broke off from the others and came roaring up behind her. *Pollard. With his mask and gun. "Okay, I'll take it off yo hands. The ballot box. That's what I'm saying I want – the ballot box."*

But it wasn't Pollard; it was Efren Summers. "Don't worry, Lurellia," he had told her at the polls, "I'll see that you get home all right." At the time she had thought it might be a good idea for him to see her home. Yet one instinctively did not trust Summers, what with that smell of stolen cattle all over him and his jowls marked with all those horrid moles. She got quickly inside the house and locked it. She could still see the caravan of cars and pickups strung out along the highway — Summers too, in the drive, looking up at the house, his face caught in the sinister glow of his cigarette. She stood just inside the front screen, with the lights out, waiting out the departure of the ungracious rustler. He was still there, staring at the house, long after the last of the caravan had drawn off into the night. She watched him, the glow of his cigarette, him just sitting there, so calm and yet so purposeful about it all, almost as though he were plotting some terrible act of desperation.

The other cars were almost out of hearing distance now, dragging a long rope of diminishing sound off through the great pine forest that separated Mt. Gizeh from the community of Vestal. She stood there for quite some little time after that, after all the sound was gone and Summers as well, with nothing but the dark and the melancholy cry of the jarflies to keep her company, thinking back on all that had happened that day—what it meant—what the future held—what the people in town would be saying—and about the curious attitude of the "young nigras," whose behavior had finally convinced her that "they really *do* want to take over the county." But how was it all to end? Was it always to be like this—robberies—beatings—even after the "nigra" officials had assumed their new duties? And was it true, as she later heard, that Pollard himself was thinking of running for the office of probate judge?

* * *

Almost a week before the climactic events of July 29, 1969, we had left Catalpa County to return to Baltimore, where I had taken a job writing editorials for the Sunpapers. During the intervening days I'd had little occasion to think about the election. Somehow it had all come to seem so remote and inconsequential, all the more so now that there was a moon landing and a mysterious drowning death at Chappaquiddick to dominate the headlines. And then one morning Catalpa County was on the front pages too, along with the moon landing, Chappaquiddick, and all the rest:

NEGROES TAKE OVER ALABAMA COUNTY

The insurgents had gotten enough of Putney's votes to gain a narrow two-hundred-ballot victory. They had won all of the six offices they had sought, taking over both the commissioners court and the board of education. But they still lacked control of the county's two major power centers: the sheriff's office and the probate judgeship. Neither Sheriff Cain nor Judge Honaker was due to seek reelection until the fall of 1970. And so again the old question asked itself: what of Putney? He was still there, working his mischief. His narrow loss this time did not mean that he would not win big the next. So it was not over yet. If the blacks were to rest easy with their new gains — more, if they were ever to get rid of Cain and Honaker and the other placeholders in the courthouse — they would somehow have to find more effective ways of nullifying Putney's influence. To some extent, then, the election seemed a little like the moon landing — more symbolic than immediately useful.

But most people didn't look at it that way, and that included my onetime drinking partner, G. Harold Edisen, chief of the *Newsweek* bureau in Atlanta. Talking to him, I got the feeling that Catalpa County had suddenly come to represent all that was meant by the Great South of legend — the South of storied romance and pillared mansion, of myth and fancy. What now was left of that South? And what now was left of all the old sin and grief? Even at this moment, as Edisen was not too embarrassed to remind me, we stood at the "climax of Southern history" and must brace ourselves for ever more terrible judgments. Now the SCLC would march from triumph to triumph, building shrewdly on what had happened in Catalpa County, extending its influence throughout the Black Belt and beyond, seizing power in a whole string of rural Alabama counties where entrenched white minorities had so long held sway, eradicating all of the old "shame" and "guilt" of Southern plantation society.

And so it went — bold predictions, big plans. But the great hope of those days would come to nothing. For many years Catalpa County would stand alone, isolated, the only predominantly black Alabama county that could also boast a predominantly black government.

No, it had not come easily and it was no harbinger. It was only what it was. And what it was was not nearly enough to suit the SCLC's bearded field marshal, Lester Ritchie. Ritchie, it seems, had thrown a big drunk during the election-night celebration and had gotten into quite a row with some of his subordinates. Almost before the first shouts of victory went up, he was already complaining about the closeness of the vote, and he was still complaining about it later at the Silver Buckle, placing most of the blame for the unimpressive showing (though he was the only one who would call it that) on George Sampkins, the young Birmingham enforcer.

Wilkins, the Silver Buckle's college-educated barkeep, would remember it best:

"... Les just kept fooling around... talking big... you know how he is when he gets to drinking... kept storming around and bragging about what he had done for the movement, all the big things he'd accomplished—how he'd practically kept the whole thing going there at one time, which he had in a way, Les had—sure, he'd done a lot in his years with the movement, organized in a lot of tough places... but, hell, he didn't know what some of those boys had been up against—how they'd practically had to drag a lot of those voters outa their houses and threaten them in a hundred different ways just to get them anywhere near the polls. Folks were still scared—plenty scared—that's right, for a truth—still scared about what Mister Charlie might say, or Mister Henry. Worried about their jobs, their place on the land—and a lot to be worried about too. But those boys got em out—did a good job to my way of thinking. But Les, he didn't wanta talk about that. Naw, all he wanted to talk about was his 'pure democracy'—*black* democracy...."

Wilkins erupted with a tremendous laugh as he set me another beer. "... Black democracy, *my* kind of democracy, white folks. Les kept wanting to know—kept shouting it out all around the place—why the black ticket couldn't've won by a big landslide—two or three thousand votes, you know. Hell, there practically isn't that many votes in the whole county. But that didn't faze Les; you know how he is when he gets a little too much to drink. He kept telling those boys how they'd fallen down on the job, because they didn't get those black folks to voting the way they were told. Sampkins, the others, they were all trying to tell him how it was out there. Sampkins, he kept saying, 'Hell, Les, let's just be glad we won. We got plenty of time to rub their noses in it.' But Les just kept talking big and throwing it up to them: 'Naw, naw, Sampkins, y'all ain't been holding up your end of the deal'. . . ."

Five years of get-out-the-vote campaigns in dozens of similar communities throughout the South had taught Sampkins that no such victory would ever come easily. But try and get all that across to Ritchie. Try and get anything across to him that evening. He kept downing whole pitchers of beer at a time, crying out madly about the deterioration of his "democratic ideals," holding the task force up to ridicule. "Yeah, Sampkins! Yeah!" There was only one way to handle Ritchie: declare him to have "done gone clean rashus" and bump him on out into the dark. The task force closed in on him, the way it had on Putney that time at the AME Zion Church, Sampkins in front, saying,

"Your ass is gonna sit in the dirt, Les. Gonna sit right down in the gravel. You gonna be picking gravel outa your ass all the way back to Atlanta. . . ."

"Looks like you don't need any more trouble tonight, Sampkins."

"Sho could use any I might get outa you."

"You talk big, Sampkins."

Ritchie stood up, clenching his fists, both fists. Soul power in the raw.

"Anytime, Sampkins. Anytime."

"By God, Les. . . ."

It was the appearance of Cyrus Blue that broke it up. The way Wilkins would remember it, Blue had come in and stood a little back from the crowd, not saying anything, just biding his time, knowing that his hour of triumph had finally come—even though he personally had yet to win an election—and waiting for the others to realize it too. He and Ritchie had never liked each other. What he saw in Ritchie was what most whites saw: a meddlesome outsider full of drunken palaver and hairy-faced lies. What Ritchie saw in Blue may have been even worse: a "trimmer" who would not shrink from working with the white man if it came to that, even if it meant denying Ritchie and the SCLC the "pure democracy" he, Ritchie, had preached about in church.

But this was Blue's moment, not Ritchie's. "I don't

know what it was," Wilkins said. "Something about him standing there like that... like it'd just then hit them what'd happened — like they'd just realized for the first time that they really *had* won the goddamn election." Wilkins wasn't even sure it had anything to do with Blue; maybe it was just a sudden dramatic conspiracy of circumstances that had brought everything into focus. "But, no, I think it *was* Cyrus. It was like they'd suddenly seen in him a lot they hadn't seen before... like it'd just hit them, you see... Like all of a sudden they'd turned and seen him standing there and said to themselves: 'Yeah... Blue... Cyrus Blue... the one that ran for sheriff that time.... Well, looks like he really *is* gonna be the sheriff this time....' "

* * *

A long time before my conversation with Wilkins — before we had heard anything from Lurellia and at a time when we knew nothing of the election except what had reached us by way of the news reports — I found myself called upon to explain the "redemption" of Catalpa County over cocktails and dinner. Our guests that evening were close students of the civil rights movement and sometimes impatient with those who would explain away the South as an unfortunate accident of history, or dwell overmuch on the many ameliorating circumstances of its racial turmoil. One was himself a Southerner and a political writer who had spent some time as a Washington correspondent before coming to the Sunpapers, and who was now working on his first book, a biographical study of a not-yet-faded presidential aspirant named Edmund Muskie. The other was an editor, tall, discreet, aristocratically thin. He was old-family Baltimore and his wife had been a Mellon. Once, many years ago, he had gotten to know F. Scott Fitzgerald through an old Princeton connection. Except that he always thought it was Fitzgerald who had gotten to know *him.* As might be expected, he drank only the finest scotch and brandy, including a certain armagnac I could never find even in the most exclusive of Baltimore's liquor stores. He dined on *escargot du frond* in and out of season and was fond of serving turtle soup to hesitating guests who had never sampled that fine old Maryland delicacy. And all who came to his table — to partake of what his wife sometimes called "a little quiet supper" —would retire in due course to the library, where it was his fashion to serve *pot-de-chocolat* in exquisitely crafted antique demitasses and where he and his guests would sit talking, with legs crossed, about all of the more important literary and social trends of the day. He was, in other words, unmistakably aristocratic in all the familiar ways: correct without being ostentatious, authoritative without being condescending, and never apologetic, not even about things that most needed apologizing for — all those times, for instance, when he had nothing but turtle soup or an exotic kidney stew to serve provincial-minded guests who would have felt more at home with hamburger or fried chicken.

So I would not apologize either, not for my inferior brand of scotch, not for the crowded and terribly ordinary row house in which we lived, not even for Catalpa County. I found myself explaining it all rather cavalierly, with my legs crossed, going into all the details — everything, all the old mores and traditions, the historical conflicts, the poverty, the many positive black and white relationships that had survived and even prevailed over the more perverse manifestations of the South's "savage ideal." No, it was not always as it seemed. The people there were not the sordid lot so often depicted in the big-city press. Quite an enlightened lot, really, for the time and place. They only wanted what was best for Catalpa County and Alabama. They didn't much care for the likes of Wallace. Some of their best friends were nigras. I went on talking about it — all the subtleties and complexities, the editor reassuringly grim, the writer suspiciously sardonic.

I was still talking about it, and even beginning to make myself heard above the Muskieite's increasingly sardonic chuckle, when Crawlie Calloway — the same — suddenly lunged front and center onto our television screen, ready to provide CBS Evening News with a thoughtful assessment of the Catalpa County election returns. My wife hurriedly summoned us into the den to witness this surprising turn of events. "He looks rather distraught," I said, in behalf of his angry apoplectic snarl. This, as I say, was before we had heard anything about Crawlie's problems with Aaron Pollard, so that I had no way of knowing for certain what was coming, though there was cause for apprehension. CBS had found him lurking at the back of his store and had coaxed him outside to face the camera. He stared balefully about and hitched up his unpressed khaki britches.

A dramatic hush fell. "Well," said Crawlie with an air of grave authority, "if you want to know what I think about the situation I think the government oughta just go ahead and turn the whole goddamn thing over to the niggers. The niggers, they're the ones that's got all the rights. The white man ain't got no rights. No use for the white man to say anything about it at all. Might as well just let em go on and do as they please, cause you can't stop em nohow now that the government's gotten into it. You ask any of the decent hard-working niggers around here and they'll tell you right quick what the situation is." The Muskieite laughed a deep sneering hollow laugh that hung in the room like a fateful omen. The editor winced with restraint. Crawlie meantime shot both hands overhead, as though surrendering to a gunman—a timely gesture to drive home his last point. "Sho, now—you just go ahead and ask any of the decent niggers about it. They'll tell you who's got all the rights now. It sho ain't the white man. Might as well just go ahead and let the niggers have it—that's what I say—the whole thing—lock, stock and barrel—and *then* see how we get along. The government's been saying the nigger was so great and deserved to have all this power over the white man. Well, we'll just wait and see—that's all. We'll just wait and see what's gonna happen now that the niggers started talking about how they gonna run everything."

But that was like CBS, to pick out your least exemplary type and hold him up as the norm. I tried to explain that too, but our guests were no longer listening. Neither apologized for not listening, and the one who had known Scott Fitzgerald did not even apologize for not accepting another drink of my off-brand scotch. The Muskieite's sardonic laugh had grown alarming. All over Alabama the lights are out.

* * *

Leave it to Ralph Abernathy to make Crawlie Calloway look like a real statesman. At least that's the way everybody seemed to feel about it after the Great Catalpa County Inauguration Day Debacle. It was all Ralph's fault, people were saying—everything that had gone wrong that day. If only he had been content to take things one step at a time... but, no, that wasn't good enough: he wasn't satisifed with just taking over the courthouse, he wanted to take over the white swimming pool too. For the people who had fought so long to keep the pool the way it was there was a certain amount of gratification in watching him make a fool of himself. Now they could stand there behind their plate-glass windows and light up their big cigars and swap jokes about it, nudging one another in the ribs and saying, "You see, I told you what it would be like all along. Just like Reconstruction."

So it was all Ralph's fault. Martin Luther King would never have done anything like that. That's what everybody was saying anyway, even the black political leaders who had always tried to stand behind Ralph when they could. Ralph, they said, was always trying to prove himself, always trying to make himself out a Big Man. But he was just a good No. 2 man; he could never take King's place. And if what the newspapers had been saying were true, he sure went out of his way to prove it on inauguration day.

All the big men of the town had been present for the inaugural ceremonies, even Sheriff Cain. The way I heard it, the sheriff made himself one swell fellow with all the black functionaries, walking around and slapping them on the back and rendering with gusto the soul-power salute he had learned from Lester Ritchie back in 1966. So maybe all those years of sitting over the domino game hadn't ruined his electioneering instincts after all, because evidently that was his only reason for being there — to win black support for his own reelection campaign in 1970.

Judge Honaker wasn't quite so forward about it all. But he too was much in evidence, assuring the new officeholders that he as well as they had only the best interests of Catalpa County at heart and that he would be ever alert for ways to help them adjust to their difficult new role. Even the malevolent circuit judge, J. Phillip Crashaw, was present for the big day. Crashaw was known far beyond the boundaries of Catalpa County for his sharp lending practices and ruthless foreclosures. But he liked to think of himself as something more than an ordinary swindler. He boasted often of his intellectual attainments, which were not inconsiderable. He had studied at the Sorbonne and had read Goethe in the original. Short and bald, with a Prussianlike swagger to his step, he could be snide or ingratiating by turns and in the latter guise occasionally presided at meetings of the Twenty Four Circle, a weekly discussion group that he had helped found. But blacks, and poor whites too, knew him mostly as a relentless and even savage creditor.

Many of his clients may have found it strange to have such a man in their presence on such a day, as strange to him no doubt as to them, except that it was his duty, as circuit judge, to administer the oath of office and make an inaugural address. And it wasn't a bad address either, given Crashaw's reputation for candor and the circumstances under which it was delivered. But could the hated judge have written a speech so full of conciliatory overtones? The answer, as it turned out, was that he could not—or, anyway, had not. The speech was actually the work of the Reverend Gilchrist, who was on excellent terms with Crashaw and had been asked to look over a preliminary draft. The preacher had found it, well, not quite what he deemed suitable for the occasion, perhaps a bit patronizing and frankly (he told me later) not far from being insulting. The judge tried again. But the second draft was no better. Why not let him, the preacher, take a hand? By all means, said the judge. Gilchrist worked at his task half the night, transforming what had been a tasteless commentary on black insufficiency into a paean of brotherhood and understanding.

"And he never stopped thanking me for it," Gilchrist would later recall. "He came to feel before his death that it was exactly what had been in his mind all along."

So it was the Baptist preacher more than anyone else who had gotten the town through its most difficult hour. But even as he did so, Abernathy, I'm told, was busy figuring out ways to disrupt the harmonious mood. As the people were leaving the courthouse he gathered some of his followers about him and said, "Okay, boys, get ready now, cause we all gonna march out to the white pool. And then you can say you've been where the white folks have been." The way led through the main part of town, up past the Baptist church and the Presbyterian church and the Episcopal church and on out the main highway through the well-to-do residential district. No one could have stopped Abernathy that day. He just marched right on out ahead of everybody, singing and praying, gaining strength as he went, his followers taunting the few whites who had gathered along the way.

"Get outa the way, whites, or you gonna make us mad!"

And so on out to the white pool, more than a thousand strong. There — amid cries of "Come on in, boys, the pool belongs to us now" — Abernathy plunged in for what he would later call a "historic swim." And a lot of white people were already laughing about it, the way he had gone strutting out there to make a plain fool of himself. But you couldn't blame him in a way. The situation at the white pool had been on his mind for a long time. The SCLC organizers had first tried to open it to blacks way back in the spring of 1965. But Mayor Swint and the city council just laughed them down. "Niggers got their own pool — a lot better pool than the white folks have got." The next year the council closed both pools as an object lesson. Let the Supreme Court try to make an issue out of that if it dared! That brought everybody around: the whites would stay on their side of town and the blacks on theirs, and the next year both pools would open on schedule. And it had been like that ever since. That's what had been bothering Ralph all that time, and he just got to thinking that if anything was ever going to be done about it, the time was now.

You better watch it, whites, or you sho gonna make us mad!

Maybe he just hadn't realized how it would look — or that his followers were more interested in ransacking the place than in taking a symbolic swim. He was already in the pool when the twelve hundred or more youths who had followed him there set to work cleaning out the concession stand.

Yeah, whites, you sho gonna make us mad.

Maybe Ralph didn't know about any of that until it was over. He was out there all that time splashing around in the pair of swim trunks he had borrowed off the locker-room wall. And then the others, full of peanuts and Baby Ruths, joined in the frolic.

"Now you can say you've been where the white folks have been!" Abernathy shouted.

The whole thing proved to be such an embarrassment that he fled town before nightfall, hooted at by some of the same people who had been sworn into office that day. But there were a lot of other people — good friends of Ralph — who didn't want to admit that he was guilty of all the things the sheriff and the mayor and all the others had been accusing him of. So they began to make excuses for him. Pretty soon somebody got out the word that Ralph wasn't to be held responsible for the swimming-pool debacle. There were even some who wanted to pretend that Ralph hadn't jumped in the pool at all. "That was Big Jesse," they said. "And everybody can tell you how much Big Jesse looks like Ralph." But Big Jesse had fled too, whoever he was. And it didn't matter, because Abernathy wasn't trying to hide anything. Back in Atlanta, he was quick to concede that it was all his doing — and a good thing too, he said, because "no just laws were broken" and also because, as he incorrectly asserted, the New Erie pool "represented the last vestiges of segregation and racism in the South." And anyway, he said, "it was a hot day and a historic occasion."

DON'T HE LOOK NATURAL

November 1969

Little Brother knew nothing of all this. He died in November, finally whupped down by the Almighty, persuaded till the last that no county could long remain solvent under black rule and that, anyway, even the black people would never willingly risk the folly of such an experiment. He sat there uncomprehendingly in the back corridor, under a wall of shelves on which Thier's *Napoleon* and a whole throng of nameless Latin grammars strove gamely to maintain hegemony against more than ten years of *National Geographic* and at least half that many of the *Saturday Evening Post*, where Xenophon's *Anabasis* and Ovid's *Metamorphosis* had already given way before a concerted rush of *Colliers* and the *American Home*. Eula was with him much of the time now, at once solicitous and dominant, talking about all the nights he had tried to get away — "Allus saying he going off to Taschahatchie City, goan meet somebody thar, goan catch the train" — and about all the other times when he had sat out on the front porch waiting for the stranger to come. "Don't know *who* he waiting fur, somebody he know up in Birmingham that time he working up thar. He say, 'Don't worry, don't worry, he be's along in a little while; he be's hyar t'rectly' . . . ."

But mostly the old man just sat there and said nothing, weak, grizzled, dying. We would often find him lying in the back hall under a swarm of blankets, the electric heater going. Miss Angie would say, "Little Brother seems better today." But he always seemed much worse, never stirring except upon some impulse that rose from we knew not where. It would seize him violently; he would leap up with a sudden wild look of anguish or panic or frenzy — a kind of rootless terror—apprehension maybe—something—I don't know what. Out would come a meaningless tumble of words as he attempted to scramble to his feet, throwing the covers off. And then whatever it was that had set him to flailing about would come crashing in on him and he would sink listlessly back into that strange ocean of silence and despair. "He be's like that all the time," Eula said. "He ain't goan be no better. God done whupped him now."

But sometimes in the evening he would still manage to make his way unaided out to the porch. And there were rare occasions when he was almost coherent.

"Ain't nothing on his mind but catching that train. Going down to Taschahatchie City and catching that train . . . Going to Birmingham . . . that's whar he allus say he going . . . down to Taschahatchie City and then up to Birmingham. He allus say, 'Well, it's fo o'clock now. Got to see if I kin catch the evening train.' Other times he would just sit there in the dark and wait for the stranger. He say, 'Well, I spect he be coming along after a little. He be's hyar t'rectly.' Or he say, 'That's him now. He coming now. I knew he be's coming along in a little while. . . .' And I ask him, say, 'Who you mean? Who you think coming?' "

But she never found out. All she could say for sure was that it was someone he had known, or thought he had known, from the time he lived in Birmingham. He was a young man then, not long out of college. He was reading law. "He wuz goan be a big lawyer in Birmingham, but you knows how his health went bad. . . ." So now he just sat on the porch and waited. Or maybe he would half rise out of his rocker and explain that he would have to be getting along now, that it was time for him to be packing his things and getting on down to Taschahatchie City.

"Miss Angie, she allus tell him, say, 'Little Brother, you better not go.' And he say, 'O yeah, it's fo o'clock—past time to be going.' " And then he would go—or at least try to go. Sometimes, with the help of the black woman, he would even get his suitcase packed and make it all the way out to the gate, even into the cab of his pickup. He would pull himself up on the running board and shove the suitcase inside and then climb in behind the wheel and sit there until, confused and again exhausted, he would turn to the black woman and allow her to help him back inside. "He try to crank it and he can't get it cranked and that's when he kind of faint and lose control of hisself."

Miss Angie would always be watching from the porch, leaning on the bannister, peering out into the cool October dark. It would be the same night after night: the black woman lugging her Anchiseslike burden back along the drive under the huge oaks and through a sagging fence on which the wisteria climbed, scentless. She would come on up through the yard past clumps of fern and quince bushes and great shaggy masses of crape myrtle and lugustrum, past small garden plots outlined with creek boulders for which we had no name now that we had stopped calling them "niggerheads." Then she would heave fully into view of the porch, Miss Angie starting to say something reassuring and not quite getting it out before the maid was already past her and through the screen and so down the long hall and back to the bedroom where a gas-flame heater hummed and purred. "I rubs his face real good wid some rubbing alcohol and gets him comfortable and say, 'Now you rest easy, boy. You goan be all right.' But he pop right back up and say, 'Well, I gots to go. It's fo o'clock. Train be coming t'rectly. . . .' "

Then one day he stopped talking about the train. Toward the last he was content simply to sit on the front porch when it was warm enough, or in the front hall when it wasn't, and wait for the stranger to come. "He allus say, 'Well, I spect he be hyar soon. He be's coming along t'rectly.' I ask him all the time who he think coming. But he jes sot thar same as ever, him and Miss Angie, and then he say, 'That's him! That's him coming now!' And maybe it was. Maybe at the very last he could actually see whoever it was he had been waiting for all this time: a tall man, faceless, driving a ramshackle two-horse buggy and wearing a faded uniform left over from the days when he had ridden with

Forrest. Little Brother would greet him out by the gate and they would stand talking for a moment and then go on out to where the buggy was parked and climb in and drive off through the woods and on down through the bottom and off into the night somewhere. Then they would be in Taschahatchie City. The buggy would again slow to a halt and the old man would get down and stand there for a long time in the cold. And then the train would come and he would climb aboard and go riding off through a country he had never seen before, past broomsedge fields and pine barrens and dark towns haunted by moonlight. And when the train pulled into the last station it would be morning and there would be a mist rising from the fields and he would look out the window and see a faded and battered sign hanging from the side of the old depot:

ETERNITY
Welcome to Everlastingness

"But his mind all come back to him at the last," Eula said, "cause God done got through whupping him, and he be's sorry fur all them bad things he done." That surprised even her — how clearheaded and penitent he was during those last hours at the hospital. She was the last to see him alive. She had sat with him all that November afternoon and into the night. "He say, 'Eula, you's a good woman. I sorry I takes all them eggs from you and all them other things. . . .' He wuz sho whupped good fo he die, and he know he been whupped too, and he see all the wrong he'd done, and he know he wuz going to meet his God, and all his mind come back to him on that last day. He say, 'Eula, you's a good woman, and I sho is sorry I takes all yo stuff and causes you so much misry. I wuzn't so very nice to you, Eula. You fogive me now.' I say, 'I already fogive you, cause I know right well you wont yo natural self.' " He was, of course, but that no longer mattered. "He say, 'you's a good woman. If it wont fo you I jes don't know whut become of me. And I wants you to take real good care of Little Sister too.' And then he jes look at me and say, 'Eula, I goan give you something.' He want me to go and get his little purse so he kin give me two dollar. But all that money had done disappeared. I tell him that, and he say, 'Eula, I sho do wants to give you some money some kind of way. When you gets back to the homehouse, you tells Little Sister I say fur her to gives you some money.' "

He stood up, the last time, bracing himself against the window sill. Everything had gone white, like snow.

"He look out the window and say, 'It snowing, Eula. It done gone to snowing.' He done already come near to die, don't you see, and everything look pure white to him, and he think it wuz snow out there. But it wont snow. I say, 'Naw-suh, that ain't snow.' But he say, 'Naw, Eula, look now. It done gone to snowing.' So I have to witness it too. I say, 'Yassuh, it sho be's snowing. Sho is. And in November too.' But it wont no snow out thar. It wont no kind of snow. It wuz jes cause everything look so pure and white, cause he done been whupped and he wuz coming near to die. He keep telling me that, saying he dying. But I say, 'Naw, you ain't dying. We going back home tomorry.' He say, 'Naw, Eula, I dying, I reckon I better sot back down.' I say, 'Well, you better *lay* down, that's whut you better do, so you kin gets well.' And he say, 'Naw, Eula, if I lay down I die.' " But he had lain down anyway and had looked up at her from the thin small pillow. "He say, 'I dying, Eula. Don't leaves me now.' I goes on working my quilt pieces. I wont goan leaves him. I tells him that. I say, 'Now, don't you worry, boy. I ain't goan leaves you.' And he say, 'You's a good woman, Eula. If I had anything hyar I'ud gives you something. Now you tells Little Sister when you gets home that I say to let you have whutever you wants.' And I say, 'You kin be telling her that. You going back home too. You goan be all right. We all go back home tomorry.' And he say, 'Eula, I sho is sorry I took all them eggs from you, and that milk, and all them things.' I tell him not to worry now, jes to rest easy cause we wuz all going back to the homehouse tomorry. He say, 'You's a good woman, Eula.' I sot in the cheer beside him, jes working my quilt pieces. He say, 'Eula?' I say, 'Whut?' He say, 'Eula, I dying.' And he jump *straight* up and grab my hand and squeeze it so tight he come near to break it. He say, 'I dying! Don't leaves me now.' And I say, 'I ain't goan leaves you. You ain't dying. You jes rest easy now.' And he jump up and he fall down, and he jump back up and I grab him and he lie back in my arms and give jes two words and then he *gone*! And he like to break my hand, squeezing it so tight, and him so skinny and thin and all, and yet he jes grip my hand as tight as any man ever hold it, and don't turn loose till he daid. I pull the bell and they all come. And they say, 'He ain't daid. He can't be daid.' They jes couldn't believes he'uz daid, cause they all thinking how much better he been, and how much clearer his mind'd got. But that wuz only cause God'uz done whupping him and goan let him see clear all the wrong he done.' "

* * *

And so again into the big parlor at the captain's house, with the bronze casket already placed among the flowers, and Little Brother shrunken inside it, and all the neighbors coming by and saying, as he had known all along they would: "My, my, don't he look natural? He sho do look natural, don't he?" And then the long ride into town, and the church already crowded when we got there, and Eula herself prominent among the mourners, fashionably sedate in her white dress and gloves, and maybe a little ill at ease too, there amid all the painted windows and alien liturgies, stirring restlessly as the rector spoke of the end and beginning of all things, of hope amid the ashes, and her wondering perhaps why none of the other mourners had commenced to "strike a moan," as was the custom in her own church, or turned to shake the "glad hands." Then came the closing prayer and the long walk to the burial ground, and Eula following at a respectful distance, thinking the *Piscopals done funeralized him proper but the Piscopal God ain't the only God cause the good Lawd ain't said nothing bout no Piscopals and He ain't said nothing bout no Baptists all He say wuz Come my little ones....*

* * *

Home at last, in the dim cold light of the autumn afternoon, the cold food waiting, the smell of the flowers not quite gone. Some of the other black people had come up to the house in our absence, and were standing by to pay their respects to Miss Angie—all the ones who had worked closely with the family over the years and had liked Little Brother in spite of his erratic and insulting ways. Sister Evalina was there with her cousins Clytie and Lurl and Lurl's oldest son Boomer. And on the same afternoon came the two Washburn brothers, June to the back door as he had been taught and Big Mose to the front. Funny about Big Mose. He had almost stopped coming by at all after losing his position at the store. He had worked there, he used to say, "from a boy on up." But a sharp decline in business during the early sixties had made it impossible for the Old Gentleman to keep him on. And it was just as well, everybody said, because by that time he had taken up the ways of the agitators and had begun to hold himself high, smoking big Havana cigars and crossing his legs in front of all the white people. And then there was the night not so long ago that he had come to Lurellia's house and rapped sharply at the back screen, identifying himself—strangely—as "Mr. Washburn."

"Who is it, you say?"

"Mr. Washburn."

"Which Mr. Washburn?"

"Mr. Mose Washburn."

"Come on in, Big Mose."

But at least it was still the back door. It might just as easily have been the front. I say that because my wife and I had once invited Big Mose to do what no other black person had ever been allowed to do—that is, to march boldly into my mother-in-law's house by way of the front entrance.

That was a long time ago now, back in early 1964, just about the time he was beginning to make his peace with the movement. We had returned one afternoon from visiting my father-in-law at the hospital in Birmingham and had found Big Mose waiting in the front yard. He had come there hoping to hear something of the Old Gentleman's condition. At first I thought nothing of inviting him in the front entrance, especially in view of Lurellia's prolonged absence. "Come on in, Big Mose." But then I realized he had never come to the front door of a white man's house and that I had asked him to make the hardest of all choices—either to disobey the "young white boss" or violate one of the South's most hallowed racial canons. It was clear, then, what we had to do: we would make the choice for him, feeling very good and liberal about it all and being very glad that we had left my mother-in-law in Birmingham.

"Don't worry about it, Big Mose. Come on in."

We wrestled him up the steps like an oversized mattress, turning him first one way and then the other before we could finally get him into the house. It was quite a scare for the big storehand. How much of a scare I found out when I invited him to join us at the kitchen table.

"Nawsuh, I be's jes fine."

He stood there sweating and fidgeting under the high bleak glare of the ceiling light, looking all around and dreading the moment that "Miz Lurellia" would come in, also by way of the front, and say, "Has there been a nigra in this door? I'm surprised that *some* people seem to have forgotten their place."

Nothing to worry about, I told him. Just go ahead and have a seat.

"Nawsuh, I jes fine. Thanks."

Well, then how about a spot of tea?

"Nawsuh, cap'n. I jes fine."

So I let it drop. Maybe it was enough for one afternoon just to get him through the front door. But I always wondered if that was what had started it all. Maybe if it hadn't been for what happened that afternoon he would never have started calling himself Mr. Washburn or smoking all those big cigars or crossing his legs so high.

On the day of Little Brother's funeral I was surprised to find that he had forgotten his airs; he seemed as congenial and as deferential as ever, just like the Big Mose I remembered from my first days in Mt. Gizeh—no matter if he did go in by way of the front door and keep his hat on after he got inside. And I learned something else about Big Mose that day: it wasn't just himself that he "mistered"; it was everybody, even my brother-in-law, whom he had helped raise. When we asked him about all that and explained that maybe the time had come to dispense with all the formality, he just laughed in that big jubilant way he had and, as though released from a thousand years of tension and uncertainty, threw both arms around the young "Mr. Holston," and shook him playfully, saying,

"I jes didn't know how things wuz, Bubba. I jes didn't know how things wuz."

The World That Farley Built

November 1970

The "cotton-patch nigger" is sheriff now. And Sedley Apperson McHardison Jones is the probate judge. The election that brought the two men to power followed by a little more than a year the 1969 takeover. It had been close that first time, thanks to the Putney vote, and it was close again. Cain and Honaker lost by fewer than one hundred votes apiece. But it might as well have been by a landslide, because the implications were now clear even to Cain himself. As much as he and the domino players and the members of the town coffee claque liked to think that what had happened in 1969 was a mere accident, made possible by the intervention of the federal courts, they now knew that other forces were at work and that the white man could no longer rely on Putney and the "decent nigras" as a source of his waning political power.

Nonetheless there was always a chance that the incumbents might have won if it hadn't been for the one thing over which neither Putney nor Sheriff Cain nor the federal judges nor anyone else had any control: George Wallace's reemergence as a candidate for governor. A disturbing development for any local white candidate who wanted black votes. But it wasn't just Wallace's return to the top of the Democratic ticket that bothered the Cains and Honakers; it was the way he got there. Wallace had adopted the pose of "statesman" in recent years and hoped he could win back the office, now held by his onetime protege Albert Brewer, without much of a struggle. He hadn't counted on Brewer being in the race at all. He had counted on running as his wife's "hand-picked" successor. But Lurleen had complicated matters by dying in early 1968, after less than two years of serving as her husband's stand-in. That left the game all in the hands of the youngish self-effacing Brewer, the man Wallace now called "Sissybritches." Brewer had served two years as lieutenant governor, an office he had won with the backing of the Wallaces, and after Lurleen's death had emerged as a likable and occasionally effective chief executive. He brought those same assets to the campaign which he hoped would win him a four-year term of his own. And he had something else going for him too: the tacit support of more than a quarter of a million newly enfranchised black voters. Besides, there had been a lot of resentment building up against Wallace since his wife's death.

People still remembered how he had treated Lurleen — making her get out and campaign as his stand-in just because the legislature wouldn't give him the succession amendment he had wanted. Lurleen was already ill with cancer, even then, and now people were saying that the campaign had merely hastened her death. With all of that anti-Wallace feeling working for him and with the help of all that black support he had not directly sought, Brewer finished first in a seven-man field, leaving the former governor in second place by more than eleven thousand votes.

Then came the runoff and a whole new strategy. Wallace dropped the pose of statesman and began describing "Sissybritches" as a captive of the "black bloc vote." Suddenly the editorial writers were all talking about the "old Wallace." It was a lurid business even by his own earlier standards. The racist propaganda began to show up everywhere, in newspaper ads, in radio commercials, and on the rumor circuit. In some papers there were full-page ads showing first-primary vote totals in black precincts (Brewer 1,781; Wallace 6) and depicting fair-skinned maidens in the company of grinning Negroes. Caption: *This could be Alabama four years from now. Do you want it*? And there was Wallace himself, talking more ominously now about the specter of a black-controlled government and at least once — forgetting perhaps that the newspapers and television cameras were present — telling an audience how "them three hundred thousand nigger votes is mighty hard to overcome." Rumor did the rest. In unsigned circulars the Wallaceites snickered at Brewer's slight build and high smallish voice. Was the governor a homosexual? Was his wife an alcoholic? His daughter a nymphomaniac?

The strategy worked a little better maybe than the Wallace people had expected. He came out well ahead this time, though by a margin much reduced from the 72,000 votes by which he had won the 1962 runoff.

"Well, it's all over," Lurellia had written. "And if George C. Wallace can feel proud of his winning, then he is less of a gentleman than I thought. Someone said he would do *anything* for a vote. And NOW I agree. ENOUGH!"

That may have been the way Cain and Honaker felt about it too. There had, of course, been no real primary in Catalpa County, because most of the new black voters had registered not as Democrats but as members of the newly organized (as of 1968) National Democratic Party of Alabama. Which meant that the main contest would have to wait until November — and that in the interim Cain and Honaker would have to find ways of winning back the support of conservative blacks who felt alienated by Wallace's racist campaign. On the day after the runoff Cain called together the domino players and said, "Well, boys, what're we gonna do?" But he already knew what they were going to do. They were going to form a separate party — the "Spotted Horse" Party" — just as the black people had already done, and thereby put a bit of distance between themselves and the Wallace ticket.

It worked well, but not quite well enough. And when it was all over even Cain seemed to lose his composure. He admitted for the first time that "the niggers've got everything their own way now." The only things that were still out of their reach, it seemed, were the white swimming pool and the bowling alley — and, as the sheriff was always saying, the bowling alley "hasn't even been built yet."

* * *

On the morning after the election the town coffee claque gathered as usual at Eddie's Grill. And the county's lame duck government returned to the courthouse, as it would continue to do each morning for the two months between now and inauguration day. And the domino players all went back to their game in the anteroom of the sheriff's office. The town, in short, resumed its customary rituals with a kind of zeal that seemed to promise relief from events too agonizing to be faced in all of their detail, or maybe it was only a way people had of reassuring themselves that the election really hadn't meant anything and that any day now someone would find a means of throwing out all the returns and restoring the white man to power.

Among the first to arrive at Eddie's that morning was Farley Meads, the one person without whose presence proceedings could hardly begin. As senior partner of the county's largest and most influential mercantile concern and as board chairman of the only bank in town, Farley Meads was the man everyone looked to in these difficult times for some word of comfort. But on this occasion he had nothing for the claque except the usual "Good morning, Eddie" and "Good morning, boys." His presence, though, was in itself reassuring. He seemed so solid and so sure of himself, everybody said later, not like the Farley a lot of people remembered, not like the Farley who had sometimes talked of cutting all of his ties with New Erie and making his permanent home in the Bahamas.

The first time he had talked about that was way back in the early sixties. For a time there Farley had not felt close to the town; he had lost his wife in a mysterious house fire and had felt somehow that people were holding him responsible. And he was not far wrong. There had been a lot of ugly rumors about all that, mostly to the effect that Farley had married beneath himself anyway and that his wife drank too much and that maybe she had set the fire herself and why had Farley been so foolish as to leave her alone there so much of the time?

Farley had scarcely recovered from the shock of losing

the woman who was beneath him, and from the rumors that seemed almost to imply that it was all for the best anyhow, when along came the civil rights demonstrations and the boycott. The store over which he presided with what my friend Edisen called a kind of "bluff geniality" lapsed into a severe economic decline. And again there was talk that Farley might throw everything over and move to Nassau. That's where he was four years later, during the initial phase of Catalpa County's black political revolution. And that's where most people thought he would decide to stay. But he no longer found that thought so comforting. A new marriage, a new home, new feelings of belonging—all that had changed Farley maybe even more than he realized, and he had come back that summer with a determination to see through to the end the role of civic stewardship for which fate had seemingly destined him. Which is not to say that he wouldn't have changed his mind even then if the county were suddenly to find itself caught up in the turbulence of Reconstruction-style "anarchy." People had feared that for a time, after Abernathy had come to take over the white pool. But in the more than fifteen months since then, the worst charge to have been brought publicly against the black-dominated government was that its expenditures had exceeded by some hundred thousand dollars the amount spent by the previous regime.

Homer Worthington had made a lot out of that in the *Democrat*. The trouble was, it was news that mattered to no one except the tiny minority of voters—whites and Putney Democrats—who paid most of the taxes. Just be glad, Farley was always reminding the claque, that these new "darky" commissioners had no power to raise taxes without legislative sanction. Home rule? There was no such thing in Alabama. And never had the white people of Catalpa County wanted it less than they wanted it now. As autumn faded the talk hovered about all the familiar topics, as if in this as in everything else the town was seeking to anchor itself more firmly in the shoals of tradition.

If it wasn't the tax rate that was up for discussion, it was

Homer Worthington's "exposés." And if it wasn't that, it might be something far more disconcerting, like all the federal job and "action" programs that had been coming in (thanks to the work of the new officeholders and their "pushy outside advisers"), and all this free federal food that was going around, and all those cheap "turnkey" housing units the government was preparing to build. And if at length the claque tired of talking about how the Great Society had come to Catalpa County, there were always the welfare loafers, black men both young and old who scorned an honest job lest it interfere with their receipt of a weekly unemployment check. And always there was Farley to provide solidity, perspective, deep thought and, at times, humor, a "bluff genial" humor that was a steadying influence not only for all of those moody fellows who could see no good at all in what the future held but also for men whose exuberant nature blinded them to all but the most "tragic" aspects of the black takeover.

And so it went through all of those sun-filled autumn days, until autumn itself grew into a mellowed age and dropped plump and overripe into the lap of winter. And then came the most startling news of all: the announcement directly from the mouth of Sedley Jones that Lawyer Meads —Farley's own brother—had agreed to stay on at the courthouse as a parttime attorney and help see the black government through a difficult transition period. Once more everyone turned to Farley, wanting to know what it was all about. How could Roger betray his own kind like that? Farley wasn't sure himself what was behind it all. But he tried to explain it the way Roger had explained it to him: wouldn't it be better, said he, for the town to have one of its own over there at the courthouse rather than leave things entirely in the hands of an untried and possibly irresponsible bunch of streetmarchers? How else were the "merchant princes" to preserve political and social stability? Would it be better for the princes simply to stand aside and watch helplessly while all they had worked for fell into egregious ruin?

The claque reluctantly fell in with his line of reasoning

—or was it Roger's? But some of the members still seemed to feel that it would have been a lot better just to let "the niggers go ahead and mess up so the whites can take over again."

I Am Not Afraid

March 1971

So it is over now, the revolution accomplished at last, and with none of the disorder and terror that have marked so many of history's other political upheavals, the streets empty of sansculottes, the Bastille untouched by a single stone. Even the swearing-in ceremonies went smoothly this time. Ralph Abernathy, still haunted by memories of his disruptive 1969 march to the white pool, wasn't anxious to bring the headline writers down on him again. His manner was conciliatory and his words unusually subdued as he and the new sheriff stood atop a mule-drawn wagon outside the courthouse and welcomed the inaugural-day throng to "freedomland."

That afternoon the celebrants crowded upstairs into the big high-ceilinged courtroom to hear more such speeches. "Yes, brothers!" said Cyrus Blue. "This is without question the liberated zone... freedomland! Catalpa County is the beginning of a new hope for America." It went on like that through most of the bright cold windless afternoon. And when all the speeches were done, when all of the shouting and applauding and barbecuing were over, the crowd had yet another victory to celebrate: the recent conviction of former Probate Judge Rufus Honaker on federal contempt-of-court charges.

And there to remind them of Honaker's glorious fall was the man most responsible for it, the relentlessly reform-minded Atlanta attorney Bryan Seaver, who had prosecuted the case for the American Civil Liberties Union. Seaver, of course, would have liked it better if he could have found himself a different victim, someone more closely identified with the old planter aristocracy. He had known and liked Honaker at the University of Alabama, where the two had been classmates, and he was very much aware that the young judge was not a typical representative of the planter class — that he had no landed wealth, no inherited position to rescue him from the ignominy of the court's judgment. But those considerations were secondary to Seaver's burning passion to carry on with the great work of the sixties. That had been his work since law school, where he had developed a zeal for liberal causes and had come to think of himself as a kind of divinely appointed avenger of crimes committed against the underclasses. A confirmed hater of the Black Belt gentry ever since his childhood days in Birmingham, he knew immediately that the Catalpa County matter was his kind of case, the kind that — during the sixties anyway — even an incompetent lawyer would have found it almost impossible to lose.

Throughout it all Honaker had denied everything and would continue to do so for as long as I knew him. A thousand times he would say it: he had acted responsibly, legally and forthrightly through the whole affair, refusing to grant ballot position to the six NDPA candidates only because no federal court had ever ordered him to do so. The three-judge tribunal assigned to the case roundly scoffed at Honaker's protestations and convicted him of both civil and criminal contempt, levying fines that together with the court costs amounted to more than ten thousand dollars.

He had hidden his feelings well enough to win favorable comment even from the pitiless Seaver, who reminded the inaugural-day crowd that his old classmate had stood before the court with "a certain quiet dignity" and on the whole was not such a bad sort as had been commonly reported:

> . . . for we know that Rufus Honaker's acts were not for himself alone. He served other men and their interests and what to them was their Southern way of life.

> That matter is over. That Southern way of life is over.
>
> Mr. Honaker should receive from you the same courteous treatment which you desired during all those years of white minority domination of your affairs. He is entitled to the full and equal protection of the law and he, too, is entitled to remain a part of this community because he is an American citizen. You can ill afford to grant him less than that same consideration you desired for yourself and your families....

He too is entitled to remain a part of this community ....But that was impossible now. Seaver must have known that. At one time Honaker had thought he might stay on in New Erie. He would return to private business or maybe open a law practice. But that was before he had fallen into the hands of the court. Now, after all that had happened, after all the humiliation, the public scorn, the betrayal, he could not even count on the Putney crowd to throw any business his way. For many years he had enjoyed close and friendly relations with many of the blacks in New Erie. He said and believed that just as all other white men said and believed it; and in his case it was probably more true than in most of the others. He had campaigned even among Negroes who were not followers of C.M. Putney and had gotten (as Cain had) almost one-quarter of the black vote in a losing election. Even among the SCLC streetmarchers he had found black men he could respect. Cyrus Blue, for instance. He had always gotten along well with Blue, and they had learned to trust each other in spite of political differences.

But maybe that had been his trouble all along. He had been too naive — too gullible — too inclined to trust people who he now knew would have found it politically impossible to speak up for him openly. That was why he had talked his attorneys into calling Blue as a defense witness. He had felt confident even as Blue took the stand that the judges would finally see the truth — some of it anyway. But all Blue said was, "Whites trust him; blacks don't." And now Honaker realized his mistake: "He couldn't have said anything else. There was too much pressure on him — too many people after him to say exactly that."

What choice, then, but to flee? His first stop would be a nearby railroad and cotton mill town, where he would serve as regional distributor for an oil and gas concern. Later he would find more suitable work as a trust officer for one of the Tuscaloosa banks. And in time he would become his own man, setting himself up as part owner of a large Northport paving firm, with the prospect of gaining the social acceptance that had been denied him as probate judge. He would no longer feel any need to explain away what had happened back there in Catalpa County, and he would no longer have to worry about vindication.

For my part I would find it impossible to believe completely in his guilt and would be forced to rely on Edisen's judgment that what Honaker needed wasn't vindication but "redemption," and that he could get it only by openly confessing his "sin" and "guilt" and by throwing himself on the mercy of those he had wronged. I would argue without much effect that Seaver and the ACLU did not seem to have had all that strong a case and that anyway Honaker had an honest face.

I called on him once more, to see again if I could satisfy myself about the matter. He had changed little. There was no discussion of vindication and certainly none of redemption. Though he betrayed no feelings of regret or bitterness, he talked still of the arbitrary and even "revolutionary" circumstances of his trial, of judges unwilling to convict themselves and therefore obliged to convict lesser men of nonexistent crimes. In others words, as Little Brother might have explained it, the court had "whupped" him once by neglecting to notify him formally of his responsibilities under the law and then had to whup him again just to prove that he "deserved the whupping in the first place."

* * *

There are no domino games at the courthouse now. All that ended for good when Cyrus Blue took over Sheriff

Cain's old office. By the time Blue came to power, he was already something of a celebrity and had begun almost at once to dress the part, abandoning streetmarching apparel in favor of wide ties, three-button suits, dark glasses. Almost from the beginning the talk was that he had gotten too big for the office of sheriff and had been neglecting his duties. But he had actually worked quite hard at the job—even if he did come in most mornings dressed like a wealthy Hungarian bassoon player. He had schooled himself in all the latest theories of the criminologists. He had studied political science and literature in the New School at the University of Alabama. And he had read all the right books. Camus. B.F. Skinner. Rollo May. But, then, he always had thought of himself as something more than merely sheriff. He had been a university lecturer as well as student, a country preacher, a political "kingmaker," and in more recent times one of the black government's chief industry hunters, traveling thousands of miles each year to sit in paneled executive suites and discourse on the advantages of Catalpa County as an industrial site.

Any other rural improverished county would have hungered for such advantages: a major north-south railroad connection, an interstate highway, navigable rivers on both its eastern and western borders, matchless resources in labor and land. But very little industry had come, probably because of the one "disadvantage" that seemed to outweigh everything else: black faces in the courthouse and what the big corporations perceived as an implied threat of unrest and governmental instability. Let an industrialist warm up to the idea of locating his business in Catalpa County, and almost immediately he would begin to hear all that talk about the white people fleeing to Australia or Scandinavia and about the Black Muslims moving in with their cattle and house trailers and alien political doctrines. Lurellia had been hearing quite a bit of it herself. The story she got was that all the black domestics and field hands were

> to quit the white people at the end of the year so
> they can't make a living — and will have to sell

their land cheap and the Negroes will be able to buy it — Now! P. told B. that Judge H. said many of the white people were going to move away from Catalpa County but keep their businesses here. I haven't talked to anybody about things. Think I shall soon. I am not afraid.

And all the while there had been a steady and growing market for news and magazine stories about the county, none of which was complete without a picture of Cyrus Blue in his dark glasses and Fu Manchu. But he had never gotten so far above himself as to neglect his preaching duties. One recent summer night he had come to preach at Mt. Gizeh's summer revival and had seemed more at home there than he had ever seemed behind that worn desk in the sheriff's office. He had put behind him all the teachings of the New School and had forgotten all about B.F. Skinner and Rollo May. Gone too was that air of reserve and wary suspicion that had sometimes made him an enigma even to his own people. He strode dramatically to the pulpit and began at once to fling himself about to the shoutings and noddings of the amen corner.

Yassuh! O yassuh! Listen to him now!

He had talked that evening about the apostle Paul and how it had come to pass in the old time that Paul was "taken away prisoner" from his native land, "a captive bound for Rome," taken away "in chains and disrepute," and how a storm had come up at sea and beat against the ship and rent the sails and toppled the masts and threw up great walls of water, and how the ship's crew had fallen back in awe and terror, "looking up with fear in their eyes and a mighty fear in their heart," crying, "Save us, father, save us from thy mighty tempest!" and how Paul alone had stood there tall and serene amid the fury of the storm, saying, "Peace, brothers! Be of good cheer!" and how before he reached the end of his journey the Lord had made him "*captain* of the ship!"

O yassuh!

And then Blue too became calm and very serene, just as

Paul had been in the old time, looking down at the congregation and gripping the pulpit, yes, quite calm now and very proud, as though the church had become an unmoored vessel and the pulpit a tiller to guide him through the storm-tossed summer night. "Yes, brothers! We must have men in the world today, men who are willing to stand tall, to be firm and stand for God, with love in their hearts, good men to stand tall in the midst of strife, and to say with Paul, 'Be of good cheer!' " And then you realized that his sermon had become unmistakably a political allegory. "Yes, brothers! In my lifetime I have seen the power of God in the world! I have seen the slave freed from his chains and I have *seen* the bottom rail rise to the top!"

O yassuh! Well?

"In my lifetime I have seen the evil altars cast down. I have seen the judgment of God brought upon the proud and the mighty. And I have seen victory visited upon the meek and the humble. Yes, brothers! I have seen the wicked brought low and the mighty cast down — big men, powerful men, men arrogant in the ways of power — all the mighty men of the earth cast down and humbled before the majesty and power of God!"

Hear him now!

"I have *seen* the power of God in the world! I have seen what God can do. . . ."

One could hear in him all the echoes of the civil rights years, the struggle and the sacrifice, the terror and ultimate triumph, the crashing to earth of discredited political systems. He had become all that Paul had been, a man to stand tall and strong in the face of adversity, to cast down the Sheriff Cains and Rufus Honakers, and to say with the apostle: "Be of good cheer." And he had become once more what he was on that cold rainy November afternoon in 1965 when he had stood in front of the Catalpa County courthouse, a young man in shirtsleeves, thin as a sliver, somber as ice, and flung about him the rich shower of oratory that was at once a taunt and a promise: *When is Alabama gonna change? When is Catalpa County gonna change? O Lord, when is this old world gonna change?*

He was still somber, still wary and troubled behind an occasional cataract of laughter. Maybe it was all those books he had been reading, or maybe it was only the Fu Manchu and dark glasses. He would glare at you a bit uncomfortably from behind his big worn desk, still unable to overcome his innate distrust of the white man. But he no longer talked only of change. At times he talked positively against it, in spite of his role as economic developer and industry hunter: "I hate to see all the change that's coming. I hate to see the land change. I hate to see us lose what we have here out of our need to become something bigger and more important."

Lose? Strange to hear that said of a county that year in and year out had ranked as the fifth or sixth poorest in the nation, strangest of all to hear it from Blue. He himself had grown up among some of the poorest of Catalpa County's tenant families, down there in the Black Warrior River bottoms. But for some reason he couldn't explain, he often found himself reminiscing about those early years, forgetting how it really was, forgetting about all the broken-down windswept shanties he lived in, the arrogance of the riding bosses, the long sweltering days in the cotton fields. "Jobs, jobs, that's what people in the county are talking about now," he says. "Jobs and industry as the quickest way to those jobs. But maybe we need to find a better way."

It was that old sense of belonging he had gotten from growing up on the land that drew him back to Catalpa County in the first place. Maybe it was the same thing that in more recent years had drawn so many other black people out of the cities and back to their native South. They had come, a lot of them, even when they knew they would find no more waiting for them than when they left. "Sure," he says, "we want people to live better in the world; we want them to have more and they can have more. But..." A sudden pause as though he had stumbled upon a thought unworthy of utterance. And then, only half aloud: "I guess people are always in search of some mystical place."

* * *

How are the mighty fallen! It is a theme much beloved

of just about all the black ministers these days, the Rev. Octavious Ponds among them. "The nigguhs do much more better," his "reverence" told me one fine spring afternoon as I got out of my car and mounted a steep wooded path to his house. The preacher was sunning himself on the porch, with an outsized Bible open on his lap and his hunting dog Black Gal beside him. "Come on up and help yoself to some of my seating." I helped myself to some of it and saw far below, through the still-leafless woods, the now-completed strip of interstate highway that in 1965 required him to give up some twelve acres of his land and left him with enough money to build the only house he had ever owned.

Actually there was little talk of civil rights that afternoon — some gloating, of course, as was only natural, some talk about how "the nigguhs do much more better than the white folks ever confess" — but mostly it was the sort of talk you might hear on almost any country porch on a warm spring afternoon, something about his hopes for his family and his congregation, something too about how he had been the first black preacher in Catalpa County to build an all-brick church, and how he now hoped to become the first to acquire a fiberglass baptismal font. He was tired of going out to the rivers and creeks every time he got ready to conduct a baptismal service. He had been too often to the city, to the big conventions, and seen how it was done there. But his deacons had told him, "Naw, preacher, we all right the way we are. It's goan cost too much to buy that fancy fiberglass pool you been wanting."

But they had all said the same thing years ago when he set out to build the brick church. At the time everyone thought it was an ordinance of God that only the white man's church was to be made out of brick and that the "nigguh" churches "all had to be made out of planks and tin and stuff." But Ponds never quit talking about that brick church till he got his way. "I just started to cry out till I got all them deacons on my side." Most of New Erie's white merchants had also lent a hand. "Went in to Mr. Willis Meads and told him, say: 'Mr. Willis, we trying to build us a fine brick church. Write yo name on the list there.' I say, 'We sho preciates yo help, Mr. Willis, even if it ain't goan be but fifty dollars.' He say, 'Fifty dollars! How bout twenty-five?' But I say, 'Nawsuh, fifty!' He wrote me the check right there. Went on down to the Hardy store. Same thing there. Then over to Barringer's. Same thing. Went up to Mr. Emptson Lord, and he say, 'Octavious, times is slow. I can't spare but twenty-five.' I say, 'Nawsuh, fifty!' He wrote it out right there."

The church netted almost six thousand dollars in that drive—six thousand to add to the five it had collected previously. Big shouting, then, on the night that preacher Ponds stood up to announce the totals. "All them deacons, they all come around to my house by the carload, say: 'Pastor, we goan sho build us that brick church.' But I say, 'Naw, we ain't goan build no brick church. We ain't got the money for no brick church. We goan build us a good wood church.' They say, 'Pastor, how much more we gotta have fo we get us a brick church?' I say, 'Well, we need bout twenty-five thousand total.' And they all say, 'Well, pastor, we just have to borrow the money then cause we sho want that brick church.' "

Many of the white men who had put in a little something toward the brick church wouldn't be around to help pay for the fiberglass baptismal font; they had long ago been ruined by the economic boycott that Ponds had helped organize. I wondered if there was any regret in him for what had happened to the decent white men like Davenport and Hardy and Lord. I gathered that there was some, but that it was mostly lost in his feeling that the Almighty had His own good reason for bringing them down along with the Cains and Honakers and Nebuchadnezzars.

Maybe there was a little bit of Nebuchadnezzar even in the most upstanding of white men. "Don't make no difference who you is, the minute you give praise to yoself and take it away from God, you is right on the eve of falling. Like Nezer was when the people of Babylon built him that big palace. God, you see, had hailed em to do that. But when it got built, Nezer he got out and strut on the wall and say, 'Did I not build this great wall?' And he just kept on making these evil expressions without honoring God's achievement till he brung hisself down. Then God strut on the wall and say, 'Nezer, you done forgot who you was, and you done forgot who I is, and now you and all yo house done come to grief.' "

A mighty good thing, then, that most of Catalpa County's black officials had heeded Pond's—or somebody's—advice about the need for a forgiving hand and a conciliatory spirit. "I tell Sedley Jones that. I say, 'Sedley, you goan be elected. I know that cause God done revealed it to me. So I wants you to go up to the courthouse and ask all them white folks up there if they is goan work for you when you is come to power.' So he go up there and ask em all that, and some of em say 'Yeah' and some of em say 'no.' And when it all come out according to God's plan and the nigguhs was in power, all them white folks cept one old lady walked out. But they all wishes they'd stayed there now, cause things is much more better now than when they was in power. Usta be folks didn't think the nigguhs was nothing. They say, 'Them damn nigguhs. They ain't nothing. They don't know how to do.' But now they see we got more sense than they got. All the leading whites is saying it: 'Them nigguhs should ought to have been in there.' That's right. The nigguhs got more sense bout how to do than the white man, when it comes to running things. The nigguhs do much more better."

* * *

Spring arrived to find the domino game established in a new home. The players had been in something of a quandary for a while, not knowing where to go after their dismissal from the courthouse. They moved first to a bench on the north side of the square and later to a boarded-up brick building vacated by Porter's Meat Market during the 1965 boycott. The sheriff was no longer a regular, nor was Calloway, whose absences had already become chronic before the game left the courthouse. He had also stopped coming around to meetings of the town coffee claque; finally he dropped out of sight altogether. People talked vaguely of his whereabouts. We knew from what Lurellia had told us that he and Janice had broken up—she had gotten the house and no one knew just how much land—and we had since heard that he was planning to remarry and leave the county for good. Another story had it that he had already left and was building a lavish beachfront home at Point Clear, still another that he was hoping to overcome the stigma of his divorce in time to enter the 1974 campaign for lieutenant governor.

But all that was before his friend Sims Krites shot himself one afternoon behind Redford's cotton gin in Taschahatchie City. Nobody knew what had gotten into Krites; people talked about his heavy losses at poker and golf, his women, his heavy drinking. But no one knew for sure what had driven him to it. I'm not sure Calloway knew either. The only time I ever saw him after that was at Ronchie's Bar in Tuscaloosa, one of those places that catches a lot of the university traffic. It was true what we had heard about the divorce. But there was nothing to the story about his remarriage or the big home at Point Clear. Politics? Yes, he had been giving it some serious thought, but the truth was that he hadn't had much stomach for it since Krites died.

"Why'd he want to do it, Macaulay? Why'd he want to go and shoot himself like that?"

And why, one wondered, had Calloway chosen to stay on in Catalpa County? He had never adjusted to the idea of black rule, and there was little to keep him there now that his divorce was final and his best friend dead. Why not go on and build that big home at Point Clear or in the Bahamas? He could afford it. He could afford just about anything he wanted in that line. He could buy his own town, his own government—and not a black face in it anywhere. But he had stayed on there with no real thought of leaving, unless it was to occupy a big political office someday.

Perhaps he had been held there by an evil magic that was somehow mixed up with the land itself, something that came up from the river bottoms like a swamp fever, and got inside a man without his knowing anything about it or even being aware of the consequences. I had been there enough to understand how it could happen; I fancied that I could see it in him even now, all the flaming passion and brooding sorrow of the land that had given him birth, and something of its savagery too, all the dark forces that had ruled there since "the year the stars fell," driving some men to madness, others to self-destruction. Was that the real explanation for what had happened to Krites?

The mystery of it all was lost on Calloway. But he was glad for a chance to talk about Krites. He wanted to talk about how it was when they were growing up together, and what a big help his old friend could have been to him in his political career, and how Krites was one of the few white men willing to stand up to King and his gang. Calloway could never talk about any of that without remembering how it was the day the crop-duster came over and belched down a spray of DDT on the civil rights marchers, a dramatic and wholesome incident to break the monotony of the daily demonstrations. It still gave him a big laugh, to think about the plane swooping low over the town and all those billows of cotton poison rolling up Taschahatchie Avenue and the demonstrators all scrambling for cover.

But the great pity was that Krites hadn't been there to see it.

"He was shacked up with Lottie Hendrix that day. You probably heard him talk about Lottie. She was the one that made all that money straightening niggers' hair. A regular fortune she made, they tell me. But she threw it all away, I guess, or maybe Krites threw it away for her. And when it was gone, there wasn't any more where it came from, cause all the niggers had started wearing those Afros by then — didn't want their hair straightened anymore— thought they looked too all-fired cute with their new Afros. And you know how it is with the white folks; most of them ain't gonna stoop to patronizing a beautician that's made her reputation straightening niggers' hair. So there wasn't anything left for Lottie around here after Krites put that gun to his head. I heard she's down in Mobile working as a waitress — turning a few tricks too, I hear. All because the niggers decided they looked better in Afros than with straight hair. Anyway, that's where Krites was the day the crop-duster came over — over there shacked up with Lottie. He sure did hate it too — always talked about what a rotten shame it was that he hadn't gotten a chance to see the niggers get a little dose of that cotton poison."

By the time I got up to go, Ronchie's Bar had filled up with an evening crop of college girls: a blur of merry faces, voices lost beneath the moody strains of "Rainy Night in Georgia"; twilight now, and no thought of politics or race problems or men driven to suicide because they couldn't figure out how to cope with a world grown too complicated, too perverse.

As I started out I had the fleeting and tantalizing thought that I would return to Ronchie's some day and find Calloway still seated down at the end of the bar, dead, of course, yet in appearance as young as ever, his head cocked at a mischievous angle, his elbows jutting out, a zombie in a white jacket and neatly pressed plaid slacks.

"Only dead man I ever knew that wore out three suits of clothes," the barkeep would say. "Been sitting up there like that for about ten years now. Folks used to ask us how come we didn't get rid of him. But I couldn't see no reason just to go and throw him out. Besides, it's good for business. You know how these young college kids are. They all get a big kick out of it—seeing a regular mummy sitting up there like that."

While I was thinking about all that, Calloway waved me back and asked me if I was sure I didn't want to hang around so we could pick up some girls and what was the white man to do now that the niggers had taken over the whole county and had I heard the real story of why Krites killed himself.

I had thought it was gambling debts and women mostly, that sort of thing. But Calloway said that wasn't it. "It was all those back taxes. Owed a bundle when them niggers came in, and they were threatening him with a big court suit if he didn't get it paid off. . ."

O Lord
it's raining
all over the world

"... They started putting the squeeze on him — talking about taking him before one of their nigger juries and making a big thing out of it. Already had the papers out on him. You can imagine how he felt — watching everything he had worked for coming apart, everything changing — the foolishness of it all — a bunch of niggers that didn't know their asses from an asset trying to put the arm on him for something everybody else had been willing to overlook for the past fifteen years. All they wanted was to get themselves a big write-up in the *Birmingham News*. It wasn't the money; they didn't care about that. Besides, Krites had been paying the interest every year. It wasn't like he was breaking the law."

I later learned that it was a story entirely without foundation. I don't know where Calloway got it; maybe Krites had made it up on himself.

"Maybe his gambling debts had something to do with it too," Calloway said, "and the liquor. You can't ever tell what gets into a man that would do something like that. But I always figured that the big thing was all those back taxes."

I was sure of it now: I would come back there someday and find him on the same barstool, grinning at me from under his cap, more erect in death than in life, shot full of embalming fluid and ten-year-old Scotch.

"He ain't hurting nothing, or costing us anything," the barkeep would say. "He don't do nothing but just set there with that big grin on his face. So the way I figured it was, why throw him out? Why not just make a regular tourist attraction out of him? Dress him up real nice, you know, so that folks'll have something to talk about when they come in. Most of em say they've never seen a dead man that could drink so much Scotch."

I again got to the door before Calloway called me back.

"Say, Macaulay, why don't you ever write the other side of it? You know what I mean: the white man's side. Look at poor old Krites. If he'd had somebody to talk to — somebody to listen to him — write it all up in the paper — maybe he wouldn't have put that .38 to his head. The newspapers, they've got to share a big part of the responsibility for his death. I guess the niggers eventually got just about everything he had. His house down there in Oak Grove, Jody got that. She's still living down there, I hear. But there wasn't anything else left by the time the niggers got through taking him to the cleaners. Why don't you boys ever write that side of it?"

I explained that it was all much too complicated to talk about now and that I'd drop by his place someday and we'd go over the whole thing.

"Tomorrow," he said.

"About four."

"Four it is."

As I again turned to go out I thought the barkeep was trying to catch my eye. But I didn't stop to go back. I knew what he was going to say anyway: "We just keep him there as something to laugh and talk about. That don't mean you're obliged to sit and talk to it."

While Fame Her Record Keeps

September 1974

For more than a year before our last trip to Mt. Gizeh the river bottoms west of the captain's house lay under constant siege. All day long you could hear the sound of it drifting up across the land, a clang of piledrivers and a roar of bulldozers and a clatter of jackhammers, as men in dusty helmets strode importantly about the valley floor, raising yet another monument to twentieth-century technological progress. The TennTom it was called, a 253-mile stretch of dams, locks and spillways that in time would connect two of the South's mightiest rivers, the slumbrous Tombigbee and the never-sleeping Tennessee, which cuts a savage swath through the north Alabama mountains.

The project had been talked about for years, in and out of Congress, beginning way back in the time of the French explorers; but only under the prodding of the Nixon administration had the construction money finally become available. Nixon himself, in the days before his disgrace, had come here to attend inaugural ceremonies. And now the builders had come, the legions of straw bosses and iron-hatted engineers, all of whom only wanted what was best for the land and who, to prove their good intentions, would dig bits of shark teeth and old bone out of the primordial mud and hang them as artifacts on the walls of their house trailers.

Would such men willingly be a party to what critics of the TennTom had been calling an ecological disaster? Their construction camp stood innocently in the shadow of the old port town where the Confederate cavalry hero Nathan

Bedford Forrest had surrendered and where Nixon had spoken. Here in the old days the cotton steamers came calling. The town had been quite a place back then, said by local boosters to have been the third largest inland cotton shipping port in the world. But that was long ago, and it had shrunken now to an inconsequential village of fewer than three hundred people, although that too was to change, and soon perhaps, with the coming of TennTom. For with the completion of all the locks and dams the river would become navigable throughout its entire length, and all the old port towns would reawaken and get about their long-neglected business.

Already the skeletal work of the first of those dam complexes had begun to emerge, off there amid the canebrakes and sloughs and palmetto flats, less than a mile from the abandoned block manufactory where Calloway and I once fished for bass and bream. Throughout all ages the valley had lain there unbroken, the river itself undefiled, timeless and mysterious and unchanging even during all those years when man first began to assert his authority over it; the old river slumbering on, tireless, inexorable, wide-shouldered, moving without seeming to move at all, while swamp owls brooded listlessly in the pines and conjure women shouted their immemorial chants to the stars. But now the whole basin was a scene of wildest disorder, as the dusty engineers rumbled about with their outsized dredges, scooping out a deep-draft barge channel that in time would replace a long meandering section of the Tombigbee known as the Great Rattlesnake Bend, where, as someone wrote, the river "in its wanderings of ten miles accomplishes not one mile direct."

Now that the work had begun, men in the valley talked of very little else. There was talk of industry coming in, jobs for everybody, prosperity of a sort no one in this part of the world had ever known—talk of oil derricks and paper mills and canning factories springing up, of warehouses and grain elevators competing with meat packaging plants and swank glass-walled skyscrapers for hegemony of the burgeoning skyline. Everywhere, in the country stores and on the streets of the little towns, you could hear it, all the big talk of boom times along the Tombigbee and how the new barge canal would open up the backcountry to merchant fleets from around the world, providing the cotton plantations and river towns with direct access to the Mobile ports and — more than that — to the great corn- and wheat-growing regions of the Midwest; all of this and more we were to have in TennTom, a mighty inland waterway — part river, part canal — that someday would be a brother and rival to the Mississippi itself.

But none of that had stopped the court suits, the injunctions, the bitter wrangling between TennTom engineers and environmentalists. Nor had all that in turn stopped the builders of the dams from getting on with what they had to do. And soon perhaps it would all be finished, the giant Mother of Dams, the sublime lock, all of it standing there far down at the end of the valley, like an alien temple amid archaeological rubble, the handiwork perhaps of some ancient Incan civilization or more likely of some forgotten species of Paleolithic man, whose own project engineers might readily have carved the whole thing out of a monstrous limestone outcropping.

One got the feeling that even the judges couldn't stop it now. And yet, as I stood there on a sandy rise above the old block manufactory, I found myself indulging a fond notion: the hope that one of the many legal challenges to Tenn Tom might yet succeed and force the Corps of Engineers to abandon the project in its entirety, lock, dam, fixed-crest spillway and all the rest, so that all of it would be left there as it was at the moment, vast and ageless and solitary, pristine symbol of man's all-conquering megalomania, abandoned now by men and machinery both, and soon to be taken by the encroaching forest, swallowed by vines and gnarled cedar, reached furtively, if at all, by faint shafts of the noonday sun; all of it to be left there, I say, and forgotten, and then to be rediscovered someday, in a distant and quite different age, by Sunday picknickers or by a party of helmeted explorers looking for a new route to the Pacific or for the ancient gold of the Aztecs.

* * *

The people of McWrenn Quarter had long been afraid that TennTom would mean the death of their village. From the time the first stake was driven, there had been talk that the ground on which their ramshackle houses stood would eventually be taken up for one of the government's "slack water impoundments." The impoundment would bring in boaters and fishermen and water-skiers and migrating flocks of brightly colored water fowl and a great deal of new money. And the McWrenn inhabitants, already the victims of one eviction, would have to move on again. But where to this time? Into one of those new federal housing complexes in New Erie? To Birmingham or Tuscaloosa?

Through the long summer afternoons, with the clang of the piledrivers resounding across the land, Clytie Venable waited for the government agent to come and bring her the news. "Maybe I can't stay here no more. Maybe they goan tell me that." Each day she and the man who came to live with her after the death of her husband sat on the front porch of the small frame house she had hauled there a little more than five years ago at a cost of some six hundred dollars plus the two hundred dollars she had already paid Bill Aspers so that she might deny him the privilege of setting fire to it.

And they waited. And sometimes a woman named Fluella Childress waited with them. She was older than Clytie, tall and spare, with an agility that had come from many years of stooping low over seemingly endless cotton rows. Only her face showed her age, a face older than any I had ever seen, beyond age even, full of all the old and abiding sorrow of chiseled stone.

And she, like Clytie, spoke always of her old life in the Flats. And about the morning that the eviction notice had come. "Done been thar all my days," she said one afternoon. "And then that letter come. I say, 'Now, whut's that fur?' All them stamps on thar. Ain't never seen no letter like that. I say, 'Well, sho looks like the government is sending us a little something. . . .' "

"That's right," Clytie said. "Usun's thought it wuz a check from the land office."

". . . I open the letter and it say 'Move!' And I say, 'Ugh, how I goan move? Whar I goan go?' Done been thar all my days. Ain't thought nothing bout no other place. Ain't never wanted to live no other place."

"Ain't none of us wanted it. My husband Will, he never did get over it."

He lasted less than a year after the eviction. And the other one, the one Faulkner would have called her "not husband," had been there ever since, a man who bore the same first name and something of the same shrunken appearance, the same unyielding reticence.

"Them old 'paper woods,' " Fluella said. "White man say, 'You all get on now. I goan grow me some paper woods.' "

"Ain't no use talking bout it no more," Clytie said. "Ain't no use even thinking bout it. Ain't nothing down thar now but pines and more pines and still more pines."

So none of them ever went back anymore. It was just too awful having to go down there along that road and see all the pines standing where the houses and garden plots and the old village school once stood. "Many a pine down thar now. Many a pine." And hardly anything else either, not even a semblance of the settlement they had known for the biggest part of their lives, nothing left now but the sloughs and backwaters and a logging road the timber company had put in, and everywhere the eerie and unnatural silence of trees grown only for "paper woods."

"Done been thar *all* my days. Didn't know whut the letter wuz fur—all them stamps on thar. Didn't know no other place. Never been no other place."

They went through it all again, talking about the morning they had received their ninety-five cent letters, and how "when the moving come up, that wuz the civil rights," and all about the land and the good times on the river, and, of course, inevitably, about the great flood of 'twenty-six.

"You could jes see that big water running. Morning come and wont no sign of water. Noon come and that water wuz ever'whar."

Sometimes the water would come up with a rush, as it had on that December morning in 'twenty-six. But most of the time it would just crawl up under the houses and sit there like a coiled snake, waiting. And then one morning it would be in the road and in the yards and maybe into the houses themselves. Then would come the good times, the best times of all in the Flats, with people moving about almost exclusively in skiffs, not only to go on shopping expeditions or to attend Sunday church services, but also to stalk the small game out in the little hills left untouched by the high water.

Or to go there on midnight adventures. Often there would be whole boatloads of merrymakers, six or eight to a skiff, sailing aimlessly off into confines ever more remote and Stygian, the lot of them swapping drinks from the jar of "wildcat" Clytie inevitably had about her — and then more drinks out on the little hills, in the light of huge bonfires, the water quiet as glass, the moon calm; one drink to follow another until the night grew reverberant with laughter and shouted insults...and at last, home again, in the cold still January morning, the skiffs darting crisply and silently from one cabin to the next, the goodbyes reluctantly said, the night soundless except for the quiet slosh of paddles and an occasional peal of laughter as more insults were swapped merrily from skiff to skiff.

"...Take me many and many a year jes to repeat the river," Clytie said, "the water rising, and rising slow like that, and usun's pushing off our skiffs into the deep water whar it run...."

As they talked of all that I could feel it too, more insistently than ever, the mystery of the land, the river, the deepening spell of afternoon, a feeling all mixed up with September, the old bronze September hills: the short days quickly gone now, summer itself quickly gone, draining off into a thousand weed-choked ravines and murky swamps, while the land shuddered beneath the repetitive clang of the piledrivers and jackhammers, each blow bringing nearer the hour appointed for Clytie's eviction. The government agent would come almost any day now, sidling up to the door with his hat off and his face done up in a smile that belied his distaste for the unpleasant task before him.

"Evening, ma'am."

"Evening," Clytie would say as she came up from the back of the house. The agent would just stand there holding his hat and explaining that while he hated to be the one to bring the news it did appear that she would have to vacate the premises because, well, the truth was that the government had big plans for this land and was anxious to proceed with the project at the earliest possible moment. "Whut plans?" The agent would juggle his hat nervously and give one of his noncommittal and slightly bureaucratic laughs. Well, he really couldn't say about that. Any further announcement would have to come from Washington. But certainly the government would do all it could to promote an orderly dispersion of the McWrenn inhabitants and to see to it that they had enough food stamps to get them through the winter.

But where was she to go? She had gotten to like McWrenn Quarter almost as well as she had liked the Flats and would find it very difficult to move again at her age. So maybe this time she just wouldn't go at all. And then one day the agent would appear again, his face twisted into a horrible grimace. There would be no pretty words this time. He and his partners would drag her out of the house and wrap her aged body in the logging chain that someone had fortunately remembered to bring and then haul her off the porch into a waiting skiff and cart her speedily across the already gathering floodwaters, the agent towering above her with that same menacing stare and saying, "Now, goddammit, now! Ain't I done told you niggers to get off this land and stay off it!"

* * *

Five o'clock. Quitting time in the Tombigbee river bottoms. The sun is still high, though already you can feel the quick coming on of the September dusk. To the west of the river, on a high bluff overlooking the Great Rattlesnake Bend, stands what little remains of the once-booming cotton port where Forrest surrendered: a couple of one-pump gas stations, a combination grocery outlet and antique shop, and the old Pritchett & Wilkes plantation store. On the front porches of the town old men still talk about the glory days of the 1840s and 1850s—about the boom-or-bust speculations, about the cock fights and gambling dens and licentious dance halls, one of which is said to have been "set on springs to give it more bounce." But nothing is left to remind one of those days except the huge neoclassical manor houses that line the side streets of the town and a little-noticed monument that marks the spot where, during the rainy April of 1865, Forrest disbanded the last Rebel command still in arms east of the Mississippi. By then the place had already lost some of its renown. The great days of the river trade could not long survive the coming of the railroads, and the town was about to fall into a prolonged somnolence from which, until recently, there seemed no hope of recovery.

But now the flush times are here again, thanks to the Army Corps of Engineers and its TennTom dredging project. Every day now the clangor drifts up from the bottoms, a confused knocking of piledrivers and battering rams, as though to mock the agrarian dream for which the indomitable Forrest fought.

Aye, waken Forrest with thy knocking,
would that thou couldst. . . .

Downriver, a houseboat stands at anchor. A turkey buzzard starts from a grove of sycamores, swooping low over the all-but-motionless water, circling, hovering. To the south and back along the road toward Mt. Gizeh lie vast stretches of bottom country, drowned in heat haze, the river motionless yet never still, its flow not yet shrunken by the huge loss of water that one day will be drained off to supply the new barge canal. The buzzard swoops again, hovers, vanishes. And the land broods: sandbanks, clumps of prickly pear, palmetto flats; a diffused sheen of sunlight seen mysteriously through the brambles and scrub pine. A Renoir pastiche. Claude Monet in Southern venacular. Smells redolent of old woods and decaying swamps; meadows, prairielands, low-lying hills all flush with the last heat of summer; the land itself a burnt ochre in color, like the wine country north of Vienna.

The old Forrest memorial stands just to your right as you come up from the river bridge. The general never intended to make this out-of-the-way port town the site of his surrender; he had never intended to surrender at all. He would halt here only long enough to regroup and fight on, to harry the enemy with guerrilla raids if necessary, employing his troops in desperate rear-guard tactics which he hoped would prevent a Confederate defeat even if there could be no chance of a Confederate victory. It is a quiet spot, this old park — nothing here but a spiked iron fence and a stone obelisk that stands out crisply against a backdrop of yucca and sweetgum and cedar. Beneath the obelisk, on knee-high pedestals, stand two crumbling Grecian-like urns, festooned with clusters of sculptured grapes; and as you peer more closely you see a worn inscription:

Nor shall their glory be forgot
While fame her record keeps.

So much else is forgotten, so much lost, yet never the memory of that last April of the war—or of all the times Little Brother sat talking about it on the front veranda at the captain's house. It all comes back now, the talk of those summer evenings, the old man reminiscing about Forrest and the retreat from Selma while out beyond the little circle of light the night insects kept up a bitter and unceasing wail, fortissimo and crescendo, a palpitant orchestral-like suite bending always to the same tragic rhythm. Yes, we would talk of April then, that last April in the already defeated land where men would not yet think of defeat, where there were thoughts only of glory still to be won, long years in Mexico or in remote mountain glens from which, implacable as ever, Forrest would repeatedly issue to harry and finally destroy the Yankee occupational forces.

Selma, the arsenal town that was the last major objective of the Union armies, was also the last of Forrest's major battles — and his most hopeless. He had only about three thousand men, most of them too young or too old for hard fighting, to throw against a cavalry force more than three times that size, said to have been the most formidable ever assembled on the American continent. He himself was a near-cripple, having lost the use of his left arm in a saber duel. But through it all he was the same "devil Forrest" General Sherman had ordered "hunted down and killed if it costs ten thousand lives and bankrupts the federal treasury."

Little Brother would laugh and grow somber by turns as he talked about how Forrest, when he came up against one of those fellows that "fit" by note, would "generally whup hell out of him before he got his tune pitched." Before the war he had been a dealer in land and cotton and slaves — in slaves mostly. He had been penniless at twenty and a millionaire before he was forty, a blasphemous untutored martinet in whom the rash hot blood of his Caledonian forebears still flowed — the very prototype of Cash's rough horse-trading type of frontiersman who scorned and eventually triumphed over the Cavalier tradition that spawned most of the legends of the plantation South.

And now, after almost four years of war, he had come at last to this old river town, ready to take the fight to the hills. On every side rose fierce cries of "On to Texas!" or "On to Mexico!" The general himself had little to say; he was often alone in those days, incommunicative, lost in thought. One evening he and his adjutant went out for a ride along the river and at length, so we are told, came to a fork in the road. "Which way, general?" Forrest wasn't sure. To Mexico — or back into the Union? For the first time in the war he seemed incapable of a quick infallible decision. But perhaps he had already begun to think the unthinkable, even before his aide-de-camp began to talk about the need for peace and reconciliation. The general sat up late that night, trying to work it all out. But there would be more talking and arguing, more long night rides, before he finally found the words he wanted.

Standing there before the old obelisk, the light of the September day going fast, one can sense again how it was on that long ago afternoon when Forrest gathered his troops about him for the surrender — how he strode slowly out of the plantation house that had served as headquarters for the Tombigbee encampment and delivered the remarkably statesmanlike farewell address that was less his work perhaps than that of his young adjutant:

> . . . Civil War, such as you have just passed through naturally engenders feelings of animosity, hatred and revenge. It is our duty to divest ourselves of all such feelings, and, so far as it is in our power to do so, to cultivate friendly feelings toward those with whom we have so long contested. . . .

He had regained the use of his arm, and there was a new lilt to his voice. His men saw him now as they remembered him from the first days of the war. A Confederate Murat, someone called him, lean and imperious, his uniform immaculate, his dark chin beard newly trimmed and his eyes hard and glittering above high cheekbones, his iron gray hair falling almost to shoulder length, after the manner of a Revolutionary-era periwig.

> . . . I have never on the field of battle sent you where I was unwilling to go myself, nor would I now advise you to a course which I felt myself unwilling to pursue. . . .

Little Brother knew most of the speech by heart. But

after all the talk was done, all the stories told, he would lapse into another troubled silence, looking up after a long while with that disturbingly quizzical tone in his voice and asking quite seriously why it was that "the North hates the South so." As usual, though, there would be no need to answer, because he would have the answer already: "Because they whupped us, that's why. Because when you whup somebody it doesn't matter what the cause of it was — you've got to go on whupping them to show that they deserved it in the first place."

* * *

Miss Angie outlived the old man by almost four years, so crippled toward the last that she was unable to get about even with the help of her metal walker. But she had changed very little otherwise. She was as extravagantly optimistic during that last summer of her life as she was the first time I ever saw her, and never lonely because she still had Eula to look after her and a thousand unseen guests to keep her company and Lurellia Holston ever at hand to run an errand or straighten out a snarled financial transaction.

After Miss Angie's death Lurellia was the only Holston left in Mt. Gizeh. And almost before we realized it she too was gone. She had finally decided to move back to her hometown of Oiler, having acquired at a good price the little house that her sister Thelma had been after her to buy ever since the days of Catalpa County's black political revolution. She had not really felt at home in Mt. Gizeh since her husband's death three years earlier. Her in-laws had never done anything to make her feel welcome, and in recent years she had not been on the best of terms with her neighbors. For a while there, after the federal government first began desegregating the Catalpa County classrooms, it had gotten so they wouldn't even nod or throw up their hands when she passed by in the road.

Lurellia's refusal to give up her teaching job as a protest against all the race-mixing had made it difficult for a lot of people to believe she was the good Christian she had always said she was. Toward the end of her working years, at a time when most other teachers were scrambling to make a place for themselves in the county's new privately endowed whites-only Tutwiler Academy, she had further compromised herself by accepting a supervisory position that took her often into the black schools and put her into almost daily contact with black principals. That did not look good at all to Mt. Gizeh's Get-A-Cow-for-Wallace-At-Any-Cost Committee, and people soon began to give her the "cold sign." The first to do so was Efren Summers, who had actually been showing much too lively an interest in her anyway, often coming to her back screen, as she said, and "behaving in a most vulgar fashion." Even though she welcomed his sudden show of indifference, she did not know how far it had gone until she chanced to run across him one morning at the bank. "He stared at me," she informed us by mail, "and without any sign of recognition spoke a freezing how-do-you-do."

Others were only a little less direct. Ethel Forbisher—old man Doc Forbisher's wife—called one night and, in a spirit of trying to help, reminded Lurellia "of the women in New Erie who were working with Negro children in Head Start and how other white people were treating them." A shame, wasn't it, what some people would do for a little money? What was it like, she wondered, to have "one of those things" in your class and have "to put up with trying to teach it something?" Was the job worth it? Maybe Lurellia would be happier clerking in a dimestore.

By then she had less than six months left until retirement, probably the most difficult six months of her entire thirty years with the school system. After losing her only assistant to illness, she struggled on alone against a mounting burden of paperwork. The ways of HEW, meanwhile, had become ever more mysterious, the courts ever more demanding, and her boss, the imperious superintendent Sensenbaugh, ever more openly hostile. But, as always, she would win through—

"Ask God to show me His will and I can do it!"

Her retirement, in the spring of 1967, came three years before her husband's death and almost four years before she finally made up her mind to return to Oiler and put forty years of ambiguous memories forever behind her. Oiler was a depressing place, one of those north Alabama mill towns that could, however, be quite nice if what one most wanted was to escape the civil rights clamor. There were few blacks and little talk of civil rights in Oiler. And the subject soon dropped out of her letters completely. She was very comfortable there, more content than we had ever seen her. But sometimes she seemed to forget all that had happened; she would think it was 1963 again and that she was back in her home in Catalpa County. She would look up at us with that look that hovered always between resignation and despair, explaining in that patiently martyred tone of hers that the "nigra situation" really did seem to be getting quite serious and that we should always be sure to keep our doors locked when we were driving through Birmingham or Atlanta and that from the way "the young nigras" were acting, one might think that they really DID want to take over the courthouse, and not only the courthouse but also the schools and the churches and the golf course and perhaps even the Heart Fund and the March of Dimes itself.

* * *

I never did get a chance to meet the woman who came to take Miss Angie "over to that other worl." A woman just past middle years is the way Eula described her, in a flowing gown and broad-brimmed hat, the most kindly and patient of Miss Angie's many visitors. She had stayed all that summer before Miss Angie's death. "Jes reading," Eula said. "Jes waiting." Each morning and again in the afternoon, Miss Angie would join the woman in the upper hall. "Miss Angie always tell me, say: 'Well, Eula, it be's time to go see the lady now.' And I say, 'Okay, gurl, I takes you thar.' She allus sot the same chair, the lady did, up thar by the big old bookcase, waiting to take Miss Angie over to that other worl." Eula knew it was the same chair from all the times she had tried to "sot" there herself. "Miss Angie say, 'No, no, Eula, don't bother the lady; don't sot that chair. Sot the straight chair.' " So Eula sot the straight chair, which she was happy enough to do under the circumstances, and awaited the pleasure of Miss Angie's unseen guest. "She always be's setting thar. Jes reading. Jes waiting. I say, 'Whut she look like, gurl?' And Miss Angie, she say, 'Eula, I don't sees her legs cause her robe it go right down to her feets, and I don't sees her feets neither.' And then she say, 'It's okay, Eula. She be's a nice lady. She be's the one whut's come to take me over to that other worl. That's another worl over thar, Eula, and she goan take me thar.' "

Then something unexpected began to happen. "She all the time start looking up at me like she done got skeared and say, 'Eula, is it time?' I say, 'Time? Time fur whut, gurl?' She say, 'Time to go over thar—over to that other worl.' She tell me the time has done come fur her to go, but she afeard she ain't goan get thar..."

Afeard?

"...Afeard the Yankees goan get her. Afeard they goan keep her from getting over to that other worl..."

Yes, of course—the Yankees. For a long time it was only the Egyptians. But now it was always the Yankees. There were whole companies of them "coming down the road...every day...every day, all the time, they coming...." They never got in the house, but they were always out in the road marching, down past the store and the captain's old one-room schoolhouse, drums beating, their voices raised in a martial air. Sometimes the sound came almost up to the porch, the roll of drums, the triumphant singing, the marching feet...

Hurrah! Hurrah!
we bring the jubilee!
Hurrah! Hurrah!
the flag that makes you free....

We were in the kitchen as Eula recounted the story, almost the last time that either of us would find ourselves in that familiar setting. The dusk had caught us there, quite suddenly, with voices and clamors of its own, falling on us like an old cloak borrowed from a dusty museum.

"Miss Angie say, 'Shut the door, Eula! Shut it and lock it *tight* cause them Yankees goan sho get in this house!' "

The unseen woman did not look up from her reading even at the sound of the approaching soldiers, not even long enough to assure Miss Angie that the Yankees were mere figments of her disordered imagination. They would sit there all afternoon and on into the evening, the one unconcerned, the other ever fearful lest she be taken off and locked up somewhere before the time came for her companion to look up and say, "Now, my dear. Now it is time to go."

In those last days the Yankees came ever more frequently and drew ever closer. "Miss Angie say, 'Eula, them Yankees near bout in! Go close that door, Eula, close it fast!' I say, 'I got it closed—locked too.' She say, 'That lady still be setting thar waiting on me to go over to that other worl, and I *sho* ain't goan get thar if them Yankees get me first.' I say, 'Miss Angie, why you think them Yankees goan get you?' And she say, 'Oh, that's whut they done befo times in the worl. They comes into the houses and takes the peoples off.' She say the Yankees wuz freeing the world, and she afeard they goan get her fo she can get over whar that other worl wuz."

Sometimes the sound of them coming would grow so loud and ominous that Eula would have to go out and run them off. "Lots of times I do that. I have to jes up and get *at* em and run them all away from hyar. Then I say, 'See, Miss Angie, they gone now. They ain't goan bother you none.' And she say, 'I don't know, Eula. I sho is afeard of them Yankees. I skeared they ain't goan let me get over to that other worl.' "

And still they came, every day toward the middle of the afternoon, while the unseen woman sat reading her book, the footsteps coming up the road, through the gate, across the bare front yard, and always the triumphant singing,

Hurrah! Hurrah!

* * *

And then one day you go back to that old house for the last time. The place stands quite empty now, as it has for the past year or more, forgotten even by the weekend sightseers for whom it once represented a rare and early form of back-country architecture. The year of neglect has left the clay road between the store and the house perilously rutted and much narrowed by the encroaching forest. And the yard has vanished beneath a fever of catastrophic growth; thickets of yucca clamber at the gate and old roses renew themselves amid a tangle of suddenly menacing and overarching wisteria that threatens to devour both the cedars and crape myrtle if not the house itself. Just as well, perhaps, that the place has finally been put up for sale, the land divided, and the mighty company that once thronged these halls rudely dispersed. Where now are Carlyle and Xenophon? Where are Tacitus, Cicero, and all their train? Where for that matter are all those other ghostly intruders, the thick-voiced aliens and gloomy satyrs, the men in aprons and funny hats, the delicately boned long-waisted young women who came so often to rearrange the jonquils in the tall vase yonder by the wardrobe that smelled of mothballs and dry cedar?

The wardrobe is gone now, to say nothing of the horse-hair sofa and marble-topped sideboard and the countless other antiques that long ago found their way into the homes of Cousin Eugene and the Dallas County plantation crowd. The scavengers came often during the last summer of Miss Angie's life, with their wooden crates and pickup trucks, making foray after foray and leaving in their wake a predictable litter of discarded Greek grammers and junk mail and old newspapers and a thousand other nameless curiosities, all piled high in the back hall as though awaiting a ceremonious burning — very little there worth the taking, not even those early issues of *Life* that would have brought quite a good price on the used magazine market if anyone could ever have found out where the used magazine market was.

As you turn to leave the dusk takes you, cool, anticipatory, full of dying footfalls and not-quite-heard voices. Outside, you pause for a moment and look back, trying to remember what Edisen had said about the sins of the planters and the crumbling of old myths — remembering, too, the verse that Little Brother had quoted so often during those last months of his life:

So sleeps the pride of former days,
So glory's thrill is o'er,
And hearts, that once beat high for praise,
Now feel that pulse no more.

But what is it about this land of lost causes and causes newly won that so obsesses you and defies interpretation? Maybe it is nothing so very important after all. Maybe it is only the smoky owl-haunted evenings, the echoes, the memory of all those summer nights when you and the old man sat there on the porch, talking about that last April of the war, the defeated Confederates — Forrest's legions — straggling west for the surrender. *They whupped us —that's why they hate us so. Because they whupped us.* But now even the echoes are gone, the house itself a forlorn relic that will soon be left to the wisteria and oleander and to the new owner whose name I have never even known.

Soon it will have become the most forgotten place of all.

Epilogue: The Correspondent

I am not sure just when it was that Harold Edisen finally settled on Catalpa County as the site for what he was still not ashamed to call his "masterpiece." But by early 1973 he was devoting himself almost exclusively to the "hard task." Temporarily taking leave of his job and family, he returned to New Erie for an extended visit and from his first day there kept a detailed journal of his findings:

> First day — Few hours in Catalpa County. Is it the place for the masterpiece? Mighty good moods and persona. Driving in dreary, drizzly day, as Highway 11 gets into New Erie the black shanty houses of Negroes perched on bluffs above the road among black branches of oaks and chinaberry trees at their bony winter worst, effect of sootiness against the dismal sky.

After long days of mingling with the townspeople and conducting exhaustive interviews, Edisen would return to spend his evenings in a crummy upstairs room at the New Erie Hotel, a floundering institution once popular as an overnight stopoff for drummers and prostitutes traveling the circuit between Birmingham and Jackson. Edisen had chosen it because he needed a special kind of atmosphere for what was to be the great work of his life. Later, when I heard people talking about the strange wild-talking man who had come there to "write up the town," I would have no trouble imagining him seated up there amid a clutter of notebooks and legal pads, sleepless and unshaven, the unsheathed overhead light shining on him, the masterpiece already beginning to take shape. Sometimes he tried to get down on paper what it was like up there. "An old linoleum light of hanging naked bulbs and old oak tables like ghosts of Hopper" is the way he described it once. "Old wooden rocking chairs alone up there, unrocked, ungossipied."

He spent almost three months in the town, mingling with both the "Brahmins" and the common folk, driven always by the hope that here in this remote corner of the world he would find all the complex tapestry of Southern life richly unfolded — here the final resolution of all its classic themes and conflicts. It was much too great a hope, yet one he never entirely abandoned in all the time that I knew him. Edisen was almost a story in himself. During my years on the *Atlanta Constitution,* I had known him as a sensitive and thoroughly likable young man who in another age or environment might have been a poet. He had not always been chief of the Atlanta *Newsweek* bureau, as he was now, and a lot of people thought he wasn't the man to succeed Corky Wiles, the former chief, when Wiles left town to take a desk job in New York. In the old days Wiles had often traveled about the South making as big a nuisance of himself as possible and then passing himself off as a correspondent for *Time.* He had even had phony credentials printed up to make the story convincing. But that wasn't Edisen's style. He was a Southerner, as Wiles was not, and deadly in earnest about almost everything and everybody. And there was something else about him too: none of Wiles's flair for dramatic stunts, certainly not that, and yet a certain expansiveness of manner, an intense curly-headed geniality that may have made him an even better reporter.

Wherever we were in those days — at lunch or dinner, on the transit after work, at one of those nocturnal cocktail parties that seemed to be always in progress — the talk would inevitably turn to the South and its politics. The civil rights revolt was then in its earliest stages. There was no "movement" as such. Everything was spontaneous and largely uncontrolled. It was the time of the freedom rides and sit-ins, a time when young people—nonSoutherners for the most part—were still in the seats of command. The Albany crusade, which marked the first real beginning of what was to become an indigenous mass movement of Southern blacks, was still ahead of us. But all the old themes were there, ready for exploitation, borrowed in part from the social reformers and academic humanists, though mostly from Faulkner and Cash and Eudora Welty; themes hackneyed even then, yet unabashedly pilfered and put forward as our own. Sometimes Edisen would get so caught up in what he was saying he would forget where he was. I often think of him as he was at such times, his whole manner urgent, volatile, half-distracted, his face bathed in a guttering flare of candlelight as he leaned over a table in the cheap Pigalle or in the bar at the Dinkler Plaza and talked about the "shame" and "guilt" of the South, about its struggle to find "redemption," about "merchant princes" and "code duellos," or maybe about a decayed aristocracy preyed upon by Snopeses. During his last days in Alabama he himself experienced a Snopesian encounter on the grounds of Pennwood, the finest of New Erie's antebellum mansions. The coming of the Civil War had interrupted the building of Pennwood, and the enormous structure was still unfinished more than a hundred years later. One afternoon the correspondent went there for a detailed inspection. As he and a companion were touring the grounds, admiring the beauty of the huge fluted columns and heroic entablatures, the owner of the place suddenly accosted them, a "hard-eyed motel owner" who, as the correspondent said, simply "could not understand that [we] were interested only in aesthetics.

"It was his property and, by God, he wanted us off it."

By that time he had already begun to doubt Catalpa County's capacity for "redemption." But for him—for both of us—the county had come to represent all we had ever known and loved and rejected about the South, its ineffably romantic quality, its haunting air of mystery and timelessness, its occasional virtues mingled with, and sometimes indistinguishable from, its sense of perverted destiny. Edisen understood all that perhaps better than I did. And that, I suppose, was why, after traveling for so many years throughout the region, he finally chose Catalpa County as the setting most appropriate for his "masterpiece."

But somehow the great themes he had meant to exploit would not come into focus. He did not quite know why. It had all seemed so simple at first, a classic story of antebellum traditions giving way peaceably before the impact of revolutionary change. The broad outlines were apparent even before he left Atlanta. And he had come there with all the best intentions, "looking for the good...the upbeat...the portrait of a community struggling to make things work.... You're okay, I'm okay...the harbinger of a New South where whites and blacks lived in peace...." But then there "fell a great silence," and, among the people he met, a "tightness about the mouth." The classically sharp portrait had dissolved into a blur of indiscriminate shades and hues. "Secrets abound," he wrote in a fit of pique. "Harper Valley PTA-type secrets would be the least of their problems. Deeper are the secrets people keep from themselves—their shames and power needs; where they deny their own highest vision." Sometimes he would pause to mull over the immense complexity of it all, the ambivalence, or to plot "escapes from the hard task." Standing at his window he would brood endlessly on all the familiar themes that had been a mainstay of the Atlanta cocktail circuit, meditating upon the "clockwork regularity" of life in the town even as he pondered the varied implications of the Southern "rape complex."

As spring came on more fully he found that he himself had become a part of that clockwork regularity. He would rise each morning promptly at six, after the arrival of the *Birmingham Post Herald* truck, and jog off through a black shanty town behind the A&P, scaring up a clamor of barking dogs and cackling hens. Later there would be prayer services at St. Leo's Episcopal Church or a game of tennis with the "pink-cheeked shy telephone man" who had been staying at the hotel. He would be finished in time for breakfast a little before nine, usually down at Eddie's Grill, where he would find the town claque already at its "ritual coffee." As always, the seven or eight regulars who appeared there pored over an agenda as unvarying as the taste of the innocuous brew that flowed from Eddie's chrome-plated coffee urn. And as always, Farley Meads would assume the role of presiding officer. The correspondent enjoyed the good-natured banter of those sessions; yet he could never feel quite right about being there, knowing as he did that these were the very men who had most stood in the way of the town's "redemption."

"No!" he shouted into his diary one night, "Catalpa County is not redeemed, not converted!" But maybe, he added, somewhat mysteriously, that in itself was "the strongest way into the future."

* * *

After the disappointments of those first days, his hopes revived tremendously when he received "more signs that God wants this to be the place for the masterpiece." What brought him to this conclusion was all the talk he had been hearing about his old friend and college mate Roger Meads, who was now in his third year as a legal adviser to the black government. That was one of two jobs that put him to working with blacks; the other was his role as deputy district solicitor, a parttime position he had held off and on for the past ten years. Since the $600 a month he got for the two jobs would have meant nothing to a man of Meads's wealth, the correspondent could only assume that his onetime "anti-hero," had thrown in with the streetmarchers for the reason he said he had: to look after the good name of the county and to protect it against the unsettling effects of inexperienced black rule. There was hope in that, of a sort, and the correspondent was proud of his old friend. Occasionally the lawyer came around to Edisen's hotel room after working hours and joined him for some convivial drinking. They would sit there until late in the evening, amid the legal pads and the "ghosts of Hopper," talking about the town, its history, its politics, the new day that had not quite dawned, the correspondent idealistic as always, the lawyer sardonic, cynical.

In his diary and later in an article (not his masterpiece) published in an Atlanta magazine, the correspondent would lavish much finely honed language on the gaunt restless-eyed Meads. But was it possible, as Sheriff Blue hinted at lunch one day, that the lawyer's altruistic gesture had served only to veil a darker purpose? Was he intentionally providing the sheriff and other officeholders with inadequate and poorly timed advice, so as to place them in awkward positions that would reflect unfavorably on their ability to govern? Was he there, in other words, only to protect white interests and speed the day when the domino players could resume control of the courthouse? Edisen knew from his own talks with Meads that the lawyer was something less than a dedicated convert to the black cause. He was still in many ways the same Meads who had helped found the local chapter of the White Citizens Council and who had once voted against George Wallace because "he was too liberal" (as was only too true, of course, in the governor's pre-"segregation-forever" days).

Meads as antihero — or only as villain? He couldn't be sure about any of it now. But perhaps Blue was being unfair. No one could doubt that the whole effect of Meads's decision to stay on at the courthouse had been beneficial to the town. Wasn't it true that his "defection" had served as a "signal" for the white community to eschew the tactics of the KKK and the Snopeses and to remain decent and civilized in the face of the black takeover? Something at least must be said for that. Could he not write that without putting too fine a literary point on it? Maybe it was also true that Meads had enough wealth and standing so that he could do as he pleased without worrying about what members of his social set might think. Still it was no small thing for a man of his aristocratic background to have repudiated the prejudices of his "caste" simply to work out an accommodation with the street-marchers. That was the story then, the major theme: the account of a man seeking to overcome his "antiheroic" past by doing penance at the altar of those he had wronged. Certainly no one else had gone nearly so far, not in those first days, least of all his brother Farley.

Farley Meads thought he had done quite enough for the county simply by refusing to run away to the Bahamas. The correspondent liked Farley even while deploring the "shame" and "guilt" that had kept him and his brother too trapped for so long in a world "much too symmetrical, finite, unchanging." Funny thing about Farley though; the way he laughed and talked you would have thought there wasn't a thing in the world for him to feel guilty about. "Good old hearty, ruddy, healthy, jutty, bulldog-faced... handsome wavy greying hair of Farley, brow wrinkled in politeness, eyes swimming behind thick glasses, mouth like J. Edgar Hoover, yet always ready for a laugh." That was Farley all right. Always ready for a joke and a big laugh. But his failures were glaring. With all of his money and power, Farley could have singlehandedly made a success of the county's economic development program. Why had he chosen not to do so? The reason was simple: Farley liked things as they were. Never mind that an economic boom would have meant more money in the hands of the "merchant princes." That wasn't nearly as important as all of those traditions that had made Catalpa County, as someone had told the correspondent, a bastion of "Greek Revival and white survival." That was what was important now. Keeping out the textile mills and rubber fabricating plants and low whites.

Toward the end of March, as he was nearing the end of his two-month sojourn in the town, the correspondent attended a Chamber of Commerce meeting presided over — naturally — by Farley Meads. Edisen waited for Farley to say something "good, positive, constructive, uplifting, and true." Instead he chose to make jokes about Tobe Little, an active chamber member whose election as one of the county's first black commissioners had climaxed a distinguished career as a distiller of illicit spirits. When the talk turned to industry, Farley's thoughts naturally turned to Tobe Little. "Well," said he, looking over at Tobe and giving a big laugh, "maybe we can find some way to legalize old Tobe and have us a regular home-grown industry. Sure — that's it. Maybe we can legalize old Tobe." The correspondent left the meeting in a mood of dejection. The mood accompanied him back to his room and hung grimly over him as he sat down to write. Why was it, he wondered, that Farley was so unfeeling? "Bluff, genial," he wrote, "but insensitive, kidding with Tobe Little about whiskey. . . still convinced this is wonderful, is communication, like Fred Cain jovially hailing Rev. Sedley Jones as jug-head old black son of a bitch."

* * *

Where, then, was redemption? The correspondent wasn't sure. But he had about decided that the only thing capable of saving Catalpa County and the South — if anything was —was a "new mythology." He had told me long ago about the death of the old mythology; the new I had not heard of until I got around to examining his diary. And he talked of it later during one of my frequent stopovers in Atlanta, leaning across the table in the little diner where we had gone for lunch and explaining how it was that he had first been seized by this "powerful new thought."

"Don't you see?" he cried. "In the South the mythology has always been the important thing. The myth of death and resurrection, the death of innocence, the passing of the myth of the Old South." He looked frantically about at the crowded diner; but it was as though the crowd were no longer there, as though the diner itself and all the traffic out along Peachtree Street were no longer there, as though he were again sitting in a cluttered room in the New Erie Hotel, trapped beneath the "old linoleum light of hanging naked bulbs."

"The problem," said he, "is that the resurrection has not been very specific. O yes, the death of it all — that was clear enough with the end of the Civil War. The myth of the end of Great Men —the defeat of the Titans. But the rebirth has not been well symbolized. That's the problem."

Would Catalpa County ever grasp the deeper implications of these metaphysical truths? Perhaps not. And perhaps it didn't even matter, because the county and its black Brahmins lacked something even more important than a new mythology. What they most lacked were home-rule powers that would enable them to adjust tax rates in a manner less favorable to the Titans and more to the liking of small holders. The Alabama legislature and the whites who controlled it decided all that — the tax rate, how much money was to be collected, how it was to be divided. Farley Meads had come to understand that quite early; maybe that's why he hadn't fled the county to take up residence in the Bahamas. He knew that the only people in Catalpa County with any real influence over economic matters were the merchants and landowners whose interests Montgomery had made it its business to protect. These were the ones, the "merchant princes" and town Titans, whose "shame and power needs" had led them to "deny their own highest visions" and, so the correspondent believed, doomed the county to an era of petty discord and fratricidal strife. The truth of it all had come home to him with profound impact as he sat there in the somber light of his hotel room: the blacks in power, yes, yet increasingly isolated, lacking either the economic power or taxing authority with which to arm themselves effectively against the Titans, or for that matter against the insurgents within their own party.

That was eventually to become the greater concern — not so much what the whites might be plotting as how to guard against the potentially dangerous usurpations of disaffected blacks. Unrest within the once solidly unified National Democratic Party of Alabama was nothing new; it had cropped up almost at the moment the blacks took power. But no one knew exactly what to make of it. Mostly it was of a piece with the old factional quarrels of movement days, deriving out of deep-seated philosophical differences rather than out of any real disagreements over issues. What it had all come down to was this: a quibbling between those who sought some sort of rapport with the Titans and those who had embraced the fanatical blacks-only tactics of the new superintendent of schools, Gordon Nesbitt. The Nesbitt faction drew much of its strength from former SCLC enforcers like George Sampkins, who had adopted New Erie as his permanent home after the 1969 takeover, and Wayne Giles, a bearded mulatto sent there by a CORE subsidiary to instruct newly elected blacks in the intricacies of public officeholding and to oversee the preparation of federal grant proposals, soon to become almost an industry in itself.

This fellow Giles was an expert in the politics of black separatism, but even the men who had sat in on his training sessions were not of a mind to think that that kind of politics would work in Catalpa County. In renouncing such tactics the NDPA leadership faction was only being realistic. Already there were some who talked about the possibility of putting together a fusion ticket for the 1974 election — whites running with black candidates as a means of encouraging other whites, who after all still controlled both the land and money supply, again to become active in county government. The new probate judge, Sedley Jones, a "shrewd actor," the correspondent called him, had been the first to invite that sort of cooperation. Roger Meads had been his first convert. His next was Hamilton C. P. Wilkes, the county's Republican tax assessor and an important member of the local "peer group." When the time came for Wilkes to seek reelection, Jones went to him, as he had to Meads, and asked him to cast his lot with the NDPA and to run with its blessings. Wilkes, who would be dead from leukemia within five years, had accepted Jones's offer as the only alternative to certain defeat, and he would argue, as Meads had, that he was far more valuable to whites in his present position than as a vanquished though proud ex-tax assessor. The correspondent lavished almost as much praise on Wilkes as he had on Meads, observing that the assessor's cooperative attitude "could end up being significant when the history of these times are written."

The correspondent had arrived on the scene in time to witness the first real confrontation between leaders of the divided NDPA and the town governing body. At issue was the location of a two hundred-unit turnkey housing complex, the largest federally funded project yet approved for the county. Blacks (and that included leaders of both factions) wanted to build the units on a broad strip of prairieland just south of the New Erie corporate limits. But Mayor Swint and his all-white aldermanic council, fearing that the residents of the proposed subdivision would vote themselves into town and take over, as was possible under Alabama law, had mounted a legal fight to prevent the units from being built. In this "quiet but desperate" issue the correspondent had found the potential for much mischief. Mayor Swint, he believed, had opposed the project on "disingenuous" grounds, pretending that the proposed development would overtax the town's water system and sewage treatment facilities when what he really feared was all those new black voters. New Erie, in its own small and insignificant way, had become a kind of mirror image of all the great cities of the land: a white enclave surrounded by black suburbs. But the turnkey project would change all that, and place the town at the mercy of the NDPA radicals. On further investigation, however, the correspondent discovered that Sedley Jones and his crowd had put forward "disingenuous" arguments of their own, acting as if housing were the only real issue when what they really wanted was "raw power" so that "they would no longer have to play the game of reconciliation."

Suddenly the correspondent grew angry. Both sides were guilty! All was lies, deceit, trickery, dissimulation. Both sides had dealt in cynical euphemisms, each seizing upon the affair as a way of enhancing its own prestige and influence rather than as an opportunity for reconciliation and rebirth, each falling victim to all of the old self-seeking inward-looking motivations and petty ambitious strivings rather than standing out for new ideals, new tactics, new myths.

Redemption? He wasn't sure it would be possible now under any circumstances. As he sat trapped beneath the glare of the unsheathed light bulbs all the old doubts came back to haunt him: "No, Catalpa County is not redeemed, not converted!" Now indeed he could see the irrevocable falling apart of all his great themes. Symbols alone there were, nice little gestures of rapprochement that had no real meaning. Perhaps it was true what the sheriff had said about Roger Meads, and perhaps the sheriff was himself guilty! What, then, was left? Were there no more frail tapers of hope? Was dissimulation to be the only enduring coin of the realm? And how could he have been so lacking in judgment as to choose Catalpa County as the setting for his masterpiece? He was not naive. No one could accuse him of that. Him? A correspondent for one of America's best-known news magazines? He had been too far and seen too much. He knew what men were and what politics required of men. What was it that Blue had said? "Sometimes it seems as if the system was made for men to destroy each other." Yes, he knew all that, perhaps in some way even more basic than the sheriff knew it. Yet he had never stopped hoping that here the "broader perspective" might prevail, out of necessity if for no other reason, forcing men to act the part of heroes and born-again antiheroes even if they had no real stomach for it and driving them at last to renounce their "shame and power needs."

Such was to have been the theme of his great work. But he could see now that it had all come to nothing. All that was left was the grim reality of the "old linoleum light," and he again sat there brooding on the metaphysical ramifications of the town's internal struggle, searching vainly for a new mythology. The Titans he dismissed one by one as men unalterably committed to the old myths, forever blind to the limitless potential of small beginnings. And he hated them all. He hated Mayor Swint, who habitually ridiculed the maneuverings of the black officeholders as "nothing but a nigger mess." He hated the Baptist preacher Irwin Gilchrist, who had repeatedly refused to grant him an interview. He hated the Junkerlike Sorbonne-educated jurist and moneychanger, J. Phillip Crashaw, whose conciliatory manner hid a deep sneering contempt for all black people. He hated Little Pepper Swaim because of all those people he had evicted from his river bottomland and because he had just recently refused to lease his father's vacant store to a group of black entrepreneurs. He hated the former sheriff Fred Cain, who he said had once cursed and insulted him on the phone. And at times he even hated bluff, genial Farley Meads, whose opposition to industrial growth had severely hampered the county's economic development program.

* * *

But most of all he hated Oliver Cromwell.

"I hate him," he told me, with the air of one about to disclose an old family secret, "him and all his dirty little Calvinistic tricks."

The little Peachtree Street diner where we had gone for lunch had begun to thin out. But the correspondent didn't notice. He was still caught up amid the clutter of his New Erie Hotel room, anxious to have me understand how he had come by his old and consuming hatred of Oliver Cromwell.

At first I couldn't understand exactly how Cromwell had figured into the Catalpa County power struggle. But that was only because I had not yet heard about Edisen's close relationship with the Rev. Wesley Teal, the new rector at St. Leo's Episcopal Church in New Erie and a man fervent in his belief that most of the evils of the Western world, including Southern racism, could be traced back to the work of Oliver Cromwell and the Long Parliament. The correspondent had come to feel the same way about it, finding much to admire in the Stuarts and much to despise in their Roundhead detractors. O yes, the spirit of the Protector had been all about him in the South of his youth — a mean niggardly white-lipped Calvinistic spirit exemplified in his mind by the institutions of segregation, country revivals, and Prohibition. And he could see the same pernicious influences at work in New Erie, dragging men down, even the town Titans, who were themselves good Episcopalians and as capable as anyone else of working up a good lively table-pounding hatred for the Protector. But he would never have thought about it quite like that if it hadn't been for Wesley Teal.

The Rev. Mr. Teal, thickly set and slightly balding, had made a profound and lasting impression on the correspondent. "A bright saucy fellow," Edisen called him, "the real live intellectual presence while I was there." Teal was a different study entirely from the man he replaced, the easygoing and splendidly noncommittal Andrew Boyes, whose black-robed ministry had so often brought him to the old Holston homeplace out at Mt. Gizeh. The Rev. Mr. Boyes would spend whole afternoons in conversation with the Old Gentleman or Little Brother and then kneel for prayer and finally get up and go away without anyone ever being able to remember anything that had been said, except that whatever it was, it had nothing to do with all the hotly controversial social issues that had broken down all the customs of the South and was even at the moment of his last visit threatening to undermine the New Erie social order.

The new rector, who had come there directly from the seminary and had taken up his pastorate prior to his ordination, was so unlike Boyes that most people predicted he wouldn't be around very long. But to the correspondent it seemed that he had appeared at a divinely inspired moment —the summer after the blacks had finally "redeemed" the courthouse from Sheriff Cain and Judge Honaker. Like so many of his kind, the rector was an odd mixture of piety and irreverence. He was a confessed integrationist, though not of the streetmarching variety, and there were vague rumors that he had been active in the labor movement. But in all matters relating to theology he was as thoroughly orthodox as the beloved Reverend Boyes had been. Maybe that's why the congregation was willing to overlook his heretical political tendencies. Teal hated Cromwell the way most of the people who came to his church hated George McGovern and Earl Warren. He luxuriated in all of the traditional grandeur of the Anglican communion, seeking in his own small way, the correspondent said, to revive something of the old Cavalier spirit that stood in such rich contrast to the "dry and pinching Puritanism" so characteristic of the Southern evangelical tradition. And the correspondent would gladly have joined in that crusade. He too reveled in "the broad-spirited Cavalier tradition coming down out of Virginia." He too enjoyed all of the old arcane church rituals, the festal days, the ennobling liturgy of a prayer book that modernists within the church had been trying to rewrite, the lovely mysterious calm of communion services held beneath the flickering lights of candelabras.

The meaning of the rector's mission had suddenly become clear to him one night during a fashionable dinner party at the home of Mrs. L.T. Barringer on Rivermont Avenue:

> Tonight I feel a masterpiece; today I have it. It came together. By chance. By God. Beginning with Mrs. Barringer's late Victorian house, the rosewood piano, her ancestors from Broussard, La. Black-haired, pale, thin lips, lipsticked, but rather pretty. Only white in town I ever heard say Negro...
>
> Then Wesley telling of dreams of black rape, of his mission to restore the Cavalier spirit, the Stuart use of power. He, too, hates Cromwell....

Back in Atlanta, away from the "old hanging naked bulbs" and the "ghosts of Hopper," he would remember all that and would feel good all over again about his decision to make Catalpa County the principal setting for his great work. He could not say truthfully that he had found anything very dramatic about it all. Nowhere had men talked of redemption and rebirth. But it may be that he had himself talked too much of those things. Perhaps he should have made a pact with himself to spend less time dwelling on the deep philosophical meaning of what some might construe as mere political accidents. The town he had once looked upon as a seedbed of idealistic rebirth had turned out to be a rather ordinary place actually, full of men and women capable of submerging their less generous impulses only long enough to support the United Appeal or the annual cancer drive, a town, in short, no different from most other American towns, with few heroes and possibly even fewer antiheroes.

But maybe that didn't really matter. Now that he'd had a chance to look back on it all, he could remember countless "small triumphs" and "encouraging symbols" that pointed the way, if not to redemption, at least to an improved racial accord and understanding. He would remember the greenskeeper who had attended sensitivity sessions sponsored by Teal's church and, after coming "into the spiritual life," had set out to reform the town, only to ruin everything by saying "nigra" in front of the new sheriff. And there was the truck driver's wife — a "salty angular, country twangy, hotdiggedy dog kind of woman" —who was so put off by the snobbishness of upper-class whites who ran the new private academy that she enrolled her three children in the black-dominated public school system and became a leader in the PTA. But mostly what he would remember was the rector's way of deriving new metaphors, new and higher orders of thought, out of the very changelessness of the town itself. People other than the correspondent had noticed the surehandedness with which the rector coaxed the town toward more conciliatory attitudes. When a black South African bishop came through on tour, Teal and almost two dozen of his parishioners were on hand to greet him. When the time came to arrange for his own long-delayed ordination, he saw to it that invitations went out to all of the more prominent black leaders. Sheriff Blue turned him down, because, as he later explained it to the correspondent, he had never had "a very high regard for the white churches of Catalpa County." But Sedley Jones came garbed in a scarlet-trimmed robe and knelt beside the same senior warden who at the start of it all had argued against the propriety of an integrated ordination ceremony.

In countless ways the rector was at work, undermining Cromwell and setting up anew the talismans of his own faith. And he was always so plump and cheerful about it all, and soothingly articulate even in the heat of argument. Maybe that was another reason he got away with so much—because he lacked "the bony sainthood, feverish quality that is the giveaway of the activist." Edisen owed the young man, who could not actually be called fat, more than he had realized at the time. They had become quite close during the correspondent's last days in the town. They often had dinner together and sometimes took long nocturnal walks during which much would be said about the Stuart dynasty and the divine right of kings and what a shame it was that Cromwell had gotten into it and how the Roundheads had come very very close to ruining it for everybody.

But the great inspiration of those days had come from his visits to two small parish churches out in the river country, where the religion of the Cavaliers had sprung up almost with the planting of the first crop of cotton. Twice each month the Rev. Mr. Teal visited the two churches to hold communion, usually on a Sunday afternoon. The correspondent had gone with him first to St. Martins-in-the-Wilderness at Town Fork and later to St. Jerome's near Taschahatchie City. St. Martins, a splendid little Gothiclike structure, with slender elongated stained-glass windows and a Germanic pitch to its roof, had stood for more than ten years on its original site near Little River before being moved in 1870 to become at once the cultural center and chief artifact of the Town Fork community. There and in the red-carpeted interior of St. Jerome's Edisen had found great joy in spite of the suspicious glares of his enemies.

He well knew who they were. At St. Jerome's his chief nemesis was a young "narrow-faced man," hulky inside an "up-to-date nicely cut doubled-breasted coat." The correspondent forgave the young man his "hard-eyed look" and quickly lost himself in the transcendant calm of the communion service. He would write fondly of what he remembered: the antique organ and the hand-carved altar on which someone had placed a spray of jonquils and jasmine, the tiny cemetery outside the window, the tall Deodora cedar near the front entrance, the soft spring rain, the light glowing on "nine rows of empty pews" and the rector talking "about the great wind, and the great earthquake, and the great fire and, in the end, the still small voice of God."

Edisen joined lustily in the singing and "for some impudent reason" suddenly remembered all the civil rights rallies he had attended in all of those other kinds of churches, all of them so much alike, broken-down frame buildings perched on blocks or pillars, often without curtains and with only the barest of furnishings, no carpeting or ornamentation of any kind, and a different set of rituals entirely—different perhaps, yet as arcane as any of those celebrated by the Episcopalians. He had found much joy in those churches too, even if the triumphs celebrated there were those yet to come rather than those that glorified the dynasty of the Stuarts and the divine right of kings. He felt that there was a lesson in that. If the black people could build creatively upon their religious heritage in order to redeem their hopes for the future, so perhaps could the rector's guilt-laden parishioners. In that alone lay hope for the Farley Meadses and for all those narrow-faced people who accosted well-meaning strangers with unfriendly stares.

He and the rector had talked about all that during their long nocturnal strolls, the need to infuse antique church doctrines with new meaning, so that what is unacceptable this year will somehow come to be acceptable the next, with no new laws having come down or new decrees promulgated. Wasn't that the lesson Wesley had been trying to impose on his congregation? Wasn't that why he had defied his church wardens by bringing in folk masses and by embracing the controversial new cult of sensitivity training? It was all part of his mission to restore the Cavalier spirit. A startling concept perhaps — to think about the pharisaical Charles I living it up at a folk mass or confessing to all the boys down at Sensitivity Training that his first loyalty was to the Pope after all. But it was by such concepts that old creeds were made to fill with new life, and change accommodated within all the old forms, and all indecent beheadings avoided, and wrangling factions reconciled, and the world made whole. Such was the rector's mission and such indeed the scope of Edisen's masterpiece.

* * *

But he would not write it after all. Somehow the "good rich hard prose" he had most learned to admire would not come. The vision that had seemed so clear that night at Mrs. Barringer's dinner party, and on all those other occasions when he and the rector were out walking the back streets of New Erie, became lost in a mire of ambiguity. Maybe what it all came down to was that he lacked the "ruthlessness" or "boldness of spirit" to tell the whole truth about the town, without worrying too much about who got hurt or what wreck of moral devastation he left behind.

He confessed all this in a tone of great secrecy as we sat there in the rapidly emptying diner. Was it possible that the strain of all those gloomy nights in the New Erie Hotel had been too much for him? As I listened to him more closely I was sure that's what it was — a spell cast by "old hanging naked bulbs" and clanking pipes and tall windows through which the night looked unfettered and "the ghosts of rocking chairs unrocked." It wasn't anything to worry about. Let him gain a little more perspective on the matter and the masterpiece would flow right out of him. But no — he was quite convinced now, after all those nights over the typewriter, that he lacked the ruthlessness to see it through. It was a weakness he had long feared in himself. Some years earlier he had dreamed a dream that made everything quite clear — if only he could have understood its whole meaning at the time. In the dream he was back in the old family store in Hazelhurst, Georgia, working for his uncle, an advancing merchant of the more disreputable type. One day a young black couple had come in hoping to return a faulty stovepipe that had been responsible for the death of an elderly relative. The young man — the future correspondent — had watched in disbelief as his uncle turned on them in high choler:

"No, goddammit, no! You ain't getting no money back. No, goddamn you! You paid yo $1.38 and got yo pipe; now get yo asses outa here."

At first the dream seemed only to confirm what the correspondent had known all along — that he wasn't ruthless enough to have been a successful advancing merchant. And then he realized it wasn't his uncle he was working for. It was William Faulkner. But it wasn't until much later that he understood what Faulkner in the guise of his uncle had been trying to tell him — not just that he lacked the ruthlessness to become a successful advancing merchant or that it had been his duty to move off to Atlanta and become a Great Writer. He had known all that anyhow. No, the real meaning of the dream was that even a Great Writer had to have something of the ruthless advancing merchant in him. And, sadly, the correspondent had discovered that he just didn't have it. Loyalties, friendships, affections — he couldn't give all that up, as Faulkner could, simply for the sake of a story. What was it that Faulkner had said? "The 'Ode on a Grecian Urn' is worth any number of little old ladies." For him the story or poem was all that mattered — how people were affected by it, nothing! The true Writer would say only:

"Okay, you bastards paid yo $1.38 and I've got my story. Now get yo asses outa here."

But the correspondent couldn't say that. He couldn't say it for the very good reason that he had gotten too close to Roger Meads, and even to Roger's brother Farley. He had, shame to say, discovered in himself the same qualities of romantic sentimentalism he disparaged in others, and had been seduced by all of the old traditions he had most wanted to repudiate. He needn't have felt too badly about it. An even more famous "demythologizer" of Southern traditions, the North Carolina journalist W. J. Cash, had betrayed many of the same lapses in his great work *The Mind of the South.*

But the correspondent still felt that he had been unfaithful to his mission. He still felt the yearning inside him, the need to express something that at bottom was inexpressible. The pageantry of the civil rights years, its impact on Black Belt society, the political and cultural realignments — it was all of it like one of those intricately woven Damascene tapestries that most pleases when it most baffles. He had found in the story of those years almost a parable of life itself, a kind of old-fashioned morality play wherein might be described all the varied and contradictory passions of "that monster manunkind": the grand and the ignoble, the proud and the disreputable, the sublime and the inane, the bold and the trivial, the liberal's irritating penchant for experiment and change no less than the conservative's outrageous clinging to all that's "accustomed, ceremonious" — yes, the obscure motifs and the salient mingled in all of their rich and shimmering complexity, a thousand imponderable mysteries there, a thousand nebulous truths struggling to be told, the sham, the deceit, the "disingenuousness" and, yes, the "shame" and the "guilt" too, and occasionally the wisdom that looked beyond all that to find redemption, and most of all the fear — not a fear readily identifiable as such, expressed rather in some other form, sometimes as violence or hatred, sometimes as "rape complex," sometimes as black subservience. Yet even in the relationship of black client to white patron he had found subtle truths that had never quite gotten told — something that went beyond mere fear. Maybe for all he knew it was something entirely apart from fear. Was it fear alone — the fear of retribution, the loss of jobs, the loss of place — that had led so many black men to vote for white political candidates? "There was some of that," he had concluded, "but not so much as the folklore would have it." A surprisingly generous assessment in view of his long captivity under the strange glaring light of his New Erie Hotel room. But reporters had to be careful about writing such "truths" lest they make themselves look bad in all of those chic New York intellectual salons where one most sought approbation.

So he would not write it either, not all of it, not in the way it should be written, if only because it was all too beastly complex or because there were too many intellectual accommodations to be made. We talked about it all again, about all the "small triumphs" and "hopeful symbols" he had found, about what the rector had said and what the town gossips had told him. But the search for "meaning" had become quite tiresome, and the loud diner quite empty, before we finally got up to go. Maybe it was only because I was so much older that the whole thing seemed suddenly so pointless. Maybe the correspondent realized it too, how pointless it had all become, even as he searched for the descriptive metaphors that once and for all would make everything quite clear. Or maybe he hadn't realized it. Maybe even now he was thinking of going back to Catalpa County someday to write the book that he could no longer bring himself to call his masterpiece.

DATE DUE